Stress and Work

a managerial perspective

Management Applications Series

Alan C. Filley, University of Wisconsin, Madison
Series Editor

Performances in Organizations: Determinants and Appraisal
L. L. Cummings, University of Wisconsin, Madison
Donald P. Schwab, University of Wisconsin, Madison

Leadership and Effective Management
Fred E. Fiedler, University of Washington
Martin M. Chemers, University of Utah

Managing by Objectives
Anthony P. Raia, University of California, Los Angeles

Organizational Change: Techniques and Applications
Newton Margulies, University of California, Irvine
John C. Wallace, University of California, Irvine

Interpersonal Conflict Resolution
Alan C. Filley, University of Wisconsin, Madison

*Group Techniques for Program Planning: A Guide to Nominal
  Group and Delphi Processes*
Andre L. Delbecq, University of Wisconsin, Madison
Andrew H. Van de Ven, Kent State University
David H. Gustafson, University of Wisconsin, Madison

Organizational Behavior Modification
Fred Luthans, University of Nebraska, Lincoln
Robert Kreitner, Western Illinois University

Task Design and Employee Motivation
Ramon J. Aldag, University of Wisconsin, Madison
Arthur P. Brief, University of Iowa

*Organizational Surveys: An Internal Assessment of
  Organizational Health*
Randall B. Dunham, University of Wisconsin, Madison
Frank J. Smith, Sears, Roebuck and Company

Managerial Decision Making
George P. Huber, University of Wisconsin, Madison

Stress and Work: A Managerial Perspective
John M. Ivancevich, University of Houston
Michael T. Matteson, University of Houston

Stress and Work
a managerial perspective

John M. Ivancevich
Cullen Chair and Professor of
Organizational Behavior and Management
University of Houston

Michael T. Matteson
Director of the Center for Health Management and
Professor of Organizational Behavior and Management
University of Houston

Scott, Foresman and Company   Glenview, Illinois
Dallas, Tex.   Oakland, N.J.   Palo Alto, Cal.
Tucker, Ga.   London, England

ACKNOWLEDGMENTS

Aesop's Fables from *The Fables of Aesop,* with an introduction by Michael Marqusee. Copyright 1975 by Paddington Press, Ltd.

Behavior Activity Profile reprinted with permission of STress RESearch Systems, P. O. Box 833, Spring, Texas, 77373. Copyright 1980. All rights reserved.

Holmes-Rahe SOCIAL READJUSTMENT RATING SCALE, reprinted with permission from *Journal of Psychosomatic Research.* Copyright © 1967, Pergamon Press, Ltd.

Social Environment Stress Model from Katz and Kahn, *The Social Psychology of Organizations.* New York: John Wiley and Sons, 1978. p. 584.

Stress Diagnostic Surveys reprinted with permission of STress RESearch Systems. Copyright 1979. All rights reserved.

Library of Congress Cataloging in Publication Data

Ivancevich, John M
  Stress and work
  Includes bibliographies and index.
  1. Job stress. 2. Executives. I. Matteson,
Michael T., joint author. II. Title.
HF5548.85.I92   658.3′001′9   80-13938
ISBN 0-673-15381-9

Foreword

The Management Applications Series is concerned with the application of contemporary research, theory, and techniques. There are many excellent books at advanced levels of knowledge, but there are few which address themselves to the application of such knowledge. The authors in this series are uniquely qualified for this purpose, since they are all scholars who have experience in implementing change in real organizations through the methods they write about.

Each book treats a single topic in depth. Where the choice is between presenting many approaches briefly or a single approach thoroughly, we have opted for the latter. Thus, after reading the book, the student or practitioner should know how to apply the methodology described.

Selection of topics for the series was guided by contemporary relevance to management practice, and by the availability of an author qualified as an expert, yet able to write at a basic level of understanding. No attempt is made to cover all management methods, nor is any sequence implied in the series, although the books do complement one another. For example, change methods might fit well with managing by objectives.

The books in this series may be used in several ways. They may be used to supplement textbooks in basic courses on management, organizational behavior, personnel, or industrial psychology/sociology. Students appreciate the fact that the material is immediately applicable. Practicing managers will want to use individual books to increase their skills, either through self study or in connection with management development programs, inside or outside the organization.

Alan C. Filley

Preface

Interest in stress has become universal in recent years. The experience of stress is not new; our cave-dwelling ancestors experienced it every time they ventured outside the protection of their caves and encountered their nemeses, the sabre-toothed tigers. The tigers of yesteryear are gone but have been replaced by such predators as role conflict, work overload, personal obsolescence, inflation, and marital disharmony. The list of individual, group, organizational, and extraorganizational stressors is extensive. This book examines some of those stressors and how people respond to them, what effects they may have on health and performance, and what can be done to prevent or neutralize negative stress outcomes.

A large body of literature on stress written by medical researchers and practitioners, clinical psychologists, sociologists, and other medical and behavioral scientists offers theories, predictions, and recommendations about stress. There is no dearth of stress-oriented publications available to the public today, as perusal of virtually any bookstores' shelves or any popular magazine rack will show.

With so much literature available, why do we wish to add further to it? The answer is simple. Virtually none of the literature has been addressed to either the student of management or the practicing manager. Much of the stress experienced by people in our industrialized society originates in our organizations; much of that which does not affects our behavior in these same organizations. The manager and the management student have been left alone to decipher, interpret, and analyze stressors, stress, and stress responses. In this book we have taken a step toward changing this. We offer an integration of theories, research, and applications from many disciplines into a framework that has relevance and clarity for those concerned with stress and work issues such as health, effectiveness and efficiency, and satisfaction. Our integrative model serves as the cornerstone for each of the ten chapters and concluding epilogue that form the structure of the book. In addition, we offer some probing self-report tests that will highlight the concepts discussed as well as pinpoint sources of the reader's own stress and individual behavior patterns.

The authors are grateful to a number of people. Dr. Hans Selye, the "father of stress," has influenced our thoughts profoundly. We are also indebted to many students, managers, and medical personnel who have allowed us to test our ideas, self-report surveys, and opinions. Paddington Press is accorded a thank-you for allowing us to incorporate ten of Aesop's fables to introduce each of our chapters. Also, we would like to thank our secretaries, Cheryl Willis and Margaret Thompson for their help in preparing the final manuscript. Their patience and positive attitudes were invaluable and well above and beyond the call of duty. Finally, Doug Floyd of Scott, Foresman is to be commended for his excellent editing.

A further personal note is in order. This is a book that never pained us to prepare. We immersed ourselves enthusiastically into the task of writing, editing, changing, and refining. In fact, we had to hold back in our expression of thought so that the end product didn't become a lengthy volume.

John M. Ivancevich
Michael T. Matteson
February 1980

Contents

The Nature of Stress   1

THE OAK AND THE REED

An Oak, which hung over the bank of a river, was blown down by a violent storm of wind, and as it was carried along by the stream, some of its boughs brushed against a Reed which grew near the shore. This struck the Oak with a thought of admiration, and he could not forbear asking the Reed how he came to stand so secure and unhurt, in a tempest which had been furious enough to tear up an Oak by the roots? Why, says the Reed, I secure myself by a conduct the reverse of yours: instead of being stubborn and stiff, and confiding in my strength, I yield and bend to the blast, and let it go over me, knowing how vain and fruitless it would be to resist.

Managerial Application • The nature of stressors are such that fighting against them may serve only to intensify the problems, while calmly composing ourselves in their midst may enable us to elude their shock.

Roseto, Pennsylvania, is a small town at the base of the Pocono mountains in the east-central portion of the state, less than an hour and a half drive from New York City. It is of interest to us in this volume because of the results of extensive medical and sociological studies undertaken in Roseto and neighboring communities during the last two decades. The Roseto story provides a vivid illustration of the rapid onset and the severe consequences of stress in modern life.

The most striking aspect of what sociologist John Bruhn and his research team uncovered was that the Rosetans enjoyed a virtual immunity from coronary heart disease (Bruhn and Wolf, 1979). The heart disease rate was less than a quarter of the prevailing rate in surrounding communities, this was in spite of the fact that obesity rates in Roseto were higher than average and that Rosetans' dietary, drinking, and smoking habits did not differ appreciably from those of other American urban dwellers.

Roseto was different from other typical American communities in several additional respects. Family relationships were extremely close and mutually supportive, and this cohesiveness extended to social and community relationships. Virtually everyone who lived in Roseto worked in the town. There were no freeways, no commuting, no traffic. A ten-minute drive to work was considered long. Family units tended to stay intact; two or even three generations often shared the same house. When children did leave home, they invariably remained in the community. Work in Roseto was steady and unemployment low. Most of the men in the town worked in jobs associated with the numerous slate quarries situated throughout the town. The tasks they performed were relatively straightforward, routine, and did not require a great deal of complex problem solving or decision making. Nor were the jobs brought home with the men in the evenings; at the end of the day work was forgotten until the following morning.

This, then, was Roseto in the early 1960s. By the 1970s when the research team returned, that picture had been significantly altered. Family units were no longer as tightly knit. Children were leaving town to attend college and either not returning or returning with a value orientation different from their parent's. There was traffic congestion. Television had significantly decreased the amount of social interaction within family units. Many of the men were commuting to work in Bethlehem and other cities, including New York. There was a new concern among workers for upward mobility. Civic involvement had decreased and with it the mutual support that Rosetans had previously given each other. In short, within a decade, Roseto had become modernized. It had been brought—somewhat unwillingly—into the 1970s.

For the first time, *stress* had become a factor in the lives of the Rosetans—stress in the form of changing values, shifting work patterns, increased life pace, loss of sources of support in the form of declining family and civic ties, traffic congestion, and a host of other alterations associated with modern urban living and "progress." This progress and the stress that accompanied it had a price. By 1971 the town had recorded its first heart-disease deaths in men under the age of fifty. By 1975 formerly relatively stress-free Roseto had lost its immunity to heart disease, and its death rate from it had reached that of neighboring communities. While the Roseto research was primarily concerned with heart disease, no doubt other stress indicators would have exhibited important changes had they been examined closely. Heart disease is simply one of a plethora of possible physiological and psychological consequences of stress.

Roseto is important because it is a stress microcosm of the United States—what took place in Roseto in a decade has been developing elsewhere for many decades. All around us are changes that are potential sources of stress; the sheer volume of change is itself a potent stressor. Many of these changes and sources of stress are related to our jobs, our careers, and the organizations in which we spend much of our time. It is this rapidly accelerating phenomenon of work-related stress which has prompted the writing of this book. There is a critical need for everyone—particularly managers—to understand the pandemic nature of work stress and its decremental role in individual and organizational health and effectiveness.

In subsequent chapters we will explore in some detail the sources of stress in our industrial society, particularly those related to jobs and organizations. We will examine the consequences, both positive and negative, of this stress and the role played by individual differences in determining levels of stress and stress effects. We will detail various stress-management techniques at both individual and organizational levels that may increase coping effectiveness, and we will delineate future research directions that should increase our understanding of the dynamic interplay between stress and work.

EVOLUTION OF THE STRESS CONCEPT

Experts do not agree about the definition of stress or its essential properties. It has even been suggested that the most remarkable fact about the term *stress* is that it has persisted and grown into wide usage, although there is almost no agreement over what it means. Before undertaking the task of defining stress, it may be useful to briefly examine the history of this ubiquitous concept.

The history of stress

A chronological history of thought on stress is difficult to set forth. The word *stress* itself predates the relevant history of the concept in which we are interested, while the concept became of interest before the word itself was applied to it. *Stress* is derived from the Latin *stringere,* which means to draw tight (Skeat, 1958). The word was probably first used around the fourteenth century, and for many years thereafter numerous variants of the word were used in English literature including *stress, stresse, strest,* and even *straisse.*

Although the word and its variants have existed for centuries, the origins of the stress concept which is the focus of this book are difficult to trace further back than the middle of the ninteenth century. At that time the French physiologist Claude Bernard suggested that external changes in the environment can disrupt the organism and that, in order to maintain the proper adjustment in the face of these changes, it was critical that the organism achieve stability of the *milieu intérieur* (Bernard, 1867). This appears to be one of the earliest—if not the first—recognition of the potential dysfunctional consequences of upsetting the balance of, or *stressing,* the organism.

In the 1920s the American physiologist Walter Cannon introduced the term *homeostasis* to designate the maintenance of the internal milieu (Cannon, 1922). While his research focus was on specific reactions that are critical in maintaining internal balance during emergencies, such as nervous irritation, he was clearly dealing with the concept of stress as it has evolved today. In his later work he adopted the term *stress* and spoke of "critical stress levels," which he defined as those which could bring about a collapse of the homeostatic mechanisms. He even grew to use the term in relation to social and industrial organization (Cannon, 1935, 1939).

The beginning of the modern usage of the term is not associated with Cannon, however, but with Dr. Hans Selye, an endocrinologist at the University of Montreal who is frequently referred to as the "father of stress." Selye's work provided the first significant breakthrough in stress research and formed the foundation for much of the subsequent work carried out up to the present. In a classic example of finding B while in search of A, Selye's efforts to discover a new sex hormone uncovered the fact that tissue damage may be precipitated by a host of dissimilar agents, including tissue extracts, cold, X rays, mechanical trauma, and nervous stimuli. Using laboratory animals in his experiments, he concluded that this tissue damage represented a nonspecific response to virtually all noxious stimuli, and he suggested it be called the General Adaptation Syndrome (Selye, 1936). It was not for another decade, however, that Selye introduced the term *stress* in his writings in referring to outside forces acting on the organism or, stated more simply, the general wear and tear of life on the body.

Probably the most significant contribution Selye made was the publication of his comprehensive volume entitled *Stress*. In this work he shifted his definition of stress to denote an *internal* condition of the organism that results in response to evocative agents. He suggested that these agents be referred to as *stressors,* thus setting the stage for much of the current terminology in the stress field (Selye, 1950). It has been suggested that this single volume has influenced research in every country "probably more rapidly and more intensely than any other theory of disease ever proposed" (Engel, 1956).

As is evident from the foregoing discussion, virtually all of the original stress researchers were medical doctors who focused in their work on physical stimuli and physiological consequences. In the past two to three decades, there has been a slight decrease in interest in the physiological study of stress and a significant increase in interest within the behavioral sciences. Consequently, there has been a subtle shift in research away from physical stressors such as mechanical trauma (i.e., injuries) toward psychological stressors such as role conflict. The stress field today, in fact, tends to be dominated by behavioral, rather than medical, researchers. This has resulted in a number of important consequences, not the least of which is increased controversy as to what stress really is.

How stress is defined

The word *stress* has been described as the most imprecise in the scientific dictionary. Like *sin,* stress means an incredibly different array of things to different people; both are short, emotionally charged words used to refer to something that otherwise would take many words to say.

Simply stated, stress involves the interaction of the organism with the environment. In our case the organism is human and the environment may be either physical properties (e.g., heat, noise, pollution) or the other organisms in the environment. While there are a multitude of ways in which stress may be defined (see, for example, Lazarus, 1966; Appley and Trumbull, 1967; Weitz, 1970; Selye, 1974; and Cox, 1978), most definitions of stress fall into one of three categories: stimulus definitions, response definitions, or stimulus-response definitions.

Stimulus definitions • A stimulus definition of stress would be the following: *Stress is the force or stimulus acting upon the individual that results in a response of strain,* where strain is pressure or, in a physical sense, deformation. Thus, as can be seen from Figure 1–1, a stimulus definition treats stress as some characteristic, event, or situation in the environment that in some way results in a potentially disruptive consequence. It is, in that respect, an engineering definition of stress, borrowed from the physical sciences. In physics "stress" refers to the external force applied to an object—say a bridge girder—and "strain" is the impact this force has on the girder. According to Hooke's Law of Elasticity, if the strain in the girder falls within the elastic limits of the girder material, then the material will remain unaffected when the stress is removed. Likewise, if the material is a human being and the strain produced falls within the individual's coping limits, no damage will result when the stress is removed.

One objection to this type of definition is that situational characteristics alone may be inadequate to predict the individual's

FIGURE 1–1   Stimulus Definition of Stress

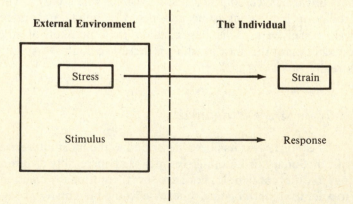

response. Thus, two individuals subjected to the same level of stress may show far different levels of strain, or one may show strain and the other not. While to a certain extent this may be explained in terms of a behavioral equivalent to Hooke's Law, it is less adequate as an explanation for temporal variations in strain in the same individual. Another problem is encountered when we take into account that stress must first be recognized as existing before it can result in strain in individuals. This presumes that some intervening process occurs that is not part of the stimulus model. Finally, as Cox (1978) points out, this approach assumes that an undemanding (stress-free) situation is the ideal condition. If this is true, why is it that most of us find forced periods of inactivity or boredom so uncomfortable?

   Response definitions • *Stress is the physiological or psychological response an individual makes to an environmental stressor,* where a stressor is an external event or situation which is potentially harmful. This is an example of a response definition of stress and is represented by Figure 1–2.

   This approach focuses upon the response the individual makes to the potential stressors in the environment. The occurrence of the stress response demonstrates that the individual has been subjected to a disturbing or dysfunctional environment. In the stimulus definition, stress is an external event; here it is an internal response which may manifest itself in a variety of visible ways.

   This approach suffers in at least one respect from the same kind of problem the stimulus approach encounters. Knowledge of the stressor

FIGURE 1–2   Response Definition of Stress

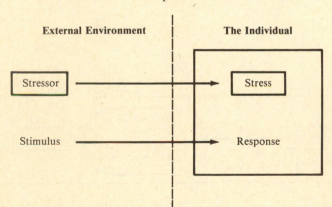

does not enable us to predict the nature of the stress response or even whether there will be, in fact, a stress response at all. Similarly, the same stressor antecedents may be associated over time with significantly different stress responses within the same individual.

Stimulus-response definitions • This, in effect, represents a melding of the two previous approaches. An example of a stimulus-response definition would be that *stress is the consequence of the interaction between an environmental stimulus and the idiosyncratic response of the individual.* It is depicted schematically in Figure 1–3.

In essence this way of defining stress emphasizes the particular nature of the relationship between the person and his or her environment. Stress is seen as more than a mere stimulus or response; it is the result of a unique interaction between stimulus conditions in the environment and the responses that arise as a result of these conditions. The idiosyncratic nature of the response is a function of intervening psychological processes that are part of the individual's make-up, i.e., individual differences. This approach is clearly less simplistic than the first two. (The single entry for individual differences in Figure 1–3 adds a deceptive simplicity to the model.) However, this approach is no more predictive and may be less so. Because it is more comprehensive it is also a great deal more difficult to deal with in practical terms. The stimulus-response definition's improvement over the first two definitions is that it recognizes the critical role of individual differences.

A working definition • Throughout the remainder of this volume, stress will be viewed as *an adaptive response, mediated by*

FIGURE 1–3   Stimulus-Response Definition of Stress

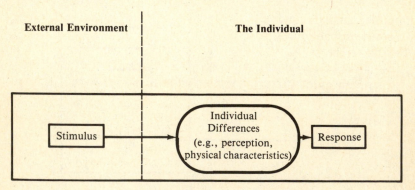

External Environment   **The Individual**

S T R E S S

individual characteristics and/or psychological processes, that is a consequence of any external action, situation or event that places special physical and/or psychological demands upon a person. The characteristics may include such variables as age, sex, race, health status, and heredity. The psychological processes might include attitudinal components, beliefs, values, and many other personality dimensions such as locus of control and tolerance of ambiguity.

The reader will have noted that our working definition is basically a form of the previously discussed set of response definitions. For the purposes of this volume we feel it is most useful to posit stress as the *response* of the individual and to identify *stimulus conditions* as stressors. This allows us to focus attention on specific environmental conditions that are potential stress producers. Whether stress is the actual consequence for a particular individual will depend on the unique characteristics and psychological process of that individual, a fact that only the stimulus-response definition took into account. An additional advantage of our working definition is the specification of an *adaptive* response. The vast majority of our responses to environmental stimuli do not require adaptation on our part and thus are not really potential sources of stress.

PSYCHOPHYSIOLOGY OF STRESS

If you were to accidentally place your hand on a red hot stove burner, a number of predictable events would occur in rapid order. There would be pain as the extreme temperature penetrated the epidermal nerve endings. There would be virtually instantaneous tissue damage as successive layers of skin were exposed to the burner and seared away. Almost immediately, you would withdraw your hand from the burner and we could probably predict that you would verbalize, in some way, your reaction to the sensation of pain.

The event just described is many things. It is an interaction between you and your environment. It is an event which resulted in physical—and perhaps psychological—injuries. Most importantly, it is an example of stress and of how we respond to our environment. All living things, including plants, respond biochemically to their environment. Human beings respond psychologically, as well. The adaptation required to cope with a stressor results in a number of biochemical alterations. These alterations may be very important—even necessary—to insure a successful response. However, they may also be inappropriate and dysfunctional. Further, the effects of the alterations may accumulate over time until significant physiological changes occur, marking the onset of illness.

What is particularly interesting about these biochemical reactions to stressors is that they are remarkably similar across a wide variety of situations. Many of the alterations that took place in the example of extreme heat as a stressor are identical to those placed in motion in response to the stressors of marital disharmony or pressing work deadlines. It is important to develop some knowledge of the mechanisms involved in this process in order to understand stress and its consequences, particularly its link with physical and psychological ailments and diseases.

Fight or flight

A snarling dog intent on warfare approaches another dog quietly sunning itself. The second dog has two options: it may stand and fight the marauder, or it may run away. In other words, the dog has to deal with the stressor by fighting it or fleeing from it.

Consider our cave-dwelling ancestors. They were conditioned in much the same way as the dog. They lived in a relatively simple environment—their major concerns were finding food and protecting themselves from the wild animals and, occasionally, one another. For our early ancestors, stress was meeting a saber-toothed tiger on the trail. If this occurred, their options for dealing with the stressor (the tiger) were identical to the dog's. They could either fight the tiger or flee from it. Once the stressor was encountered, a number of bodily changes took place to prepare them to deal with this threat. But they still had only two ways of responding.

These bodily or biochemical changes were essential to prepare our ancestors for the challenges with which they were faced. They prepared them to either fight or flee, depending upon which course of action seemed most appropriate. The problem that we encounter today is that the human nervous system still responds the same way to environmental stressors, although the environment is radically different. The tigers are gone and with them the appropriateness of the fight-or-flight response. Yet it is that response for which the body is prepared. When a supervisor turns down an employee's request or gives him or her a difficult or disagreeable job assignment, the employee can neither physically attack the supervisor nor run away. Social conventions and organizational expectations rule out either course of action. Instead, the employee is expected to respond in a dignified, calm, and accepting manner.

To demonstrate the inappropriateness of the fight-or-the-flight response in this situation, return to the cave dwellers and examine the outcome of their experience with the tiger. Assuming for a moment that they were successful in dealing with that stressor, they are either safely back in their caves (flight) or they have killed the menace (fight). Either way, the biochemical alterations which occurred were useful to them in coping with the stressor, and once the threat was dealt with, the stress was relieved and their bodies returned to normal. Such is *not* the case with an employee who encounters a stressful situation with a supervisor. Since neither fighting nor fleeing is an acceptable alternative, the fight-or-flight response does not contribute in any way to alleviating the stress. Of critical importance is the fact that the body prepares for something that doesn't happen. Thus, unlike our ancestors', our bodies do not return to normal nearly as rapidly. It is under these conditions of prolonged fight-or-flight readiness that stress begins to have a detrimental effect on health.

The basic problem, then, is that we have a programmed response to environmental stressors which is, far more often than not, inappropriate to coping successfully. The biochemical changes involved are part of the general stress response, known as the General Adaptation Syndrome.

The General Adaptation Syndrome

It was Dr. Hans Selye, the researcher who provided the foundation for most of the current thinking and research in the stress field, who first conceptualized the General Adaptation Syndrome, or G.A.S. (see, for example, Selye, 1976). Selye considered stress a nonspecific response to any demand made upon the organism. He labeled the three phases of this nonspecific defense reaction the *General Adaptation Syndrome*. Selye called it *general* because the consequence of stressors had effects upon several areas of the body; *adaptation* refers to its stimulation of defenses designed to help the body adjust or deal with the stressor; and *syndrome* indicates that individual pieces of the reaction occur more or less together, and in fact, are at least partially interdependent. The three distinct phases are those of alarm, resistance, and exhaustion.

The *alarm stage* is the first and perhaps most important of the three. It is during this phase that significant alterations in biochemical structure occur. When a threat or stressor is encountered, the "alarm" is sounded and the body's entire stress system is mobilized. This mobilization activates the body's energy reserves. While virtually every major organ system is involved, one of the first changes is increased pituitary secretion of adrenocorticotropic hormone, which in turn causes a step-up in corticoid secretions such as adrenalin. (It is the increase in circulating adrenalin, for example, which allows the amazing feats of strength sometimes displayed in emergency situations.) Adrenaline in turn acts upon muscle and fat tissues, causing them to release various chemicals that they store. The liver subsequently converts these chemicals into glucose, which is used directly by the heart and other organs as an energy source.

Other results of the alarm stage include increases in respiration, heart rates, and blood pressure; increases in blood cholesterol; decreases in digestive processes while blood is diverted to needed areas; activation of blood-clotting mechanisms, a safety device in case of injury; and a heightening of all senses, including pupil dilation. If the threat is extremely short-lived, the G.A.S. may not proceed beyond this stage. In fact, a person may very well be in the alarm stage of the G.A.S. and, if the threat is highly transient or of insufficient intensity, not be consciously aware of the response at all.

If the stressor is not short-lived, however, and if it can potentially be dealt with, the second or *resistance stage* is entered. During this period resistance against the stressor increases. The stage is characterized by the identification of the organ or system that is best equipped to deal with the kind of threat represented by the stressor. The changes associated with the alarm stage disappear and are replaced by changes characteristic of whatever adaptive strategy the individual adopts. While resistance to a particular stressor may be abnormally high during this phase, resistance to other, unrelated stressors may be unusually low. This is due both to the general effects of the G.A.S. and to the fact that finite resources are concentrated on one defense perimeter, leaving others exposed. Conceptually, if not physiologically, this helps explain why individuals are more illness-prone during periods of emotional strife than at other times. There may be a limited amount of adaptive energy available, and concentrating on one stressor leaves us with increased vulnerability to others.

The final stage is that of *exhaustion*. Prolonged and continual exposure to the same stressor may eventually use up the adaptive energy available, and the system fighting the stressor becomes exhausted. At this point many of the activities associated with the alarm stage return. One consequence of this stage is that the responsibility for fighting the stressor may be shifted to another system or organ in the body, and the G.A.S. cycle is repeated. Another consequence, however, is that there is no alternative system with which to defend against the stressor, and the individual dies. It should be noted that the completion of this three-phase response is not necessarily bad. As Pelletier (1977) points out, some stressors may serve to excite the organism out of an inappropriate reponse and to transfer defense responsibilty to other areas better suited to dealing with a particular stressor.

It is important to keep in mind that the activation of the G.A.S. places extraordinary demands upon the body. Clearly, the more frequently the G.A.S. is activated and the longer it remains in operation, the more wear and tear the body is subject to. Like any other machine, the body has limits beyond which it cannot continue to function. The more frequently an individual is in a fight-or-flight mode, the more susceptible that individual is to fatigue, disease, disability, aging, and death, *and,* from a management standpoint, to the performance decrements that are associated with these phenomena.

CONSEQUENCES OF STRESS

The mobilization of the body's defense mechanisms are not the only consequences of contact with a stressor. Stress effects or consequences may be many and varied. Some consequences may be primary and direct. Others—perhaps most—may be indirect and represent secondary or tertiary outcomes. Some are, beyond a reasonable doubt, stress consequences; others are simply hypothesized to be stress linked. Some may be positive, such as enhanced drive and increased self-motivation. Many are dysfunctional, disruptive, and potentially dangerous. Cox (1978) presents a taxonomy of stress consequences that includes the following:

1. *Subjective effects:* Anxiety, aggression, apathy, boredom, depression, fatigue, frustration, guilt and shame, irritability and bad temper, moodiness, low self-esteem, threat and tension, nervousness, and loneliness.

2. *Behavioral effects:* Accident proneness, drug use, emotional outbursts, excessive eating or loss of appetite, excessive drinking and smoking, excitability, impulsive behavior, impaired speech, nervous laughter, restlessness, and trembling.

3. *Cognitive effects:* Inability to make decisions and concentrate, frequent forgetfulness, hypersensitivity to criticism, and mental blocks.

4. *Physiological effects:* Increased blood and urine catecholamines and corticosteroids, increased blood glucose levels, increased heart rate and blood pressure, dryness of the mouth, sweating, dilation of the pupils, difficulty in breathing, hot and cold spells, lump in the throat, numbness and tingling in parts of the limbs.

5. *Organizational effects:* Absenteeism, poor industrial relations and poor productivity, high accident and labor turnover rates, poor organizational climate, antagonism at work, and job dissatisfaction.

Cox' list is not all-inclusive; neither does it limit itself to those consequences over which there is universal agreement. It is representative, however, of ills which are frequently associated with stress.

Similarly, it should not be presumed that stress is always—or even frequently—a precursor to these consequences. Clearly job dissatisfaction, increased blood pressure, inability to make decisions, apathy, and any of the other phenomena identified above may be totally unrelated to stress. No knowledgeable medical or behavioral scientist would claim otherwise. However, the possiblity that stress may be either a primary causitive or contributing agent to these effects cannot be ignored.

Physical health

Of all the possible consequences of stress, the physical health effects are perhaps the most challenging, controversial, and dysfunctional. Those who boldly hypothesize a link between stress and physical disease are, in effect, suggesting that an emotional response is responsible for producing a structural change in an individual. It is not our purpose to review here the medical literature dealing with this topic. Suffice it to say that virtually no one would deny a link between stress and disease.

Most current medical textbooks, in fact, attribute anywhere from 50 to 70 percent of illnesses to stress-related origins. The nature of that linkage and how much of the variance it can account for in the etiology of various diseases are the principal questions today.

In the health effects part of his taxonomy (omitted in the preceeding discussion), Cox (1978) includes asthma, amenorrhea, chest and back pains, coronary heart disease, diarrhea, faintness and dizziness, dyspepsia, frequent urination, headaches and migraines, neuroses, nightmares, insomnia, psychoses, psychosomatic disorders, diabetes mellitus, skin rash, ulcers, loss of sexual interest, and weakness. There is a great deal of overlap between this list and the so-called *disease of adaptation*.

Selye's diseases of adaptation represent the broadest, most widely used general classification of stress-induced physical health outcomes (see, for example, Selye, 1950, 1976). The conceptual basis for adaptive diseases is relatively simple. Stress responses are essentially attempts by the body to change or adapt to external environmental conditions. An effective stress response represents a successful adaptation. But the body does not always respond perfectly or appropriately. When it fails in its response, or when it adapts inappropriately, the result is a negative physical outcome or a disease of adaptation. Selye's adaptive diseases include diseases of the heart and blood vessels, kidney diseases, certain forms of arthritis, and inflammatory skin disorders. Once again it is important to note that neither Selye nor anyone else is arguing that these illnesses are exclusively, or even usually, the by-products of stress. It is interesting, however, that many of these afflictions, such as coronary heart disease, have shown an increase in incidence rates over the last few decades—increases which parallel the growing complexity and quickening pace of American life.

A variety of studies point to a correlation between stressful situations and physiological changes in the individual. These projects have ranged from massive, loosely controlled field studies to small, tightly controlled laboratory projects. Many of these deal with job or job-related factors. The work of Kiritz and Moos (1974), for example, showed that members of highly cohesive work groups who cooperate with one another while performing a difficult task produce far fewer fatty acids than groups working on difficult tasks and *not* cooperating.

Perhaps the most significant of the potential stress-physical illness relationships is that of coronary heart disease. Although virtually unknown in this country sixty years ago, cardiovascular illnesses today account for half of all deaths in the United States, including accidental ones. The disease is so pervasive that American males who are now between the ages of forty-five and fifty-five have one chance in four of dying from a heart attack in the next ten years.

Traditional risk factors such as obesity, smoking, cholesterol, and high blood pressure can account for no more than about 25 percent of the variance in the association with coronary heart disease. There is growing medical opinion that stress may be important in the remaining 75 percent (see, for example, Lehmann, 1974). Add to the coronary heart disease toll the outcome of other stress-related diseases, and a picture emerges of stress as a highly involved, potentially lethal factor in the state of this country's health. The costs in decreased industrial efficiency, lost production, and replacement expenses, not to mention human happiness, are extremely high.

Even a brief overview of health consequences of stress such as this one would be incomplete without mention of the mental health effects. In his pioneering work during the 1950s and 1960s, Kornhouser (1965) studied extensively the mental health of industrial workers in the Detroit area. What he failed to find was as interesting as what he did find. What he *did not* find was a relationship between mental health and such factors as salary, security, working conditions, and similar variables. Instead, clear associations between mental health and job satisfaction emerged. Poor mental health was associated with frustration growing out of not having a satisfying job. Numerous studies since then have lent further support to Kornhouser's earlier findings.

In addition to frustration, the anxiety and depression that may be experienced by those under a great deal of stress may manifest itself in the form of alcoholism (an estimated 15–20 percent of the adult population are problem drinkers), drug dependency (over 150 million tranquilizer prescriptions are written in this country annually), hospitalization (over 25 percent of the hospital beds are occupied by people with psychological problems), and, in extreme cases, in suicide (one of the more rapidly increasing causes of deaths in the last twenty-five years.) Even the relatively minor mental disruptions produced by stress, such as inability to concentrate, reduced attention span, and impaired decision-making abilities, may have significant organizational costs in the form of reduced efficiency and effectiveness.

STRESS AND WORK

For most employed individuals, work is far more than a mere forty-hour-a-week commitment. Even if the actual work time is forty hours, by the time work-related activities such as lunch during work, travel time, and preparation for work are added in, a minumum of ten hours a day, and more likely eleven or twelve hours are spent in job-related activities. And this represents just the forty-hour-a-week job. Many people stay longer hours at the office, take work home in the evenings, and regularly return to the office on the weekend, spending sixty to ninety hours a week on work-related activities. That may represent as much as 70 percent of nonsleep time—including weekends—being devoted to job pursuits.

Not only do we spend a great deal of time at work; many people find a substantial portion of their satisfaction and identity in their work. Consequently, their work and nonwork lives are intertwined and interdependent. The distinction between work-related stress and nonwork-related stress is, then, an artificial one at best. Sources of stress on the job spill over into a person's nonprofessional life, affecting stressors and stress there. As a consequence of stressors experienced during the working day, the manager may come home irritable, noncommunicative, or even abusive toward his or her spouse, thereby subjecting the marriage relationship to strain. This strain may be a source of subsequent stress that in turn negatively affects job performance and causes even more work-related stress.

Stressors at work can take many forms. Frew (1977) identifies eight sources of work-related stress: the unwritten psychological contract regarding the individual's expectations of what the job will provide; the stressors surrounding careers and career development; the negative impact on the family of job demands; the trauma of change, particularly as it relates to human obsolescence; organizational obsolescence; stress arising from attempts to cope with job demands; coping with expectations of superiors; and the ideology of the organization.

Our own view suggests that five major categories of stressors are relevant. One, *extraorganizational* stressors, are the events and situations outside the person's immediate work life which nonetheless influence work stressors and performance. These include disruptions such as marital problems, financial difficulties, political uncertainties, and larger quality-of-life concerns.

Four *intraorganizational* categories comprise the remaining stressor sources. Three of these—individual, group, and organizational stressors—refer to the level or initial source of the stressor. Thus, role overload may be an individual level source of stress; intragroup conflict may be a stressor at the group level; aspects of climate or the manner in which jobs are designed may be organizational level sources of potential stress. Finally, the physical environment in which work is performed may give rise to stressors such as excessive noise or insufficient lighting. The available research suggests that the four categories of intraorganizational stressors and the various extraorganizational stressors interact.

Stress at work affects performance. Potential stressors multiply as organizations grow in size and complexity, as jobs specialize more, and as human obsolescence becomes a greater threat than mechanical obsolescence. We live today in the most technologically advanced and industrialized nation in the world. Yet, in recent years our productivity per person has ranked behind those of Japan, France, Canada, West Germany, and Italy. The explanations for this phenomena are many and varied, but a growing number of investigators concludes that a partial explanation may be found in the increasingly stressful environment and in the average person's poor ability to deal with these stressors in a manner which does not cause significant disruptions to the individual's personal and organizational systems.

COSTS OF STRESS

Our overview of the nature of stress would be incomplete without mentioning the costs of the stress problem. It is virtually impossible to pinpoint stress costs. We can estimate, for example, how much alcoholism costs industry each year (approximately $20 billion), but it is much more difficult to know what portion of that cost is stress-related. Or we can estimate that $18–25 billion is lost each year due to absence, hospitalization or death of executives, but we have no accurate measures of what percentage of those costs may be the result of stress-induced or stress-aggravated illnesses. Even the United States Clearing House for Mental Health Information's recent report that U.S. industry had a $17 billion annual decrease in its productive capacity over the last few years due to stress-induced mental dysfunctions must be taken as a speculative figure.

The truth of the matter is that no one knows the dollar cost of stress. Based on a variety of estimates and projections from government, industry, and health groups, we would roughly estimate the costs of stress to be approximately $75–90 billion annually. This estimate, which approaches 10 percent of the United States gross national production, is probably a conservative one. It attempts to take into account the dollar effects of reductions in operating effectiveness resulting from stress in the form of poorer decision making and decreases in creativity. It also reflects the costs associated with mental and physical health problems arising from stress conditions, including hospital and medical costs, lost work time, premature deaths, and replacement costs.

We must also take into account costs associated with accidents, some of which are stress-related. Sabotage may result from frustration born of stress; absenteeism and turnover often reflect the stress of dissatisfaction, and a host of other variables may contribute—perhaps only indirectly—to stress costs.

Many of the greatest costs of stress in organizations today are expressed, not in terms of errors made, but of opportunities missed. Perhaps someone under too much stress didn't respond creatively or wasn't able to see the potential in a situation or decided to play it safe and stay a follower rather than risk being a leader. Costs associated with these events are literally incalculable. Who can say how much more an organization might profit with just a 3 percent increase in creativity or a 5 percent increase in the quality of decision making?

One other aspect of the costs of stress which has not been mentioned is the cost in terms of reductions in the quality of life. These clearly affect the dollar costs just cited. Aside from that, they are important considerations in their own right. The strain placed upon interpersonal relationships—particularly marriage and family relationships—is but one example. The transient nature of friendship bonds and the increasing levels of dissatisfaction with work and careers are other examples. It is, of course, impossible to place dollar figures on happiness, but if it were possible, we might find that the previously cited cost figures would seem insignificant.

There are, however, benefits, as well as costs, associated with stress. Though our primary focus will be on the negative aspects of stress and what managerial action can eliminate or minimize them, the reader should realize that stress is also a positive force in our lives. The satisfaction we feel from accomplishing a difficult goal, for example, is stress-based. That is, the behavior which led to attaining the goal consisted of one or more adaptive responses to external environmental stimuli. Without stress there would be no motivation, and probably very little creativity. In Chapter 10 we will discuss this notion of "good" stress further. In the meantime, it is important to keep in mind that stress can be beneficial and even necessary.

PLAN OF THE BOOK

In this chapter we have attempted to provide a brief overview of stress by examining its historical origins, various definitions, psychophysiological properties, and costs. Chapter 2 will build upon this introduction and present a framework, or conceptual model, for examining stress and work. The model will integrate the two major approches to studying stress—medical and behavioral. In Chapter 3 the problems involved in diagnosing or measuring stress will be presented and the current state-of-the-art in stress measurement will be discussed, once again from both the medical and behavioral perspectives.

Because mental and physical health is so important to human happiness, as well as organizational efficiency, Chapter 4 will examine the stress-disease link in some detail. The mechanisms involved in moving from a psychological event (stress) to a physiological outcome (disease or poor health) will be traced, as will the various health disturbances that may be associated with stress.

In Chapters 5, 6, and 7, the major categories of stressors developed in the model will be investigated. Chapter 5 will deal with environmental and individual level stressors; Chapter 6 with group level and organizational level stressors; and Chapter 7 with extraorganizational stressors. In Chapter 8 the critical role in the model of individual differences will be examined. A major objective of this chapter is to provide a rationale for the differences in stress responses to the same environmental stimuli by different people or by the same person at different times.

Chapter 9 reviews the critical relationship between stress and work performance and examines the role of stress in both facilitating and hindering effective performance. Chapter 10 discusses stress management, develops a rationale for the importance of stress management, and looks at individual and organizational approaches for dealing with stress. Finally, the Epilogue identifies some unresolved questions about stress and work and points to future areas for research.

Throughout the book, our underlying thesis is that if individuals and organizations increase their awareness of the stressors operating on the job *and* develop plans to deal with those stressors, not only will organizational efficiency increase, but so will the quality of life of the people in those organizations.

REFERENCES

Appley, M. H. and R. Trumbull. *Psychological Stress*. New York: Appleton-Century-Crofts, 1967.

Bernard, C. L. *Rapport sur les progrés et la marche de la physiologie générale.* Paris: Baillière, 1867.

Bruhn, J. G. and S. Wolf. *The Roseto Story: An Anatomy of Health.* Norman, Oklahoma: University of Oklahoma Press, 1979.

Cannon, W. B. "New evidence for sympathetic control of some internal secretions." *American Journal of Psychiatry* 2 (1922): 15.

Cannon, W. B. "Stresses and strains of homeostasis." *American Journal of Medical Science* 189 (1935): 1–14.

Cannon, W. B. *The Wisdom of the Body.* New York: W. W. Norton and Co., Inc., 1939.

Cox, T. *Stress.* Baltimore: University Park Press, 1978.

Engel, F. "A critique of some concepts relating to the etiopathogenesis of the disease of adaptation." Proceedings of the World Congress on Medical Psychology, Buenos Aires, 1956.

Frew, D. R. *Management of Stress.* Chicago: Nelson-Hall, Publishers, 1977.

Kiritz, S. and R. Moos. "Physiological effects of social environments." *Psychosomatic Medicine* 36 (1974): 96–114.

Kornhauser, A. *Mental Health of the Industrial Worker.* New York: John Wiley and Sons, Inc., 1965.

Lazarus, R. *Psychological Stress and the Coping Process.* New York: McGraw-Hill, Inc., 1966.

Lehmann, P. "Job stress: Hidden hazard." *Job Safety and Health* 2 (1974): 4–10.

Pelletier, K. R. *Mind as Healer, Mind as Slayer.* New York: Delacorte Press, 1977.

Selye, H. "A syndrome produced by diverse nocuous agents." *Nature* 138 (1936): 32.

Selye, H. "The general adaptation syndrome and the diseases of adaptation." *Clinical Endocrinology* 6 (1946): 117–230.

Selye, H. *Stress.* Montreal: Acta Inc., 1950.

Selye, H. *Stress Without Distress.* New York: J. B. Lippincott Company, 1974.

Selye, H. *The Stress of Life.* Second edition. New York: McGraw-Hill, Inc., 1976.

Skeat, W. W. *A Concise Etymological Dictionary of the English Language.* Oxford: Oxford Press, 1958.

Weitz, J. "Psychological research needs on the problems of human stress." In *Social and Psychological Factors in Stress.* J. E. McGrath, ed. New York: Holt, Rinehart & Winston, 1970.

FOR FURTHER READING

Albrecht, K. *Stress and the Manager.* Englewood Cliffs: Prentice-Hall, 1979.

McLean, A. *Work Stress.* Reading, Mass.: Addison-Wesley, 1979.

Weitz, J. *Social and Psychological Factors in Stress.* New York: Holt, Rinehart & Winston, 1970.

A Model for Examining Stress and Work

2

THE TWO FROGS

One hot sultry summer, the lakes and ponds being almost everywhere dried up, a couple of Frogs agreed to travel together in search of water. At last they came to a deep well, and sitting upon the brink of it, began to consult whether they should leap in or not. One of them was for it, urging that there was plenty of clear spring water, and no danger of being disturbed. Well, says the other, all this may be true, and yet I cannot come into your opinion for my life; for if the water should happen to dry there too, how should we get out again?

Managerial Application: • It is important in any endeavor to carefully and systematically weigh the consequences of any action one takes. Look before leaping is a maxim worthy of remembering in analyzing stress in organizations.

Throughout the history of medicine, health has been viewed as a condition of equilibrium and illness as the disruption of a balanced condition. The concept of a balanced state dominated Hippocratic medicine in the fifth and fourth centuries B.C. and persists today in many forms. Although the Hippocratic conceptions of balance are irrelevant to modern medical practice, the concept of bodily balance helps us understand the complicated interplay of biological and physiological mechanisms (Mechanic, 1978).

In this chapter we will discuss both the medical approach to studying how stress affects bodily balance and the behavioral approach to examining stress, and we will highlight similarities, differences, and overlap in these two approaches. Finally, an integrative model will serve as the author's framework for examining stress and work. The model will specify how variables interact with each other and the boundaries of the framework. It will integrate the medical and behavior variables relevant for managers and will draw from many stress models available in the literature that do not treat stress and work from a managerial perspective.

THE MEDICAL APPROACH TO STRESS

The traditional role of the physician is to evaluate the complaints presented by patients, to interpret the symptoms, to assess what effects these symptoms have had on the patient and may have in the future, and to manage the case so that the patient can benefit (Mechanic, 1978). The training of doctors to treat illness—biological, emotional, or toxin-induced—emphasizes diagnosis. Medical diagnosis precedes any prescription for correcting a problem or preventing some potential future episode.

Medical practitioners rely on theory and diagnosis so that the proper course of action for treating an illness is made obvious. If a scientifically derived theory of disease is confirmed, the diagnosis will provide a valid prediction of the course the disease will take. It will imply its etiology; and it will suggest the course of treatment needed.

The physician and stress

The diagnosis of stress by medical practitioners is often determined by discussions between patient and doctor. The doctor recognizes excessive stress through questioning, observing the patient's facial expressions and physical movements, and by examining the patient's current physical health. Physicians believe that the symptoms of stress occur in a wide variety of combinations. However, two distinct types have been identified—*endogenous* (which has no clear relationship to environmental stressors) and *reactive* (a response to a specific stressor or a combination of stressors). Medical practitioners watch for both of these in their interaction with patients.

Although doctors in many medical specialties treat patients with stress problems, psychiatrists and proponents of psychosomatic incidence are involved the most with stress. Stress has become generally accepted by many medical practioners, especially psychiatrists, as a link in the etiological process of mental illness. The concept of mental illness encompasses the so-called psychoneuroses, psychoses, personality disorders, psychosomatic illnesses, and acute and chronic brain disorders. The individual experiencing an episode of mental illness is classified by the doctor after observation as a "disturbed" person.

Many crucial questions remain concerning the contribution of stress to mental illness, such as when stress occurs, how much stress is needed to create a disturbance, and the nature of the stress that precipitates illness. As yet, medicine offers no clear-cut or perfect answers to the problem of stress and disturbance.

Psychosomatic medicine and stress

Psychosomatic medicine is characterized by many theories and research efforts based on different theoretical orientations (Graham, 1972). The term *psychosomatic* specifies relationships between psychological processes or behavior and somatic structures or bodily organs. Although the theories differ, they share the assumption that discomforting life events (i.e., stress) play a role in causing or contributing to illness.

Psychosomatic medicine practitioners assume that all psychological and social experience is related to a person's physiology. Although we are aware that our feelings are associated with bodily changes, it is quite another thing to demonstrate that these feelings produce bodily disequilibrium or increase susceptibility to diseases. For example, it is well recognized that for some people stress increases stomach acidity. This acid build-up in the stomach can erode its walls, producing an ulcer. However, other factors besides stress may contribute to the condition. Some people's stomach walls are susceptible to acid erosion, or a person may be physically run down and more likely to secrete stomach acid. So in psychosomatic medicine one proceeds cautiously in attributing physiological changes to psychic factors.

In the United States, interest in psychosomatic disease has occurred largely within a psychoanalytic framework. A leading proponent of this aproach was Franz Alexander (Alexander, 1950). The basic assumption of the psychoanalytic approach is that stress can manifest itself in a number of linked open systems. Stress in one system may be transferred to other systems.

Another psychosomatic approach to understanding stress, disease, and interactions is the life-situation approach, exemplified by the research and writings of Harold Wolff. Wolff reports that noxious substances applied to the body will set off offensive and defensive reaction. He has demonstrated clinically that such reactions can be generalized from physically threatening life situations to socially threatening ones. He assumes that when such conditioned responses occur frequently—in a variety of situations perceived to be socially and personally defeating—symptom formation and tissue damage can result (Wolff, 1953). Wolff believes that:

> The stress occurring from a situation is based in large part on the way the affected subject perceives it; perception depends upon a multiplicity of factors including the genetic equipment, basic individual needs and longings, earlier conditioning influences, and a host of life experiences and cultural pressures. No one of these can be singled out for exclusive emphasis (Wolff, 1953).

Although the work of Alexander and Wolff has been useful, theories of psychosomatic illness are still not well defined. The field of psychosomatic medicine continues to rely on reports of gross correlations between situations, people, and disease without the degree of specifications necessary to further research understanding.

Psychosomatic medicine is no more or less informative than other branches of medicine attempting to examine stress, illness, and disease linkages. The predominant view among medical practitioners is that stress should be examined the way other precursors of disease are. Physicians generally suggest that the study of stress needs to follow the traditional medical sequence used in diagnosis:

Specified Stress ⟶ Reaction of the Person ⟶ Structural Change (Pathology)

But the medical literature on stress contains many gaps, questions, and controversies. There is a need to integrate the medical concept of stress with other scientific approaches, so that a more precise understanding of stress may be developed.

THE BEHAVIORAL SCIENCE APPROACH TO STRESS

A *behavioral science* is defined as a body of systemized knowledge about how people behave, the relationship between human behavior and the total environment, and why people behave as they do. In essence, behavioral science is the study of how people solve problems. In the past three decades the behavioral sciences have made an evergrowing contribution to the practice of organization management. One reason has been the increased interest by management in solutions to organizational problems, which have become more confusing and demanding.

Behavioral researchers in organizations have conducted empirical studies of such topics as dyadic superior-surbordinate relationships, group behavior, motivation, leadership, intergroup conflict, communication, decision making, organizational and job design, and organizational change. More recently, stress at work has received attention from behavioral scientists. They are asked to apply their knowledge, creativity, and scientific procedures to provide management with information regarding how stress affects employee behavior, performance, and health.

Some behavioral scientists view stress in terms of its origin; others see it as an accumulative and interactive process; and others concern themselves with studying how different people respond to stress. Most behavioral examinations of stress have lacked a consistent definition of stress. Terms such as *emotional arousal, anxiety, frustration, depression, tension,* and *pressure* have been used interchangeably. This inconsistency has resulted in confusion and unnecessary delay in the practical application of research findings.

The ambiguity and confusion concerning stress suggests that additional clarification is needed among behavioral scientiests. Unfortunately, behavioral scientists are trained in many different disciplines, and this diversity does not lend itself to unified efforts to attack problems involving stress and work. Although a universally accepted definition of stress has not emerged from the behavioral sciences, there is some agreement on the variables that should be studied to understand the stress and health linkages (House, 1974). Five classes of variables are found in comprehensive reviews offered by behavioral scientists:

1. Social conditions conducive to stress;
2. Individual perceptions of stress;
3. Individual responses to stress (physiological, affective, and behavioral);
4. Lasting outcomes of perceived stress and responses to it;
5. Individual and situational moderators.

These are the classes of sociopsychological variables that behavioral scientists have attempted to measure and integrate in order to examine stress and work. Self-reports have been the most common method of collecting data. Occasionally, interviews have been used to supplement or substitute for self-reports. The behavioral scientist, like the physician, relies on diagnosis to tap the factors contributing to stress. Therefore, reliable diagnosis is as important in the behavioral sciences as in medicine.

BEHAVIORAL MEDICINE: AN INTEGRATIVE APPROACH

Behavioral medicine is a new field concerned with the development of behavioral science knowledge and techniques relevant to the understanding of physical health and illness. It is also concerned with the application of its knowledge and techniques to prevention, diagnosis, treatment, and rehabilitation (Schwartz & Weiss, 1978b). Behavioral medicine attempts to maximize communication between disciplines, biomedical scientists, physicians, and behavioral scientists. The techniques of psychology, internal medicine, physiology, cardiology, epidemiology, sociology, anthropology, and psychiatry all need to be focused on stress and work relationships. Behavioral medicine may well prove to be the key to understanding and treating stress.

Leaders in behavioral medicine believe that the following problems can be solved by joint behavioral-medical research efforts:

1. Psychosocial factors contributing to physical health and disease, including social psychology, personality, and psycho-

physiological studies investigating social, behavioral, and emotional stresses and their consequences.

2. Development of behavioral diagnostic techniques, including psychophysiological assessment procedures (e.g., in stress testing).

3. Behavioral contributions to the treatment and rehabilitation of physical disorders, including stress management (Schwartz and Weiss, 1978a).

These and other problems are important enough to society, organizations, and individuals to warrant using the combined talents and diagnostic skills of medical and behavioral scientists. So behavioral medicine does not oppose behavioral or medical approaches but attempts to integrate the two approaches.

The theory, research, and practice now available on stress and work can be brought together to provide practicing managers with guidelines for managing stress among subordinates and themselves. Currently, the theory, research findings, and practices are spread over diverse medical, behavioral, and popular press publications, thereby hampering the manager's acquisition of usable knowledge. Managers are expected to derive optimal performance from employees, despite disruptive stressors which affect subordinates. So organizations need applied models, guidelines, and techniques for managing stress and work.

Unfortunately, neither the medical approach to stress, with its disease orientation, nor the behavioral approach, which has a predominately psychiatric tone, provides a managerial overview. Jargon needs to be replaced with meaningful, work-related concepts and ideas, and a model of stress is needed that integrates the medical and behavioral approaches.

THE NEED FOR A FRAMEWORK
TO STUDY STRESS

Motivation, leadership, and organizational design theories are concerned with people, behavior, and effectiveness. The theories in these areas vary in their theoretical boundaries and how they are structured. Herzberg's two-factor theory, for example, focuses on the individual employee's intrinsic and extrinsic preferences, while project management design theories deal with structural arrangements and how individuals are affected by them. Differences in theories' perspectives arise not only from the focus, but also from the questions asked, how the questions are answered, and the backgrounds and values of the theorists.

In our work, theory functions in several ways. First, it is a way of seeing, a manner of perception. Second, it is a way of explaining observations, though it also suggests observations to the observer. Third, a theory is a method of simplifying so that managerial implications can be drawn. Fourth, theories are not always exhaustive explanations of the causes of phenomena or the relationships among them. The notion of incompleteness must be clarified so that incorrect expectations are not developed. Finally, *theory* and *model* are words we use interchangeably. A model is a formalized theory or a specific interpretation of a theory. In this book, theories and models are used to generate predictions or understanding concerning stress and work.

The goals of a stress model

Any theory of stress and work must address two goals of science: prediction and understanding. In discussing *prediction* we are concerned with the value of one or more units in the model or the state of the entire system being studied (e.g., the person, the group, the organization). The emphasis in prediction is on *outcomes*. *Understanding* emphasizes the interaction of variables in a model. How do variables interact? Why do they interact? When is the interaction most important?

Managers have not had models that predict stress and work outcomes while also improving their understanding of the phenomena involved. A working model of stress and work is needed to provide managers with some explanation of how and why someone becomes stressed and how people respond to stress. A tested and verified model could describe stress reactions, suggest prescriptive sets of actions, and predict and explain the casual linkages between variables in the model. As we have emphasized in our discussions of the medical, behavioral science, and behavioral medicine approaches to stress, there is no such tested or verified model available to managers.

The typical manager already has a set of beliefs about stress and work, and in a rather loose sense, these beliefs constitute a theory. It is likely that the manager's theory is based primarily on experience. However, even though a manager's theory of stress is probably incomplete and relies primarily on personal experience, it does influence his or her actions in managing stress. Consequently, managerial experiences need to be incorporated into a management-oriented model.

The medical approach and the behavioral approach to stress and work attempt to piece together experience, research findings, variables, and practices that are more general than individually based theories of stress and work. Thus, no model of stress will parallel exactly the experience of a single manager, nor can it be accepted as the final model. The goals of an integrative stress model that we have adopted are these:

1. The model should improve managerial understanding of stress and work relationships.

2. The model should use terminology and concepts that make sense from a managerial perspective.

3. The model should appeal to managers in general and not a specific or a small group of managers.

4. The model should *not* be viewed as the complete or final solution to issues concerning stress and work.

5. The model should integrate medical and behavioral science variables that are relevant to managers.

6. The model should suggest courses of action that managers can take to counter stress in subordinates and in themselves.

7. The model should offer suggestions for testing and research on stress and work variables.

8. The model should incorporate individual, group, and organizational as well as extraorganizational variables that are potentially related to organizational outcome variables.

These goals serve as the basis for reviewing current models in the stress and work literature, critiquing the models, and developing a model that fits into the behavioral medicine approach. The goals are organized concisely in Table 2–1. We concluded after reviewing the literature that there were no stress and work models available that integrate the medical and behavioral approaches and provide managers with usable principles and guidelines.

EXISTING MODELS OF STRESS

There are numerous medical and behavioral models that attempt to explain stress. A number of the available models were formulated by

TABLE 2–1   Goals of Stress and Work Model

Goals	Reason for Goal
Improve managerial understanding	Managers need to work with employees who are stressed and achieve performance goals acceptable to their superiors.
Use understandable terminology and concepts	So that a common and unambiguous dialogue can occur between those studying, working with, and researching stress and work.
Appeal to managers in general	General appeal will help all managers not just a select group. It will also help promote the notion of managing stress in organizations.
Should be viewed as one way of looking at stress and work and not the final answer	Final answers in the field of organizational behavior and management are viewed suspiciously. There are so many factors and individual differences to consider that final answers are not feasible.
Integrate medical and behavioral variables	Stress and disease, and stress and behavior are both important to managers. Medical and behavioral researchers study variables that should be considered.
Suggest courses of action to managers	The manager must create conditions or alter conditions so that stress doesn't totally incapacitate subordinates. Action is needed once stress problems are identified.
Suggest testing and research	Theory must be tested before it can have wide acceptability. Thus, testable propositions and actual research are needed to verify and to accomplish the reliable diagnosis needed by managers.
Incorporate individual, group, and organizational variables	Individual, group, and organizational variables all affect stress and work. Each level needs to be included in a model attempting to present a realistic picture of stress and work.

researchers, who used them to guide their own studies on stress. The models reviewed here were selected as representative and also as understandable frameworks to be used in our own development of an integrative stress model. Each of the models has provided valuable insight into stress and stress research.

A biochemical model

Dr. Hans Selye developed a biochemical model of stress. The general features of the model were covered in Chapter 1. Briefly, this model is concerned with the analysis of stress at the physiological and biochemical levels. Selye defines stress as "a state manifested by a specific syndrome which consists of all of the nonspecifically induced changes within a biological system" (Selye, 1956). A nonspecifically induced change is one that affects all, or most parts of a system. Recall that Selye describes these nonspecifically induced changes in terms of the General Adaptation Syndrome—alarm, resistance, exhaustion.

Selye's research on stress is outstanding and comprehensive. Unfortunately, managers would be unfamiliar with his medical vocabulary, and he does not discuss group or organizational variables in the model.

A psychosomatic model

The psychomatic model has been alluded to earlier. It is based on the premise that the tensions and strains in one system of the body have pathological consequences for other bodily systems. For example, a manager who is anxious and fearful about receiving a year-end performance evaluation may experience significant physiological changes during the waiting period—say a week—before the actual session. These internal changes may cause significant alterations in the organic processes of the body: blood vessel and digestive tract constriction, an increase of red blood corpuscles into the body's circulatory system, an increase in the flow of epinephrine (adrenaline), and an increase in the sugar content of the blood. The psychosomatic model attempts to track how these and other physiological reactions are set in motion by psychological processes. It also attempts to determine which physiological reactions and psychological processes are linked.

Dunbar, Alexander, and Grinker did not apply their psychosomatic model to stress and work. Nor did they present their findings in a manner from which managers could benefit. In short, the psychosomatic model is not a framework from which managerial courses of action emerge (Lachman, 1972).

The combat model

Basowitz and his associates developed a model of stress based upon a study of soldiers in combat (Basowitz, Persky, Korchin, and Grinker, 1955). They defined *anxiety* as a conscious and reportable experience of intense dread. These feelings typically arise when the integrity of the organism is being threatened. In theory, any stimulus is viewed as a potential threat to the organism and could produce anxiety.

In the combat model, stimuli are placed along a continuum. At one end are stimuli that have meaning only for a single individual or a few people. At the other end of the continuum are stimuli that, because of their intensity and explicit threat to vital functions, are likely to overload the capacity of most people to cope. Basowitz uses this idea to designate as stressful certain kinds of combat stimuli, without regard to response. Such stimuli are assumed to be stressful, even though the researchers recognize that they may provoke differing individual responses. This model has been used to explain the responses of groups of combat soldiers who are simultaneously subjected to conditions of extreme duress.

The Basowitz model implicitly assumes that what is stressful for one person must be stressful for another; it fails to recognize individual differences. Furthermore, it has little relevance for managers. Organizational dimensions that managers have to cope with are not mentioned or developed in the combat model.

The adaptation model

Mechanic formulated a model of stress response among graduate students involved in Ph.D. preliminary examinations (Mechanic, 1962). In his model, stress is designated as the discomforting responses of persons in particular situations. Mechanic proposed that whether or not a situation is stressful depends upon four factors: the ability and capacity of a person, skills and limitations produced by group practices and traditions, the means provided to individuals by the social environment, and the names that define where and how an individual may utilize these means.

The adaptation model shows that when people feel unprepared to meet a situation they experience intense discomfort. Such feelings may result from a lack of appropriate knowledge and skills, the uncertainty of the situation, or particular personal traits such as low self-confidence. In general, persons who have strong skills and preparation are more likely to feel and act confident than those who do not.

The adaptation model does not specifically deal with organizational or work situations. The preparation of students for comprehensive examinations is somewhat different from that of employees preparing a sales presentation, a budget, or a human resource staffing plan for an executive committee. In addition, Mechanic ignores how people perceive the situation. Perception of stimuli and situations is an important facet when studying stress and work relationships.

The disaster model

Janis has proposed an explanatory model of stress that examines psychological responses of individuals to traumatic events (Janis, 1954). The variables and relationships presented in the model are based on Janis' research of victims of air-raid attacks during wartime and patients before undergoing major surgical operations. Janis' disaster model consists of three main segments— the disaster event, the psychological responses of individuals to the disaster, and the intrapsychic and situational determinants of these responses.

Exactly how a person responds to the disaster event depends upon such factors as previously formed expectations concerning the ways in which danger situations can be avoided, the amount of prior training a person has in relevant protective strategies and tactics dealing with the danger, chronic levels of anxiety and the strength of the person's dependency needs, and the person's perception of his or her role in the situation.

The Janis model deals exclusively with events of an extreme traumatic nature. Most work-related events do not cause this level of trauma. The Janis model offers managers no specific hints for dealing with organizational or job-type stress among subordinates.

The occupational model

A model that attempts to integrate the existing data on the relationship of occupational stress to heart disease is proposed by House (1974). He uses existing research findings on the role of social and psychological factors in the etiology of chronic diseases, especially heart disease. Figure 2–1 presents the House model. The solid lines indicate presumed causal relationships among variables. Dotted arrows from the

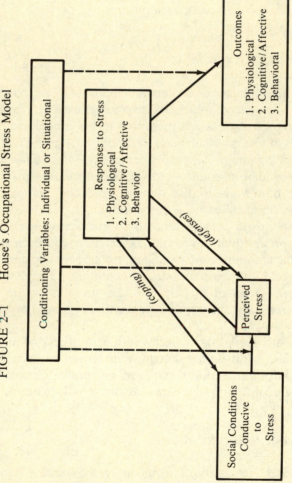

FIGURE 2-1   House's Occupational Stress Model

box labeled "conditioning variables" intersect solid arrows, indicating an interaction between the conditioning variables and the variables in the box at the beginning of the solid arrow in predicting variables in the box at the head of the solid arrow.

House's model indicates that the experience of stress is a subjective response resulting from the interaction of social conditions and particular personal characteristics (e.g., abilities, needs, and values). Characteristics of social situations (such as harmonious working relationships versus high-conflict relationships with co-workers) may also condition the degree to which a potentially stressful situation actually results in perceived stress. In short, the model proposes that the relationship between social conditions and outcomes like heart disease is mediated through the individual's perception of the situation, and that the perceived meaning of objective conditions depends on both the nature of the person and the nature of the social situation.

The model also implies that a number of individuals who experience the same degree of subjective stress will seldom all manifest the same type of outcomes such as coronary heart disease. How the individuals adapt to the situation is the crucial point. Responses to perceived stress may be physiological, psychological (cognitive/affective), and/or behavioral.

House offers his model as a heuristic device for clarifying and integrating existing research and suggesting new areas for further research. The model does not present specific organizational variables. It is more general than job specific and does not offer managers guidelines for understanding stress and work relationships. It is a model, however, that attempts to illustrate how occupational stress plays a significant role in the etiology of coronary heart disease and, probably, other chronic diseases as well.

Social environment model

A series of studies at the Institute for Social Research of the University of Michigan has resulted in a social environment model of stress. The model provides a framework for research on the effects of work role on health and has served as a basis for continuing studies of stress and work (French and Kahn, 1962).

Figure 2–2 presents the social environment model. The figure specifies six sets of variables. The categories of relationships and hypotheses are represented by arrows, which also indicate the directions of causality.

FIGURE 2–2   Social Environment Stress Model

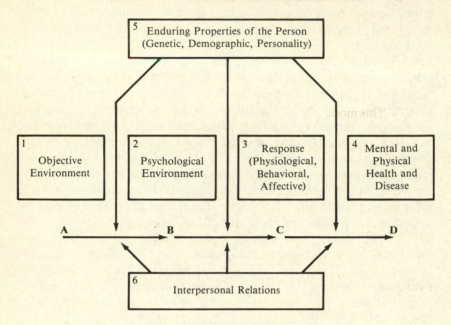

Hypotheses of the A → B category have to do with the effects of the objective environment on the psychological environment (as the individual experiences it). For example, some employees who have to work on project teams and report to more than one superior (a fact in the objective environment) often report that they are confused by their relationships with superiors (a fact in their psychological environment).

The B → C category relates facts in the psychological environment to the immediate responses in a person. For example, the perception that one is confused with superior relationships often results in increased tension about the job. The C → D category relates the effect of such responses about the job to criteria of health and illness. The relationship between job tension and coronary heart disease is an example of the C → D category.

The three categories of hypotheses must be qualified by moderating variables, represented by the vertical arrows in Figure 2–2. These hypotheses show that relationships between objective and physical environments, between psychological environments and responses, and between responses and criteria of health are moderated by enduring individual characteristics and by interpersonal relations. For example, the extent to which an employee experiences job tension because of confusion in his or her relationship with a superior depends upon the person's personality, goals, previous experiences with the superiors, and other individual and interpersonal characteristics.

The environment model attempts to develop a comprehensive theory of mental health. The model is used to sequence research projects, beginning with efforts to understand the objective work environment and ending with studies of health and disease.

This model is substantially more relevant for practicing managers than any of those already discussed. It attempts to integrate medical and behavioral approaches to study stress and work, and in testing the model, different occupational groups are used in field settings. Unfortunately, its developers pay little attention to how extraorganizational variables such as family conditions, the individual's financial situation, and the general economy affect the relationships displayed in the four hypothesis categories. We contend that separating the work role and the external organizational role is unrealistic. An employee's work role is affected significantly by his or her extraorganizational roles and vice versa.

Another factor of importance to managers that is not highlighted in the social environment model is performance. Concern for performance is implied when individual responses are being considered, but more emphasis seems warranted in light of the importance of the job performance of subordinates.

The process model

McGrath has proposed a process-oriented model of stress (McGrath, 1976). He views a *stress situation* as a four-stage, closed-loop cycle. It begins with conditions or circumstances in the sociophysical environment. If the situation is perceived by the person as leading to some undesirable state if left unmodified, then it becomes a stressful situation. The person then chooses some response alternative with the intention of changing the situation (making it less stressful).

Figure 2–3 presents the process model of stress. The four stages in the model (A, B, C, and D) are connected by four linking processes. The first stage linking A and B is called the *cognitive appraisal process*. In it, a person appraises a situation (accurately or inaccurately). The second process link, B and C, involves *decision making*. It involves relating the perceived situation to the available alternatives and choosing a response or set of responses to deal with the undesirable features of the situation. The third link is the *performance process,* which results in a set of behaviors that can be evaluated in terms of quality and quantity. The

FIGURE 2–3   The Process Stress Model

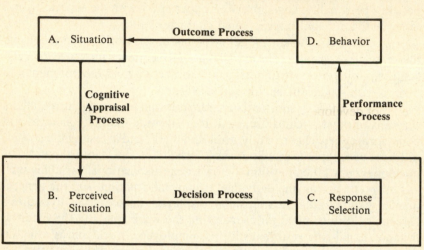

fourth link is between behavior and situation and is called the *outcome* process. The extent to which a chosen response results in desired behavior depends on the performer's ability to execute and the extent to which the behavior results in desired (or undesired) changes in the situation. This, in turn, depends on the level of performance as well as the performance of others working with the person (teammates) and the performance of others working against the person (opponents).

McGrath is concerned primarily with the performance of tasks in the organizational context. He makes no attempt to integrate medical and behavioral variables. Furthermore, the model emphasizes the individual and does not incorporate group factors that influence the various processes displayed in Figure 2–3.

AN OVERALL CRITIQUE OF SOME EXISTING STRESS MODELS

Each of the models described has made a significant contribution to improving the theory and research on stress and their practical application. These models have enabled theorists to examine relationships more thoroughly and have guided researchers in testing important hypotheses. Without these models it would have been more difficult to approach stress and work as we have in this book. Many of these approaches have provided building blocks for our own integrative medical-behavioral model of stress and work.

The purpose of this section is to analyze the existing models in light of the eight goals for a stress and work model presented earlier in Table 2–1. These goals pay particular attention to providing managers with practical ideas and guidelines for understanding and coping with stress and work. It is important to recognize that most of these models were not developed for managers. Thus, the limitations of these models are primarily created by the managerial perspective we elect to adopt.

One of the major factors that inhibits the use of existing models is the difference in approaches used to define stress. Different referents of the stress concept can be found across the models. Mechanic defines stress in terms of responses that individuals make to situations. Basowitz defines it as a quality of a situation that is independent of the reaction of individuals to stress. Selye defines stress as an intervening state which is the internal reaction to stressors or noxious stimuli. None of these interpretations specifically address stress and work relationships as encountered by managers.

Only the occupational, social environment, and process models use terminology and concepts with which managers are familiar. Selye's model incorporates many medical terms unfamiliar to managers, while the psychosomatic model uses terms familiar to a psychiatrist, but unfamiliar to most managers. Because of terminology and concept clarity problems, the appeal to managers of most of the models would be moderate to low. An important criterion used by managers in adopting or reviewing any model is whether it has practical application value. This type of value is enhanced if the model is couched in familiar terms.

Another limitation of most of the existing models is that they fail to integrate the medical and behavioral science variables that have organizational applications. In fact, most models do not attempt to integrate medical and behavioral variables at all. Although some integration is attempted in the psychosomatic model, it is done without focusing on work behavior and outcomes. On the other hand, McGrath's process model is work oriented, but it fails to incorporate health or medical variables. Janis' model has little relevance to managers because it is concerned with extremely traumatic wartime and surgical events. Since most of the models do not integrate medical and behavioral variables that are relevant, they fail to suggest courses of action for managers dealing with stress in subordinates and in themselves. Only the process and social environment models offer some implicit suggestions to managers.

Table 2–2 presents a summary of how each of the existing models meets the goals we established for our model of stress and work. The table illustrates that some of the models do not offer managers what they require to explain and cope with stress and work. The social environment model comes closest to meeting our requirements for a useful model. However, even this excellent model fails to suggest managerial courses of action, and it also fails to incorporate extraorganizational variables, which we believe should not be excluded from discussions of stress and work.

AN INTEGRATION MODEL OF STRESS AND WORK

We have attempted to develop an integrative model that incorporates features of the medical, behavioral, and behavioral medicine approaches to stress, as well as various features of other existing models. In developing the model a managerial perspective served as the cornerstone. Included as *units* (parts) of the integrative model were: the antecedents to the stress situation, which are referred to as *stressors* (each of these stressors were work related to employees in general, managerial and nonmanagerial), an interpretation or assessment of the extent to which the presence of antecedent conditions result in stress to individuals (perceived stress), the effects or responses to the operation of stressors (outcomes), and the results of those outcomes (consequences). The model also incorporates moderator variables that affect the relationships between stressors, perceptions, outcomes, and consequences.

Figure 2–4 presents the integrative model and displays the nature and direction of various relationships between the units. For illustrative purposes, examples of variables are provided within each unit. The variables presented should not be construed as exhausting the examples that could be included in such a model. They represent variables which have emerged from the theoretical and empirical bases.

As shown in Figure 2–4 each unit is divided into a number of levels designed to facilitate organizational research and reflect intuitively and/or empirically attractive divisions. The rationale for the intraorganizational division of stressors into individual, group, organizational, and physical levels is that although no level is more important than another, each warrants special attention. Likewise, with respect to perceived

TABLE 2–2   Comparison of Existing Models on Goals for Stress and Work Model

Goals of A Stress and Work Model	Selye Biochemical Model	Psycho-somatic Model	Basowitz: Combat Model	Mechanic: Adaptation Model	Janis: Disaster Model	House: Occupational Model	Social Environment Model	McGrath: Process Model
Improves Managerial Understanding of Stress and Work Relationships	No	No	No	Some	No	Some	Yes	Some
Uses Terminology and Concepts Managers Can Easily Understand	No	No	No	Some	No	Some	Yes	Yes
Appeals to Managers in General	No	No	No	Some	No	Some	Yes	Yes
Model is Viewed As Complete	Yes	Yes	No	No	No	No	No	No
Model Integrates Medical and Behavioral Science Variables That Are Relevant and Meaningful to Managers	No	No	No	No	No	Some	Yes	No
Model Suggests Course of Action to Managers	No	No	No	No	No	No	Some	Some
Model Offers Suggestions for Testing and Research on Stress and Work Variables	No	No	No	Some	No	Some	Yes	Some
Model Incorporates Individual, Group, Organizational, and Extraorganizational Variables	No	No	No	No	No	No	No	No

No designates that the model does not generally accomplish the goal; *Some* designates that to some extent the model does accomplish the goal; *Yes* designates that the model generally does accomplish the goal.

FIGURE 2–4   A Model for Organizational Stress Research

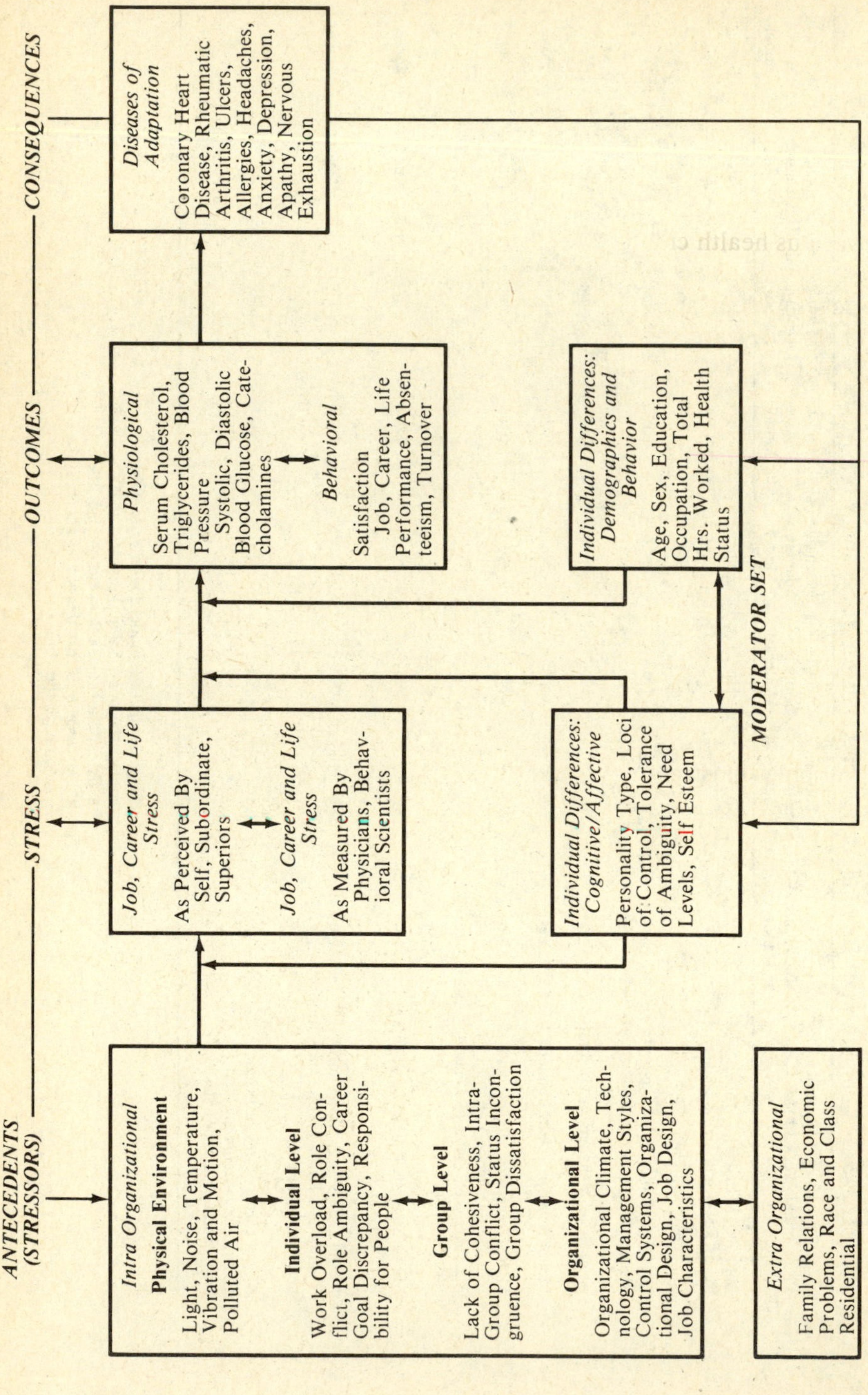

ANTECEDENTS (STRESSORS)

STRESS

OUTCOMES

CONSEQUENCES

Intra Organizational
Physical Environment
Light, Noise, Temperature, Vibration and Motion, Polluted Air

Individual Level
Work Overload, Role Conflict, Role Ambiguity, Career Goal Discrepancy, Responsibility for People

Group Level
Lack of Cohesiveness, Intra-Group Conflict, Status Incongruence, Group Dissatisfaction

Organizational Level
Organizational Climate, Technology, Management Styles, Control Systems, Organizational Design, Job Design, Job Characteristics

Extra Organizational
Family Relations, Economic Problems, Race and Class Residential

Job, Career and Life Stress
As Perceived By Self, Subordinate, Superiors

Job, Career and Life Stress
As Measured By Physicians, Behavioral Scientists

Individual Differences: Cognitive/Affective
Personality Type, Loci of Control, Tolerance of Ambiguity, Need Levels, Self Esteem

Physiological
Serum Cholesterol, Triglycerides, Blood Pressure Systolic, Diastolic Blood Glucose, Catecholamines

Behavioral
Satisfaction Job, Career, Life Performance, Absenteeism, Turnover

Individual Differences: Demographics and Behavior
Age, Sex, Education, Occupation, Total Hrs. Worked, Health Status

MODERATOR SET

Diseases of Adaptation
Coronary Heart Disease, Rheumatic Arthritis, Ulcers, Allergies, Headaches, Anxiety, Depression, Apathy, Nervous Exhaustion

stress, extraorganizational life stress interacts with organizationally related job and career stress.

The model distinguishes between physiological and behavioral outcomes. The relationship between the physiological outcomes and a disease such as coronary heart disease has been established in the medical literature. However, the relationships between the behavioral and physiological outcomes and between the behavioral outcomes and various health criteria are less clear. These two sets of relationships are extremely important to managers, since they can influence the development and maintenance of organizational conditions (e.g., job design, reward systems, leadership style) which minimize dysfunctional stressors.

Finally, the model introduces individual differences by providing for cognitive/affective and demographic/behavioral differences which may moderate various relationships in the model. There is a gap in both the medical and behavioral research of how important individual differences are in understanding stress and work and health relationships. Consequently, the moderators represented in Figure 2–4 are tentative and should be viewed as representative of the possible range of moderators in the two moderator categories.

Before discussing each of the units in the model in greater detail, some caveats are in order. To begin with, this model is not final, and programmatic research projects are being conducted to verify the units and relationships specified in Figure 2–4. Furthermore, the specific variables illustrated are neither exhaustive nor unquestionably appropriate; they are used to capture the managerial perspective we wanted to illustrate. The model is not intended to imply that the outcomes and health criteria are the only ones of interest to management. Finally, the importance and difficulty of accurately measuring the variables displayed in each of the units should be made clear. The measurement of all of the variables shown is important because management will depend on such measures to develop appropriate courses of action.

Stress and disease

As stated in Chapter 1, many medical researchers propose that the chemical stress reaction within the human body contributes to most health breakdowns and that it is linked to many other disorders. The list of diseases claimed to be linked to stress or aggravated by it has been referred to as "Who's Who in American Disease" (Albrecht, 1979).

However, the nature and extent of the relationship between stress and such diseases as peptic ulcers, hypertension, coronary heart disease, and cancer is not well understood. The extent to which organizational stressors contribute to the etiology of the diseases shown in Figure 2–4 is a question that requires further investigation.

Perceived stress

There is a significant difference, frequently overlooked in the existing models just discussed, between *stress* and *stressor*. The antecedent stressor is a necessary prerequisite to the experience of stress. Stress, however, does not necessarily follow from a stressor. The greater part of stress research in the medical and behavioral literature has attempted to link stressors with outcomes. However, whether or not an antecedent stressor is stress-provoking depends in large measure upon the perception of the individual exposed to it. As Figure 2–4 shows, perception is influenced by various individual difference moderators.

Managerial understanding of individual differences is important. For example, one subordinate may view a stressor or set of stressors as a challenging opportunity to display skills in coping with them; another may perceive the same stressor variables as threatening or irritating. These different perceptual conclusions may explain why attempts to link stressors directly to outcomes have produced contradictory results.

A consideration of the source of the perceptions within the various categories and levels of perceived stress is important in the model. Clearly, the individual is the most direct and knowledgeable source of information of the extent to which stressors result in perceptions of stress. However, the individual is not the only source of such perceptions. Just as second parties are frequently better observers of our behavior than we are, it may also be true that others' perceptions of the degree of stress we are undergoing represent valid data in assessing total stress. The manager who is able to identify behavioral and job performance changes in a subordinate and correctly associate such changes with particular stressors, even when the person is consciously unaware of these changes, demonstrates the value of second-party assessment.

Stressors and outcomes

From a managerial perspective, any aspect of organizational functioning linked to negative behavioral outcomes is undesirable. When absenteeism and turnover are high, performance is lagging, and worker satisfaction is low, the attendant organizational dysfunctions provide serious consequences for managers. These dysfunctions are often interpreted as a result of poor management. In some cases the performance problem may be caused largely by extraorganizational stressors such as marital conflict or financial difficulties. Figure 2–4 hypothesizes the important relationship between intra- and extraorganizational stressors. Except for researchers using the social environment stress model, few investigators have examined the type of intra- and extraorganizational stressor-outcome variables shown in the integrative model.

Relationships between stressors and physiological outcomes are important for a number of reasons. Most significant are the implications for the individual's general health. The work time lost, the dollars involved, humanitarian feelings about the health of others, and the epidemic proportions of some diseases create sufficient reasons to study stressor-outcome relationships. However, organizational behavior and management researchers lag far behind their medical counterparts in developing strategies to understand and deal with these relationships.

Individual differences

Two different sets of individual differences are hypothesized to moderate the relationships in Figure 2–4: cognitive/affective and demographic/behavioral. Behavioral scientists have maintained that individual personality differences explain some of the variance observed in employee behavior. Medical researchers also emphasize the importance of individual differences, especially in their studies of the etiology of heart disease. Thus, some of the more researched and publicized cognitive/affective individual differences are recommended for further testing in our integrated model.

Demographic and behavior variables were included because of the findings of researchers focusing on coronary heart disease. Many demographic variables have been implicated in heart disease, such as heredity, sex, and family medical history. The role these and other demographic individual differences play in stress and work is important enough to be examined further.

Propositions based on the integrative model

As already stated, the value of a model lies in the ability to predict and *understand*. Current research and models in the stress and work area do not permit precise predictions. A more attainable goal appears to be improved understanding among managers concerned about the type of variables shown in Figure 2–4. This understanding can begin by examining propositions that could be refined into hypotheses as quality research accumulates on stress and work variables. The following hypotheses appear to be the prime candidates for testing so that the integrative model can eventually become more predictive in organizational settings:

1. Stressors at the individual, group, organizational, and physical levels play a significant role in the outset of various diseases for some individuals and not others.

2. Emotional, physiological, and behavioral responses viewed as indicators of job, career, and life stress are significantly influenced by the person's perception of the stressor(s).

3. The same antecedent stressors may result in increased levels of stress in some individuals, have little or no effect on stress levels in others, and serve to reduce levels of perceived stress on still others.

4. Stressors are related to physiologic factors and behavioral outcomes.

5. Physiological factors or conditions can be improved (from a medical perspective) by decreasing the number and intensity of stressors that are perceived as dysfunctional or excessive by an individual.

6. Individuals differ in their susceptibility to stress and consequently to health breakdowns as a function of differences in personality facets.

7. Some individuals are capable of responding positively to job, career, and life stresses at different points of time and cannot respond positively to stress conditions at other points of time as a function of personality and/or demographic variables. This ability can be developed into a predictive stress vulnerability index.

8. Some physiological variables (e.g., high serum cholesterol, imbalanced catecholamines) will be negatively associated with job satisfaction and performance.

9. After programmatic testing and use of rigorous research designs, causal inferences will be made that behavioral variables "cause" the alteration in physiological variables.

10. Life, career, and job dissatisfaction and low levels of job performance will be associated with higher incidence of health breakdowns.

These ten propositions and others to be developed from the integrative model need to be tested using rigorous research designs. The testing will require the joint efforts of medical and behavioral researchers under the guidance of researchers using the behavioral medicine approach. Whichever approach is used, there must be a primary concern with the managerial use of the findings. The integrative model with its managerial perspective offers the orientation needed by managers to perform their jobs more effectively and to cope with stress and work in a dynamic and proactive manner.

REFERENCES

Alexander, F. *Psychosomatic Medicine, Its Principles and Application.* New York: W. W. Norton and Co., Inc., 1950.

Albrecht, K. *Stress and the Manager.* Englewood Cliffs, N.J.: Prentice-Hall, Inc., 1979.

Basowitz, H., Persky, H., Korchin, S.J., and R.R. Grinker. *Anxiety and Stress.* New York: McGraw-Hill, Inc., 1955.

French, J.R.P., Jr. and R.L. Kahn. "A programmatic approach to studying the industrial environment and mental health." *Journal of Social Issues* 18 (1962): 1–47.

Graham, D.T. "Psychosomatic medicine." In *Psycho-physiology.* N.S. Greenfield and R.A. Steinbach, eds. New York: Holt, Rinehart, & Winston, Inc., 1972, 839–924.

House, J.S. "Occupational stress and coronary heart disease. A review and Theoretical Integration." *Journal of Health and Social Behavior* 15 (1974): 12–27.

Janis, I. "Problems of theory in the analysis of stress behavior." *Journal of Social Issues* 10 (1954): 12–25.

Lachman, S. *Psychosomatic Disorders: A Behavioral Interpretation.* New York: John Wiley and Sons, Inc., 1972.

McGrath, J.E. "Stress and behavior in organizations." In *Handbook of Industrial and Organizational Psychology.* M.D. Dunnette, ed. Chicago: Rand McNally and Company, 1976, 1351–1395.

Mechanic, D. *Students Under Stress.* Glencoe, Ill.: The Free Press, 1962.

Mechanic, D. *Medical Sociology.* New York: The Free Press, 1978.

Schwartz, G.E. and S.M. Weiss. "Yale conference on behavioral medicine: A proposed definition and statement of goals." *Journal of Behavioral Medicine* 1 (1978a): 3–12.

Schwartz, G.E. and S.M. Weiss. "Proceedings of the Yale conference on behavioral medicine." DHEW Publication No. (N1H) 1978b, 78–1424, Government Printing Office, Washington, D.C.

Selye, H. *The Stress of Life*. New York: McGraw-Hill, Inc., 1956.

Wolff, H.G. *Stress and Disease*. Springfield, Ill.: Charles C Thomas, Publisher, 1953.

FOR FURTHER READING

Appley, M.H.E. and R. Trumbull. *Psychological Stress*. New York: Appleton-Century-Crofts, 1967.

McQuade, W. and A. Ackman. *Stress*. New York: E.P. Dutton and Co., Inc., 1974.

Scott, R. and A. Howard. "Models of stress." In *Social Stress*. S. Levine and N.A. Scotch, eds. Chicago: Aldine Publishing Co., 1970, 259–278.

Selye, H. "Confusion and controversy in the stress field." *Journal of Human Stress* 1 (1975): 37–44.

The Measurement of Stress: Medical and Behavioral Perspectives

THE EAGLE AND THE CROW

An Eagle flew down from the top of a high rock, and making a stoop at a Lamb, seized it with her strong talons, and bore aloft her bleating prize to her young. A Crow, observing what passed, was ambitious of performing the same exploit and darted down upon a Ram; but instead of being able to carry it up into the air, she found she had got her claws entangled in its fleece, and could neither move herself nor her fancied prize. Thus fixed, she was soon taken by the Shepherd, and given away to some boys, who eagerly enquired what bird it was? An hour ago, said he, she fancied herself an Eagle; however I suppose she is by this time convinced that she is but a Crow.

Managerial Application • It is impossible for any person to truly measure the stress being experienced by someone else. Inaccurate measures can sometimes be dangerous and result in problems.

Measurement is an important concern in understanding the affects of stress on all aspects of a person's life. It can be argued persuasively that obtaining adequate measures of the variables presented in the integrative model shown as Figure 2–4 is the major problem in studying stress and work. Theories in medicine, the behavioral sciences, and behavioral medicine contain variables that either cannot be measured at all or can be measured only approximately, for example, motivation and creativity. So managers should not expect perfect measures of stress, since such data are unavailable. This chapter will first discuss measurement from a medical and behavioral science point of view. Then some specific measurement characteristics, procedures, and methods will be discussed. It will become apparent that the measurement of stress among individuals is still rather crude due to the complexity of people and the lack of a generally accepted conceptual basis. Measuring stress involves a wide range of procedures ranging from self-report scales to the use of catheters to draw blood samples for analyses of hormone secretions.

MEASUREMENT IN SCIENCE

Measurement is an important issue in all science, not just medicine or the behavioral sciences. Scientifically grounded theories predict relationships between measured variables, for example, between the temperature in a blast furnace and the quality of iron ingots formed, or between blood pressure and heart rate. The variables we are concerned about in our integrated model of stress must be measured validly before relations between them can be studied and before management strategies of coping with stress can be developed.

There have been tomes written on the nature of measurement in science. The generally accepted definition is that *measurement* consists of rules for assigning numbers to objects in such a way as to represent quantities of attributes. The term *rules* indicates that the procedures for assigning numbers must be explicitly formulated. In some cases the rules of measurement are obvious. This is the case when using a yardstick to measure the size of a room. What should be done to measure the length and width of the room is obvious, and consequently it is not necessary to study a set of procedural manuals to perform the measurement. But obvious measurements are quite rare in any science. For example, measuring a person's blood chemistry, e.g., glucose p̄ cho, albumin, uric acid, and so forth is a mystery to most people. In the same way the rules for measuring the stress response of employees are at the present time not intuitively obvious.

In science the term *standardization of measures* is often used. Essentially, a measure is said to be standardized if different people employ the measure and obtain similar results. Thus, a measure of job stress is well standardized if different researchers who employ the measure obtain similar numerical results for job stress. Similarly, a test of blood pressure is well standardized if different examiners find the same blood pressure readings.

In the definition of measurement, the term *attributes* indicates that measurement is concerned with some features of objects (Nunnally, 1970). In essence, one does not measure objects—one measures an object's attributes. Thus, one does not measure a person, but rather the performance or the skills of the person. Nunnally (1970) points out that although the object-attribute distinction sounds like hairsplitting, it is important. First, it emphasizes that measurement involves making abstractions. An attribute concerns relations between objects on a particular dimension. A chestnut and a gray race horse may weigh the same, and two gray race horses may have different weights. The attribute *weight* is an abstraction that must not be confounded with all the particular features of a horse, e.g., color, weight, or times during practice runs.

A second reason for pointing out that measurement always concerns a particular attribute is that it forces us to examine the nature of the attribute before it is measured. In some instances the attribute may not exist. For example, the mixed results obtained in numerous efforts to measure an attribute called task-goal specificity make it doubtful that there is such an attribute in goal-setting programs. It may be that a measure of task-goal specificity may involve a mixture of attributes rather than only one attribute.

In our definition of measurement we emphasized that numbers represent quantities. Quantification concerns *how much* of an attribute is present in an object; numbers are used to communicate the amount. *Quantification* is a term often used interchangeably with *measurement*.

Measurement is closely related to counting. What one does in any measurement is count similar units. Height is measured by counting equal units of extension (centimeters, meters, inches, feet, or yards). Body temperature is measured by counting equal units in the form of degrees. The amount of liquid consumed on a hot summer day can be determined by counting the number of ounces or liters.

Our definition emphasizes that *rules* for quantification are important. In establishing rules, the crucial consideration is that they be unambiguous. The rules may be developed from previous experience, common sense, guesses, or a sound conceptual model. However, the proof of measurement in science lies in how well the measure serves to explain important phenomena. Consequently, any set of rules that unambiguously quantifies properties of objects constitutes a measure and has a right to compete with other measures for scientific and practical usefulness (Nunnally, 1970).

THE ADVANTAGES OF MEASUREMENT

Most people respect scientific measurement. Placing men on the moon, improved delivery of medical care, economic growth, and educational enhancement have been significantly affected by the use of measurements. If scientific measurements were not available, the world would certainly be poorer, and hunches, intuitive opinions, and subjective appraisals would be the rule. The advantages associated with scientific measurement would be lost in a sea of guesswork and hopes.

Communication

Communication among researchers is essential. Each researcher builds on what has been learned in the past, and through communication the comparison of findings, models, and propositions can be invaluable in advancing knowledge. The communication between researchers can be enhanced if standardized measures are used. Suppose, for example, that in a training program experiment the effects of instruction on performing a task are being analyzed. It is assumed by the researcher that a particular mode of instruction would make the participants perform better. Exactly what "perform better" means must be clarified for other researchers. If a standardized measure of performance on the task were available, scientists could formulate and share more precise findings. If the means and standard deviations of scores for the different groups of participants (and nonparticipants) were reported, for example, detailed communication with others about the study would be possible.

Objectivity improvement

Another advantage of measurement is that it reduces the need to guess when observing a phenomenon. An important feature of science is that any statement made by one scientist should be independently verifiable by other scientists. For example, if there is no standardized measure of what constitutes job stress, two researchers could disagree widely about the job stress experienced by an employee. It would be difficult to test theories concerning job stress that were based solely or mostly on subjective opinions.

The endless array of models with hypothesized attributes is a major problem. The difficulty of measuring the attributes has resulted in many of the models' (see Chapter 2) going untested. The results of relations between measured variables in any model of stress requires the use of the most objective measurement possible. Unless more and better quality objective measures are used, guesswork will continue to be offered in place of scientific observation.

Quantification

The numerical results provided by standardized measures yield two major advantages (Nunnally, 1970). First, numerical indices make it possible to report results in finer detail than would be true if subjective opinions were used. A second advantage of quantification is that it permits the use of powerful statistical and mathematical analyses. Without the use of multivariate analyses, it would be impossible to test most of the stress and work models discussed in Chapter 2. Furthermore, mathematical notation enables one to formulate the specific deductions about attributes in a model for experimental examination.

Time

Once developed, good measures can save researchers and managers time. For example, suppose an organization has thousands of employees working on various jobs. Rather than interview employees individually to ask them what job or organizational factors cause them stress, a representative sample could be obtained with a self-report questionnaire. In a study of the effects of a job redesign on the satisfaction of employees, it is far more economical to employ standardized measures (e.g., the Minnesota Satisfaction Questionnaire) than to have managers attempt to guess the amount of job satisfaction among subordinates.

An important point in saving time is that reliable and valid measures must be used to acquire accurate information. Of course, self-report questionnaires are not always valid and should be used cautiously, preferably with other types of measures of an attribute. In fact, many scientists hold self-report measures in low esteem because of the lack of reliability and validity.

The communication, objectivity, quantification, and time characteristics of measurement are important to the development and use of theories in any field of science. The medical doctor must communicate objectively and efficiently with other practitioners. The applied behavioral scientist is also concerned with clearly and objectively communicating with peers and practitioners. Measurement offers scientists and practitioners a vehicle for understanding the real world in terms of purposes and operations.

MEASUREMENT IN MEDICINE

The practice of medicine relies on measurement for diagnostic and predictive purposes. Some of the measurement occurs on a one-on-one patient-doctor basis, while other measures are collected via multiphasic screening, automated multiphasic health testing, health maintenance examinations, and so forth. All of these methods of measurement have the ultimate goal of providing medically and economically effective health surveillance. In most cases the use of measurement in medicine is intended to be a screening process to distinguish the early sick from the well.

The physician

The modern physician has been trained to use the scientific method to learn about patient wellness and illness. The physician examines the patient, asks questions, and observes nonverbal communication to assess a patient's wellness or symptoms. Today many physician-conducted physical examinations are selective in that a lot of the details and tests are performed by nurses, technical specialists, and others. The physician relies on hard data from laboratory and physical measurements analyzed by specialists. In addition to these hard data the doctor uses subjective impressions of the patient's complaints and attitudes.

The physician collects data, diagnoses, then treats. The data collected are both objective (analysis of blood sample) and subjective (discussion with patient). The public has bestowed upon medicine an objective measurement aura. That is, the physician is viewed as a collector and interpreter of hard data which are always accurate because they are objectively obtained. Of course measurements in medicine are not always accurate. The physician's assessment of a patient's anxiety or stress from nonverbal cues may be totally inaccurate. In simple terms the physician may not be skilled in the interpretation or gathering of interview responses or in observing nonverbal communications. Even laboratory tests of blood samples can be inaccurate. Thus, although the physician is concerned with communication, objectivity, and quantification, he or she is often unable to measure an attribute accurately because of observation deficiences, masked symptoms, poor testing procedures, or the lack of knowledge in an area.

The Medical Research Approach to measurement

In some medical cases and personal situations, a comprehensive medical approach to measurement is used. For example, in some cases historical, biochemical, and physiological measurements are obtained, processed, and presented to a doctor for review. We have designated this the *Medical Research Approach* (MRA) to measurement. The patient then meets the physician to discuss the results of the testing and measurement. A description of what is called a *medical research model of measurement* follows (Duff and Lipscomb, 1973).

In this model the patient reports to a station in a clinic, hospital, or office where a history is taken and blood and urine samples are obtained. The history is used to identify abnormality of function and to provide the doctor with key words to direct attention to a potential problem area. Some history forms ask twenty questions, while others ask as many as three hundred questions.

A carefully selected set of measurements is taken by technicians at a physiological test station in the MRA by technicians. Measures of height, weight, hearing, vision, blood pressure, temperature, and heart and lung efficiency are collected (Duff and Lipscomb, 1973). These are fairly objective and accurate measures used by the doctor to form diagnostic opinions and treatment strategies.

Multiple biochemical measurements are performed on blood and urine samples. Again, this information is used by the physician in consultation with the patient. A benefit of using historical, physiological, and biochemical measurements collected by technicians is that the physician can spend more time with the patient. Additionally, the MRA enables the physician to use multiple measures to review the patient's problems.

The use of medical instrumentation

The collection of multiple measures by medical personnel has been facilitated by the use of medical instrumentation. In medicine the term *instrumentation* often denotes equipment, machines, and tools. On the other hand, in the behavioral sciences *instrumentation* is used in many cases to designate questionnaires, interviews, or other observational devices used to collect data. A major function of medical instrumentation is the measurement of physiological variables. In medicine a variable is any quantity whose value changes with time (Cromwell, et al., 1976). Examples of physiological variables are body temperature, the electrical activity of the heart (ECG), arterial blood pressure, and respiratory airflow.

The measurement of physiological variables is required in both the diagnosis of disease and monitoring the impact of treatment. In either case, measured *values* are compared with normal values obtained through measurement of the same values in large numbers of healthy people.

In order to be useful to a physician diagnosing a patient's problems, a physiological variable must undergo a significant change from its normal values. Equally important, it must be easily measurable and the method of obtaining the measurement must cause a minimum of discomfort to the patient (Cromwell, et al., 1976). Some physiological variables are easy to measure (e.g., indirect measure of blood pressure), while others are difficult and require complex electronic equipment for their measurement (e.g., direct measures of brain wave activity).

Some physiological variables such as body weight change their values rather slowly and therefore require less frequent measurement. Others, however, vary at a rapid rate, and their measurement requires sophisticated instrumentation. The electrical activity of the heart (ECG measure), for example, varies rapidly and must be traced for at least one complete cardiac cycle.

Thus, measurement in medicine involves the use of historical, physiological, biochemical, and personal data. The data are often analyzed by the physician and/or sophisticated electronic equipment and computers. In medicine, as in other fields of science, objectivity, quantification, communication, and time economy are sought-after characteristics of measurement.

MEASUREMENT IN THE BEHAVIORAL SCIENCES

Research in all areas of behavioral science—psychology, sociology, and cultural anthropology—is dependent on measurement. Measurement problems in some areas have proved to be extremely difficult. For example, the manager applying behavioral science techniques finds it difficult to measure employee's attitudes toward managers or their perceptions of pay. These measurement problems are no more difficult than those faced by physicians assessing heart function or brain wave activity, but they are generally considered more complex because self-reports are often the only measures employed.

Most behavioral science research involves the measurement of variables. Some common variables assigned numerical values are age, job tenure, job satisfaction, leadership style, organizational climate, role conflict, employee productivity, absenteeism, and personnel turnover. These are variables meaningful to managers in their attempts to improve the quality of work life for subordinates.

Although some variables in the behavioral sciences are easy to measure, others are far removed from receiving numerical values. Measuring the job performance of a middle-level manager is extremely difficult. Furthermore, standardized measures of work phenomena are rare. For example, job satisfaction is measured by a variety of self-report instruments, including the Job Descriptive Index (JDI), the Minnesota Satisfaction Questionnaire (MSQ), and the Faces Scale. Unfortunately, little communication between researchers using the different job satisfaction measures occurs. In addition, little research has been performed comparing measurement characteristics of the various satisfaction measures (Gillett and Schwab, 1975).

The behavioral scientist measuring job satisfaction or personal values is involved in assigning numbers to objects. This type of assignment is also practiced by the medical scientist in measuring blood pressure or other relevant variables. In the behavioral sciences major attention is paid to the *levels of measurement* used in making the assignment. Scales or measuring instruments are used to assign numerals or symbols to aspects of objects or events. While many forms of scales exist for measuring, four types are usually discussed in the behavioral sciences—*nominal, ordinal, interval,* and *ratio.*

In the behavioral sciences the term *observation* is used. This term is sometimes misunderstood. Does it mean that behavioral scientists look at workers on an assembly line or in an office, form impressions of what they see (or think they see), and then conclude something about the behavior observed? Yes and No. The scientist makes observations by measuring variables or gathering information to measure variables (Kerlinger, 1979). An experimental scientist manipulates an independent variable—say job characteristics—by giving members of two experimental groups two types of job characteristics (e.g., feedback and autonomy) in order to "observe" their different effects on job performance. The observation in this example is of behavior that is assumed to reflect performance. The purpose of the observations is to obtain measures of the dependent variable job performance. The observant manager may notice that job performance in the two groups is different after the job characteristics have been altered. These hunches or opinions are important in science, but they are insufficient. The manager needs to know how much job performance changed.

The manager's habits, experience, needs, motives, and other influences on perception tend to result in error unless precautions are taken. This is where measurement enters the picture. The difference between casual observation and measurements based on scientific observation lies in the reliability factor. Managerial observers can be consistent (reliable) from one time to another when they use measurement.

Consequently, measurement in the behavioral sciences involves the use of scales that provide the researcher or practitioner with information about some particular feature of objects. As in medicine, objectivity, quantification, communication, and time economy are characteristics of behavioral science measurement. Table 3–1 presents the characteristics and some examples of measurement as practiced by medical and behavioral science researchers. There are many similarities displayed in Table 3–1. A major difference in the measurement activities of medical and behavioral scientists involves the collection of physiological and biochemical measures versus the collection of cognitive/affective

TABLE 3–1 Measurement Characteristics in Medical and Behavioral Science and an Example

	Medical Science	Behavioral Science
Objectivity	*Some.* Physician often interprets patient's answers and makes subjective judgements about visual cues.	*Some:* Researcher often provides opinions, interpretations, and suggestions.
Quantification	*Yes.* Historical, physiological, and biochemical indices are used.	*Yes:* Different levels of measurement are used to quantify observations made.
Communication	*Yes.* Physicians have developed medical jargon and scientific style that pertains to the medical field. Use language that examines contributing factors or precursors to disease or illness episodes. Little communication with behavioral sciences.	*Yes:* Researchers have developed scientific methods and research designs to study phenomena in laboratory and field settings. Concerned about independent, dependent, and moderator variables. Little communication with medical sciences.
Time Economy	*Yes.* Physician has started to rely on specialists to run tests. He or she then interprets the test results. The physician is then able to spend more time in consultation with patient.	*Yes:* Use of sampling plans and self-administered surveys so that large groups of observations can be made. There are, however, numerous problems associated with the use of self-report surveys.
Measurement Example	Blood pressure is measured by use of a sphygmomanometer. A cuff is placed around the arm of the patient. The cuff is inflated, arterial blood flows past the cuff only when the arterial pressure exceeds the pressure in the cuff. Systolic blood pressure in the normal adult is in the range of 95 to 140mm Hg, with 120mm Hg being average. Normal diastolic pressure ranges from 60 to 90mm Hg, with 80mm Hg being average. The patients blood pressure is compared to normal values.	Job satisfaction is often measured by the use of a self-report questionnaire such as the Minnesota Satisfaction Questionnaire. Employees are asked to respond to questions designed to reflect satisfaction with specific job related factors such as pay, type of work, security, and opportunity for advancement. Individual responses are often aggregated to yield a group score which is compared to other group scores or is used as a baseline measure.

measures. The medical researchers primarily probe physiological and biomedical factors, while most behavioral researchers rarely examine these kinds of variables. On the other hand, behavioral scientists continually probe the emotions, feelings, knowledge, and attitudes of people. Some medical specialties such as psychiatry probe these cognitive/affective variables, but for the most part, medical experts focus on physiological and biochemical measurements.

THE IMPORTANCE OF RELIABILITY AND VALIDITY IN THE MEDICAL AND BEHAVIORAL SCIENCES

Any measurement, whether it is of blood pressure or job satisfaction may vary with respect to reliability and validity. It is very important in medicine and the behavioral sciences to use reliable and valid measures. The reliability of a measure may be found in its repeatability. In many shopping malls there are blood-pressure cuffs that shoppers can use to determine their systolic and diastolic measures. A major problem with these "pay as you measure" cuffs is unreliability. One does not typically receive consistent readouts, even when they are taken only seconds apart. Medical doctors would not tolerate such inconsistent tests of blood pressure. The physician insists on using instrumentation that yields the most consistent or reliable results possible.

In the behavioral sciences checks are made to determine if measures such as job satisfaction are reliable. A major method of checking reliability is to give the same self-report survey or interview more than once to the same people. A check is then made to determine if the outcomes are consistent across testing periods. This is a *test-retest* reliability procedure. Other forms of reliability checks such as *split-half* and *internal consistency* (coefficient alpha) are also popular when using questionnaires.

The *validity* of a measure is the extent to which it actually indicates what it is supposed to be measuring, which is called the *criterion*. It is important in science to validate a measure by showing that it relates consistently to the criterion. Validation is often accomplished in medicine by using norms developed from large groups of healthy people. For example, average or normal blood pressure readings for adults range from systolic 95 to 140 mm Hg to diastolic 60 to 90 mm Hg. If it is known that a person has a blood pressure of 160/100 (which could be determined directly by percutaneous insertion of a short cathether into a blood vessel) and the measure taken actually yields 160/100 on the cuff reading, the test is considered valid. The direct measure and the indirect measure yielded the same or similar results of what the medical community defines as arterial blood pressure.

In the behavioral sciences too much reliance is often placed on *face* validity. In many magazine articles you are invited to "test your stress level." Many of these scales seem to measure what they are supposed to (they have face validity), but they have not been validated. A useful way to validate is to find separate groups of people known to be high versus low on the characteristic being measured. A measurement scale is considered valid only if it accurately differentiates between the high and low groups.

THE ISSUE OF DIRECT AND INDIRECT MEASUREMENT

At times medical and behavioral science researchers measure physiologic, biochemical, or behavioral variables directly. However, in many cases direct measure is impossible to obtain. When direct measures are not available the researcher, physician, or manager rely on measurements that are indicative of the target or variable (Sheridan, 1976).

An illustration of the difference between indicative (indirect) and criterional (direct) measures could be the voting in an election. Before the presidential election, for example, there is no way to measure the number of votes for a candidate. Pollsters use preelection sample polls to predict how many votes a candidate will receive. The pollsters' tally of preelection responses provides an *indicative* or *indirect measure*. The voting itself is the *criterional* or *direct measure*. It is important to be aware of the distinction between direct and indirect measurement. The cuff measure of arterial blood pressure is an indirect measure, while direct measurement would require the use of invasive methods such as using a catheter inserted directly into an artery or vein.

In the behavioral sciences there is a tendency to present measures as necessarily valid. However, the validity of indirect measures is open to serious question and should be tested. Indirect measures are widely used in the behavioral sciences because it is difficult to measure directly variables such as values, needs, self-actualization, and commitment.

A major type of indirect measure is the verbal measure. Suppose a manager is doing a study of the frequency of reprimands he uses with male and female subordinates. If the real focus of the study is the reprimands, a direct measure would be made. However, if the manager were interested in whether he discriminated against women, the frequency of reprimands would have to be considered an indirect measure.

Some behavioral scientists dislike indirect verbal or self-report measures of attitude and behavior because of reliability and validity problems. It is easy to get a verbal or self-report measure of a person's job satisfaction, but it is impossible to be perfectly certain that the resulting measure reflects nonverbal or personal behaviors and attitudes.

Direct behavioral measures are difficult to obtain in the behavioral sciences. For example, if one is interested in studying job factors influencing satisfaction, it might appear easy to measure satisfaction by asking people to scale their level of satisfaction on some instrument. However, direct measurement requires that behaviors be selected that are considered indicators of job satisfaction. For example, frequencies of absence, turnover, and grievances have been used as behavioral surrogates in studies of job satisfaction. By assessing these variables, inferences are made about a person's level of job satisfaction.

Sometimes behavioral surrogates clearly reflect the topic of interest—the number of calories consumed in a study of dietary practices, for example. At other times, as in the case of a complex topic like stress, it may be difficult to identify accurate behavioral surrogates.

STRESS MEASUREMENT: THE STATE OF THE ART

Based on our discussion of the basics of measurement in the medical and behavioral sciences, we can now examine a limited number of ways that stress is measured. Among the various methods used to collect stress measures are questionnaires, interviews, and physiological tests. Numerous measures of stress are offered by researchers, managers, physicians, and authors of popular press articles. It is not our intent to criticize unfairly the measures that are available to assess stress. We do want our readers, however, to consider the issues of objectivity, communication, quantification, time economy, reliability, and validity when examining the sample of measures presented.

The popular press

There is no shortage of measures of stress available in books, magazine articles, and newspaper clippings. Many of the authors of these writings invite readers to test "your" current stress level. Unfortunately, these measures have not been subjected to reliability and validity checks. They are easy and fun to complete, but authors need to at least caution readers about the psychometric quality of any of these self-report questionnaires.

An example of a self-report test of stress is presented in Table 3–2. The person is asked to check those events that have happened during the last few months and for each "yes" answer score *1* point. The points are added, and a scoring key with a description is provided. Medical and behavioral scientists would ask about the reliability and validity of the Table 3–2 measure.

Social Readjustment Rating Scale (SRRS)

Thomas Holmes and Richard Rahe (1967) developed a life events scale called the Social Readjustment Rating Scale. They studied the clinical effects of major life changes of over five thousand patients suffering from stress-related illness. As a result of copious interviews and questionnaire responses, Holmes and Rahe were able to assign a numerical value to each life event, ranking them in order of magnitude. The participants in the development of this scale included executives, doctors, students, and athletes.

After developing the scores for each life event, the medical histories of patients were examined. It was found that those who had a high score on the life change index were more likely to contract illness following the events. In research to validate the SRRS, it was found that 80% of the people with scores over three hundred and 53% of the people with scores between 150 and 300 suffered some form of stress-related illness. On the other hand, these illnesses were found to occur in less than a third of the people with scores over 150. The SRRS is presented in Table 3–3.

TABLE 3–2   A Self-Report Test of Stress Level

1. Have you increased your alcohol, smoking, or eating recently?	Yes	No
2. Are you having problems with co-workers?	Yes	No
3. Do you argue frequently with your wife (husband)?	Yes	No
4. Are you having money problems?	Yes	No
5. Are you having problems with your boss?	Yes	No
6. Have you had sexual difficulties?	Yes	No
7. Do you feel uncomfortable about inflation?	Yes	No
8. Do you have trouble with your in-laws?	Yes	No
9. Are you exposed to loud noises frequently?	Yes	No
10. Do you feel tense?	Yes	No
11. Have you had problems paying taxes or with the IRS?	Yes	No
12. Are you having trouble with your children?	Yes	No

Give yourself 1 point for each *Yes* answer

   1–3   Your stress level is low and probably controllable.

   4–6   You have moderate amounts of stress which can be coped with by good rest, some exercise, and a good diet.

  7–10   You have high stress and need to do something like relax or exercise to reduce the level before it hurts you physically.

 11–12   Your stress level is at a danger level and you may be susceptible to a major illness.

The SRRS has been used as a rough estimate of the degree of stress a person is suffering at the time of testing. A review of the SRRS indicates that less than a quarter of the stressful events are job related and of the forty-three events, only ten are decidedly negative in wording. The vast majority of life events are worded neutrally.

The notion advanced by Holmes and Rahe that adaptive change causes increased stress seems reasonable. However, the SRRS does not account for a person's capacity for meeting and dealing with stress. For example, divorce may be very stressful for one person who is opposed to the divorce, but for someone else, it may be a relief from an extremely stressful existence. Despite this shortcoming the Holmes-Rahe SRRS appears to be a more reliable and valid instrument than most of the popular press stress-oriented instruments available.

TABLE 3–3   The Social Readjustment Rating Scale*

Instructions: Check off each of these life events that has happened to you during the previous year. Total the associated points. A score of 150 or less means a relatively low amount of life change and a low susceptibility to stress-induced health breakdown. A score of 150 to 300 points implies about a 50% chance of a major health breakdown in the next two years. A score above 300 raises the odds to about 80%, according to the Holmes-Rahe statistical prediction model.

Life Events	Mean Value
1. Death of spouse	100
2. Divorce	73
3. Marital separation from mate	65
4. Detention in jail or other institution	63
5. Death of a close family member	63
6. Major personal injury or illness	53
7. Marriage	50
8. Being fired at work	47
9. Marital reconciliation with mate	45
10. Retirement from work	45
11. Major change in the health or behavior of a family member	44
12. Pregnancy	40
13. Sexual difficulties	39
14. Gaining a new family member (e.g., through birth, adoption, oldster moving in, etc.)	39
15. Major business readjustment (e.g., merger, reorganization, bankruptcy, etc.)	39
16. Major change in financial state (e.g., a lot worse off or a lot better off than usual)	38
17. Death of a close friend	37
18. Changing to a different line of work	36
19. Major change in the number of arguments with spouse (e.g., either a lot more or a lot less than usual regarding child rearing, personal habits, etc.)	35
20. Taking on a mortgage greater than $10,000 (e.g., purchasing a home, business, etc.)	31
21. Foreclosure on a mortgage or loan	30
22. Major change in responsibilities at work (e.g., promotion, demotion, lateral transfer)	29

Life Events	Mean Value
23. Son or daughter leaving home (e.g., marriage, attending college, etc.)	29
24. In-law troubles	29
25. Outstanding personal achievement	28
26. Wife beginning or ceasing work outside the home	26
27. Beginning or ceasing formal schooling	26
28. Major change in living conditions (e.g., building a new home, remodeling, deterioration of home or neighborhood)	25
29. Revision of personal habits (dress, manners, associations, etc.)	24
30. Troubles with the boss	23
31. Major change in working hours or conditions	20
32. Change in residence	20
33. Changing to a new school	20
34. Major change in usual type and/or amount of recreation	19
35. Major change in church activities (e.g., a lot more or a lot less than usual)	19
36. Major change in social activities (e.g, clubs, dancing, movies, visiting, etc.)	18
37. Taking on a mortgage or loan less than $10,000 (e.g., purchasing a car, TV, freezer, etc.)	17
38. Major change in sleeping habits (a lot more or a lot less sleep, or change in part of day when asleep)	16
39. Major change in number of family get-togethers (e.g., a lot more or a lot less than usual)	15
40. Major change in eating habits (a lot more or a lot less food intake, or very different meal hours or surroundings)	15
41. Vacation	13
42. Christmas	12
43. Minor violations of the law (e.g., traffic tickets, jaywalking, disturbing the peace, etc.)	11

The Michigan Stress Assessment

In 1962, French and Kahn presented a model which attempted to identify major variables that play a sociopsychological role in the etiology of coronary heart disease. In Chapter 2 this stress model was referred to as the social environment model. The model includes the objective and subjective environment that a person experiences. These two sets of independent variables are measured by use of tally sheets and self-report questionnaires. For example, to obtain *objective* work load data, a person's secretary was asked to record her observations of the frequency of phone calls, office visits, and meetings received by the boss. An example of the tally sheet is presented in Figure 3–1.

Questionnaires were used to acquire information for the subjective environment indices of stress. Included as subjective stress variables were measures for role ambiguity, subjective quantitative work load, role conflict, responsibility for persons and responsibility for things, participation, and relations with work group.

A sample of the items used to measure responsibility for people and things is presented in Table 3–4. The respondent is asked to answer these questions on a scale from 1 (very little) to 5 (very great). Caplan (1971) and Sales (1969) have used these scales in studies examining stress. They imply that the Michigan measures of stress are reliable and meet acceptable construct validity standards. Reliabilities reported for the subjective scales are in the .70 to .85 range. Factor analysis was used in the studies to determine the construct validities (which they considered acceptable) of the scales.

Note that the Michigan measures of subjective environment are indirect. They are also what are referred to as *perceptual measures*. The respondent is asked about his or her perceptions of subjective environment stress. Although these measures have not been subjected to rigorous validation testing, they have been and continue to be used by many behavioral scientists examining stress. They seem to be the most widely used measures of perceived stress found in the behavioral science literature.

Medically based stress measures

The popular press, SRRS, and Michigan stress measures rely on verbal reports, tally sheets, and self-report data to acquire, for the most

FIGURE 3–1   Objective Work Load Tally Sheet

Example of
TALLY SHEET

My boss arrived at _____ A.M., P.M. (circle one)
                 (time)

I am beginning this tally at _____ A.M., P.M. (circle one)   Today's date _____
                          (time)

Time	Phone IN	Phone OUT	Office Visits (with 1 other person)	Meetings BOSS ARRANGED	Meetings OTHER ARRANGED	Other such as lunch, break, time unable to observe boss, etc.
8						
9						
10						
11						
Noon						
1						
2						
3						
4						
5						

It is _____ A.M., P.M. (circle one), and this tally is ended for today.

TABLE 3–4   Responsibility for People and Things Items (Caplan, 1971)
             How Much Stress Exists For:

		Very Little				Very Great
P	The responsibility you have for the work of others	1	2	3	4	5
T	The responsibility you have for initiating assignments and projects	1	2	3	4	5
T	The responsibility you have for budgets and expenditures	1	2	3	4	5
T	The responsibility you have for carrying out assignments and projects	1	2	3	4	5
T	The responsibility you have for equipment and facilities	1	2	3	4	5
T	The responsibility you feel toward accomplishing the general goal of your division or directorate	1	2	3	4	5
P	The responsibility you have for the futures (careers) of others	1	2	3	4	5

P = Responsibility For People
T = Responsibility For Things

part, indirect assessments of stress. Some researchers in the behavioral and medical sciences claim that these are not measures of stress. So, skepticism among researchers about the quality of the available and widely used measures is the rule rather than the exception. A typical question asked is, "How do you know that you are measuring stress?"

Among variables that medical scientists have used to examine stress responses are cortisol and growth hormone. Cortisol and growth hormone are secreted by the adrenal cortex. The adrenal cortex is stimulated by pituitary gland secretions (ACTH). Rose, Jenkins, and Hurst (1978) collected blood for cortisol and growth hormone determinations from air traffic controllers (ATC). The researchers collected blood samples from the ATC while they performed their job activities. During each day of blood collection, a small catheter was inserted in the vein of each man's forearm, and this catheter was attached to a sigmamotor pump, permitting continuous collection of blood. A total of 16,792 samples of blood were withdrawn from approximately five hundred ATC over the course of the study.

Rose et al. (1978) reviewed previous research on cortisol and growth hormone secretions and found that higher levels of these secretions in the blood indicated increased stress. They then incorporated measures of these secretions in their air traffic controllers study. They took multiple measures of these secretions while the ATC worked. Notice the vast number of samples drawn and analyzed by the researchers. They did not rely on a limited number of samples, but elected to use many measures at various times to acquire a more precise picture of secretions.

The results of the cortisol analysis indicated that, on the average, ATC showed very substantial differences among themselves with regard to total daily cortisol, peak cortisol, and maximum cortisol. It was found that there was a tendency for maximum levels to be higher while the controllers were on the job.

The blood samples drawn during work also allowed Rose et al. (1978) to analyze the growth hormone content of secretions. Only 2% to 3% of all samples showed levels of 5.0 mg/ml or greater, the threshold commonly used in the medical literature to indicate a significant level of secretion. It was determined that the high growth hormone secretors, although displaying emotional sensitivity to work load, performed well on the job.

The state of the measurement of stress includes direct and indirect measures, perceptual and physiological measures, and some concern about reliability and validity. The most direct measures of one aspect of stress are cortisol and growth hormones. On the other hand, the most indirect measures seem to be the Yes-No scales found in the popular press. Perceptual measures are popular in the behavioral sciences, while physiological and biochemical measures are employed in the medical sciences.

It is not surprising that perceptual, physiological, and biochemical measures are obtained, since these are what medical and behavorial scientists have been trained to use to study variables. A problem with all of the measures presented above is that, if managers are going to derive value from the measurement of stress data, they must understand what is being discussed. While there is a great deal of confusion, managers today seem to be more impressed with physiological measures of stress, probably because they are associated with the medical field. There are other reasons why medically derived measures of stress have more stature among interested parties such as managers.

First, there is a generally low regard for self-report scales. Introspective surveys are subject to distorting influences that diminish the reliability and validity of the measures. But every type of physiological response is subject to erroneous assessment and inference. Paying more attention to reliability, validity, and measurement characteristics could improve the quality and image of any self-report measure of stress.

A second reason for the popularity of physiological measures is that self-report perceptual measures have often failed to produce convincing results. Correlations between perceptually measured and clinically judged stress have tended to be low, ranging from .10 to .30, (Caplan, 1971).

Another reason is the possibility that processes (stress responses) below the level of complete awareness can only be identified by physiological measurement. Does the person feel stress manifested as hormonal secretions, increases in blood pressure, and the dilation of blood vessels? One is not able to assess these important responses to stress by using only self-report measures, verbal expressions, or visual observations.

A fourth reason is the tendency of many behavioral scientists to assume that their measures are less precise and scientific than medically derived physiological measures. This, of course, is subject to debate since measurement, even in the medical field, is far from pure science. The availability of commercially produced physiological measuring devices, specialists available to perform tests, and sophisticated computer processes should encourage the increased use of psychophysiological measures in the future among those concerned about measuring stress accurately.

REFERENCES

Caplan, R. "Organizational stress and individual strain: A social-psychological study of risk factors." Dissertation, University of Michigan Microfilms, Ann Arbor, Michigan, 1971.

Cromwell, L., et al. *Medical Instrumentation for Health Care*. Englewood Cliffs, N. J.: Prentice-Hall, Inc., 1976.

Duff, W. R. and H. S. Lipscomb. "A Health Testing Concept: Simple-by-design." In *Health Evaluation: An Entry to the Health Care System*. D. F. Davies and J. B. Tchobanoff, eds. New York: Intercontinental Medical Book Corporation, 1973.

French, J. R. P., Jr. and R. L. Kahn. "A programmatic approach to studying the industrial environment and mental health." *Journal of Social Issues* 18 (1962): 1–47.

Gillet, B. and D. P. Schwab. "Convergent and discriminant validities of corresponding Job Descriptive Index and Minnesota Satisfaction Questionnaire Scales. *"Journal of Applied Psychology* 60 (1975): 313–316.

Holmes, T. H. and R. H. Rahe. "The social readjustment rating scale." *Journal of Psychosomatic Medicine* 11 (1967): 213–218.

Kerlinger, F. N. *Behavioral Research: A Conceptual Approach.* New York: Holt, Rinehart and Winston, 1979.

Nunnally, J. C., Jr. *Introduction to Psychological Measurement.* New York: McGraw-Hill, Inc., 1970.

Rose, R. M.; Jenkins, C. D. and M. W. Hurst. Air traffic controller health change study. Federal Aviation Administration Contract, Department of Transportation, 1978.

Sales, S. "Organizational role as a risk factor in coronary disease." *Administrative Science Quarterly* 14 (1969): 325–336.

Sheridan, C. L. *Methods in Experimental Psychology.* New York: Holt, Rinehart and Winston, 1976.

FOR FURTHER READING

Best, C. M. and N. B. Taylor. *Physiological Basis of Medical Practice.* J. K. Brobeck, ed. Baltimore, Md.: The Williams and Wilkins Company, 1973.

Campbell, J. P. "Psychometric theory." *In Handbook of Industrial and Organizational Psychology.* M. D. Dunnette, ed. Chicago: Rand McNally and Company, 1976.

Geddes, L. A. and L. E. Baker. *Principles of Applied Biomedical Instrumentation.* New York: John Wiley and Sons, Inc., 1975.

Keppel, G. *Design and Analysis: A Researcher's Handbook.* Englewood Cliffs, N. J.: Prentice-Hall, Inc., 1973.

Stone, E. *Research Methods in Organizational Behavior.* Santa Monica, Calif.: Goodyear Publishing Co., Inc., 1978.

Weiner, H. *Psychobiology and Human Disease.* New York: Elsevier, North-Holland, Inc., 1977.

Stress and Health   4

AESOP AT PLAY

An Athenian one day found Aesop entertaining himself with a company of little Boys at their childish diversions, and began to jeer and laugh at him for it. Aesop, who was too much a wag himself to suffer others to ridicule him, took a bow unstrung, and laid it upon the ground. Then calling the censorious Athenian, Now philosopher, says he, expound the riddle if you can, and tell us what the unstrained bow implies. The Man, after racking his brains a considerable time to no purpose, at last gave it up, and declared he knew not what to make of it. Why, says Aesop, smiling, if you keep a bow always bent, it will lose its elasticity presently; but if you let it go slack, it will be fitter for use when you want it.

Managerial Application • Neither the minds nor the bodies of individuals are made to endure unremitted tension. Like the bow, people under constant stress lose their elasticity.

      Chester Comer awakens at 7:00 A.M., having overslept by forty-five minutes. Panic-stricken, he realizes he will be late for the second time in as many weeks. In his effort to hurry he cuts himself while shaving, scalds his tongue on too hot coffee, and worries what the boss will say. On the freeway, unable to change lanes, he is caught behind a slow-moving vehicle. He honks, stays within inches of the other vehicle, and mutters uncomplimentary remarks about the other driver, unconsciously tensing his entire body and tightening his grip on the steering wheel.

      Once at the office he finds dictation from yesterday still not transcribed and chews out his secretary without waiting for her explanation of the delay. Overhearing the exchange, Chester's boss explains that the secretary had been handling a special assignment for him and reprimands Chester for his discourtesy. Upset over the reprimand, Chester slams down his coffee cup, spilling coffee over important papers on his desk. Later that day, preoccupied with his thoughts in a staff meeting, he fails to recognize that a question is being directed at him and suffers the embarrassment of having everyone's attention focused on him as the boss suggests that if Chester would pay attention, he might have a better idea of what was going on in the company.

      That evening, after several more incidents, Chester drives home an hour late. Tired, tense, and irritable, he is short-tempered with his children, upsetting his wife, which in turn provokes an argument. Chester ends up spending the night on the couch, staring at the ceiling until the early hours of the morning. Consequently, he oversleeps again, awaking tired and irritable.

      Chester has had a bad day and indications are the upcoming day may not be much better, with Chester starting off tired and irritable. There are at least three aspects of Chester's day which are worth noting. First, Chester encountered a number of situations that were potentially stress-provoking: he overslept; he injured himself; he was caught in traffic; he found work undone that he expected to be completed; he was reprimanded by a superior; he was embarrassed in front of co-workers in a staff meeting; and he argued with his spouse. Undoubtedly, a number of other events transpired during that day that also carried stress-provoking potential.

      The second aspect of Chester's experiences that is of importance is that Chester probably transferred those potentially stressful occurrences into actual stress. That is, Chester let what was happening get to him. This is important for two reasons. First, it precipitated additional stressor situations. For example, because Chester let himself become upset over the fact that he overslept, he cut himself while shaving and scalded himself on hot coffee. In other words, because Chester was stressed, he contributed to the introduction into his environment of stressors which might otherwise not have been present. Thus, by being under stress, Chester became more stressed. Second, Chester might have dealt with his environment more productively, reducing his stress and even eliminating some stressors.

The third and perhaps most important aspect of Chester's day is that Chester has helped create for himself a continuing state of stress. He has, in effect, encountered a number of fight-or-flee situations in the space of twenty-four hours. At the onset of each such encounter, his body responds with the expected—although entirely inappropriate—response. So physiologically, his body is in an almost constant state of preparedness for fighting or fleeing. This takes its toll on Chester and contributes to his fatigue at the end of the day. Most importantly, however, is that repeated on a day-in and day-out basis, those chronic physiological stress reactions can contribute to long-run and even permanent damage to Chester's system. What will inevitably happen, if this turns out to be a typical day in the life of Chester Comer, is that he will become a victim of some type of stress-related affliction.

In this chapter we will examine stress-related afflictions. We will see how the duration of the stress experience is an important variable, and we will look at our physical responses to stress. The potential role of stress in chronic diseases will be outlined, the diseases identified, and the relationship between stress, work, and health outcomes will be discussed. Finally, we will examine the role of causation in the stress-disease link, emphasizing the importance of not drawing premature cause-and-effect conclusions.

DURATION AS A VARIABLE IN STRESS SITUATIONS

Each of us encounters a number of stressful situations every day. Most of the time the stress reactions elicited are so mild that they go unnoticed by us. Nonetheless, even those of us leading the most relaxed and stress-free lives possible will probably experience some of these stress reactions every day. It is when the situations are perceived to be major that the reaction to them becomes a potential problem, inviting negative health consequences. The severity of the situation or of the response may not be nearly as important, however, as the duration. We have all experienced events which were intensely stressful for a brief period of time. A near collision on the freeway is an example. We may feel our heart skip a beat, experience noticeably increased respiration and heart rate, and become weak-kneed. These are all indications that major turmoil is taking place in our internal system. Yet, once the threat has passed our system returns to normal very quickly.

That isolated stress event, in spite of the internal havoc it raised, probably resulted in absolutely no long-lasting physical damage to our system. On the other hand, if we were constantly in a state of agitation, serious health dysfunctions might be expected. There are a couple of ways individuals experience constant or chronic stress. One is to be continually exposed to a number of short-run stressors, as our friend Chester was. The other way is to experience a stressful event that is of long-term duration.

In an effort to identify stressful social situations which might lead to negative health consequences Schwab and Pritchard (1950) recognized that the duration of a stress event plays a critical role in determining the possible consequences of that event. Accordingly, they evolved a typology of stress events which includes three categories of stress situations classified according to the duration of the event:

Short stress situations. This category includes the many, usually mild, stress situations almost everyone faces daily. It includes experiences such as being caught in traffic, sitting next to someone who is smoking, and receiving criticism. Their common denominator is their duration. They are events lasting from seconds to, at the most, a few hours. Not only is their duration of little significance, so is their influence. Unless we experience a continual chain of these events, the stress they provoke is unlikely to contribute to any negative health outcomes. So, while Chester's bad day is not likely to be significant by itself from a health standpoint, numerous similar days over many months may lead to important physical problems.

Moderate stress situations. This category includes events which last from several hours to a number of days. Included here would be periods of work overload, temporary absence of family members, new job responsibilities, a continuing unresolved disagreement with a boss, co-worker, or family member, and other events of moderate duration. From a health perspective, the importance of this category is the role these events may play in precipitating the onset of physical problems where a predisposition already exists. Two independent Canadian studies (Kavanagh and Shepard, 1973; Levene, 1974) have demonstrated a temporal relationship between moderate stress situations and heart attacks in men predisposed to coronary difficulties.

Severe stress situations. These are the chronic stress situations. They may last weeks, months or even years. They involve such disruptions as sustained reactions to the death of a loved one, protracted financial difficulties, prolonged physical illnesses, and inordinate and sustained demands in a work situation—any extended exposure to a situation which the individual finds threatening or intolerable. While there is no certainty that exposure to one of these severe stress situations will lead inevitably to negative health outcomes, an increasing amount of evidence strongly implicates severe stress as a precursor to such outcomes. How exposure to a stressor can lead to the bodily changes accompanying an illness or disease is the topic of the next section.

PHYSICAL RESPONSES TO STRESS

It may seem somewhat strange for a management-oriented book dealing with an organizational phenomenon to devote attention to the question of the physiology and endocrinology involved in a psychological event. We feel, however, that it is important—even essential—to deal with this topic for two related reasons. First, while physical consequences are certainly associated with psychological stimuli, acceptance of this fact requires a leap of faith on the part of many people. To the extent that the mechanisms linking stress and physical health can be understood rationally rather than accepted as an article of faith, acceptance of the relationship between the two will be increased.

Second, an increase in the understanding of any phenomenon should serve to increase the likelihood that the phenomenon will be dealt with efficaciously. When an automobile displays symptoms of malaise, a driver who is even vaguely familiar with the principles of how the internal combustion engine operates is in a better position to recognize the onset of a problem and diagnose it properly than someone who lacks even this rudimentary knowledge. Likewise with the stress-health relationship. The greater the understanding of that process, the more likely it will be that proper diagnosis, leading to appropriate remedies, will be made.

No attempt is made to present a detailed treatise on the physiological consequences of exposure to stressors. What follows is an extremely concise overview of some of the more significant bodily responses in stress situations. We urge the reader to move through this brief section closely to better appreciate the major theme of this chapter and a dominant thrust of this book—the stress-disease link.

Homeostatic regulation

The human body is a living open system and as such shares numerous characteristics with similar systems. One of these critical characteristics is *homeostatic regulation*. *Homeostasis* refers to the maintenance of constancy or equilibrium in the internal bodily system. It is homeostatic regulation, for example, that is responsible for the maintenance of a certain proportion of salt content in bodily fluids, regardless of changes in the absolute volume of fluids.

A critical aspect of the role played by bodily homeostatic mechanisms is the maintenance of internal equilibrium or balance in the face of external disturbances. As long as our environment remains constant, little or no effort is required to maintain balance. When our environment changes, however, it falls upon our internal balance regulators to adjust. Such properties as body temperature, glucose levels, and blood pressure may be adjusted to respond to environmental changes. Just the relatively simple procedure of maintaining proper internal body temperature in the face of a change in external conditions sets off a sequence of events including changes in respiration, cardiovascular functions, and endocrine gland activity. Moreover, body temperature changes influence the state of wakefulness and may affect other psychological states as well. In short, in an effort to maintain a state of internal balance our homeostatic regulatory mechanisms may involve a number of bodily systems.

Stressors are one important form of external environmental conditions which bring the homeostatic mechanisms into action. In a very real sense, the stress response is simply an outgrowth of the body's attempt to adapt to a changing environment. If the attempted adaptation is appropriate and successful, it very likely goes unnoticed and produces few, if any, negative side effects. If it is unsuccessful or inappropriate, the result is noticeable (via a feeling of discomfort, tension, anxiety, frustration or the like) and, if chronic, apt to produce undesirable side effects. While many aspects of homeostatic regulation are not fully understood, we have a pretty clear picture of what happens internally as we attempt to adapt to an external stress.

What happens when we respond to a stressor

The physiology of the body's response to stressors is in reality a description of how the body mobilizes in order to protect itself. Stress effects may be beneficial as well as harmful, but that does not alter the fact that bodily changes inevitably occur in stress situations. The stress response is quite complex; the major body systems involved include the brain, the autonomic nervous system, and the endocrine system. The primary objective of these systems in a stress situation is to maintain or restore the equilibrium discussed earlier which is threatened by the "invading" stressor. Figure 4–1 details the chronology of the major responses involved.

The initial stage of the stress response begins in the brain with the perception of the stressor. The brain is a highly complex organ, and no

FIGURE 4–1   The Stress Response

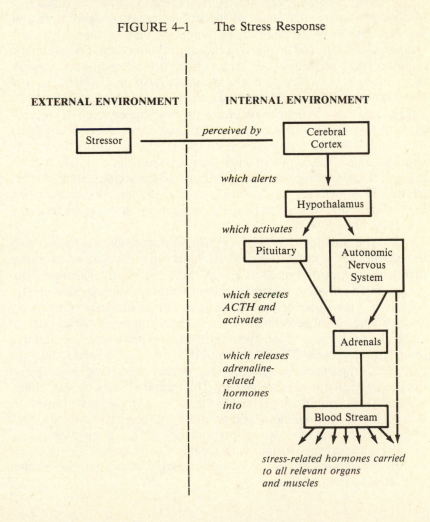

clear line of physiological separation can be drawn between and among the parts. Nonetheless, it is clear that all external stimuli are received in the brain, which in turn activates other appropriate body systems. The section of the brain which is chiefly responsible for beginning the response chain is the *cerebral cortex*. From an evolutionary standpoint, the cortex is the newest section of the brain, and it is the organ most directly involved in behavior and conscious mental processes. It is in the cortex that the perception of a stressor is registered. It is also the cortex that is responsible for controlling the *hypothalamus,* perhaps the most critical organ of all involved in the stress response.

The hypothalamus, which is located in what is called the mid-brain, is involved in a host of visceral and regulatory processes. It is partially responsible for regulating emotions such as fear, rage, and euphoria, and it is also involved in the control of body temperature and appetite. Most importantly, in terms of our stress response, it activates the autonomic nervous system and regulates the pituitary gland, central gland in the endocrine system. Thus, when an individual is exposed to a stressor, such as the imposition of a short deadline or a run-in with the boss, the stressor is perceived and placed in context through the mechanisms of the cerebral cortex. The cortex in turn activates the hypothalamus. The hypothalamus then activates the adaptive mechanisms of the autonomic nervous system and the endocrine system. It is the ability of the hypothalamus to respond to psychological stimuli (in the form of stressors) which gives it such a central role in the stress response processes.

The *autonomic nervous system* is responsible for controlling various functions which traditionally have been thought to be under involuntary control, such as gastrointestinal, cardiovascular, and reproductive activities. (Current evidence strongly suggests that certain aspects of these functions are at least in part voluntarily controlled.) When an individual perceives a stressor, the autonomic nervous system, under the stimulation of the hypothalamus, initiates a series of adaptive or defensive moves. This is accomplished via two separate, but not independent, parts of the system—the sympathetic nervous system and the parasympathetic nervous system. The former arouses various bodily systems which are part of the changes the body undergoes as it prepares to defend itself. The individual experiences the results of this system's arousal through increased heart beat, sweating, a knot in the stomach and other sensations we associate with threat of some type. The parasympathetic system has an almost opposite responsibility, namely calming and relaxing the organism.

The *endocrine system* plays an integral role in the stress reaction. The endocrine system consists of numerous glands which produce a variety of hormones. The hormones pass into the blood stream and serve as chemical regulators of physiological activity. In a stress situation there is a very close interplay between this system, the autonomic nervous system, and the hypothalamus.

Two endocrine glands, the pituitary and the adrenals are of special interest. The pituitary is connected directly to the hypothalamus via vascular connections. About the size of an acorn, the pituitary regulates hormone production and activity within the entire endocrine system. When this gland learns, via the hypothalamus and the autonomic nervous system, that a stress situation exists, it discharges hormones into the bloodstream that in turn activate other parts of the endocrine system. These hormones prepare the body to deal with (adapt to) the stressor by increasing blood flow, respiration and so on. (The reader will recognize these reactions as part of the body's fight-or-flee response discussed in Chapter 1).

One of the sets of glands of the endocrine system activated—by far the most important one—is the adrenal glands. The adrenals are acted upon by the pituitary's adrenocorticotrophic hormone (ACTH) and in turn produce the hormones adrenaline and noradrenalin and a family of related hormones called corticoids. Everyone is familiar with the occasional news stories in which someone at the scene of an accident lifts a car off a victim, although in a nonstressful situation that same individual would be unable to lift that great a weight. This temporary increase in muscle power is brought about by the action of the adrenals. The increased secretion of adrenaline alerts the body to be on guard against whatever threat it is experiencing.

Thus the body's response to a stressor is a complex, coordinated, neurochemical mobilization of all available adaptive mechanisms to meet the stressor. Numerous changes take place, some noticeable to any observer, some sensed only by the stressed individual. Some go unnoticed and take place without conscious awareness on the part of the person "under attack." These responses include, among others, release of stored sugars and fats into the blood stream to provide energy, increases in respiration and heart rate to provide more oxygen, increase in blood pressure to insure adequate blood supplies to crucial areas, activation of bloodclotting mechanisms to help protect against physical injury, tensing of muscles to prepare for rapid movement, heightened hearing and vision, and changes in stomach acidity. Some activity, rather than being intensified, tends to decrease. Thus, digestive processes slow, and bowel and bladder muscles relax.

This complex pattern of events requires that significant amounts of energy be expended. If we remain in a defensive posture for long periods of time or, over a long period, repeatedly activate our defenses for shorter periods of time, serious negative consequences may result. The length of time the body can supply increased amounts of adrenaline, for example, is limited, and the available adrenaline can become depleted. In an extreme case of adrenaline insufficiency, death results. Less extreme reactions include lowered resistance to stress, depression, loss of motivation, and emotional instability.

Other consequences of the stress response are recognizable as being counter to health and well-being. For example, the stress response elevates blood pressure, and a chronic stress response may lead to chronic elevation in blood pressure. One rather unfortunate aspect of our body's response is that it prepares us to fight or flee, and while that may have been very appropriate for dealing with the tigers of yesteryear, fight or flee responses are simply not relevant for most of our 20th century stressors. Thus, our body has no satisfactory release for the state of preparedness. An exception to this general rule is reported by Wolf and Shepard (1950) in the case of a patient with high blood pressure who was constantly agitated because of disagreements with his brother-in-law. Ultimately, by beating up his brother-in-law, he was able to reduce his blood pressure by forty points. This frequent inappropriateness of our stress response partially explains the link between stress and disease.

STRESS AND DISEASE

As previously indicated, a major difficulty with the body's stress response is that neither fight nor flight are appropriate reactions to most modern-day stressors. Fighting with a boss or subordinate or fleeing from a job (by being absent or quitting) are more likely to intensify stress than relieve it. Consequently, the physical preparedness that the stress response provides is inhibited and may become chronic. The relationship between this chronic stress and other variables related to disease is expressed in the following formula developed by Lagerlof (1967):

Disease = $f(S) \times (C) \times (F)$ where,

S = emotional stressor

C = the individual's constitution or general state of health

F = other factors such as environmental conditions, medical history, etc.

This formula has at least three unknowns that help explain why some people develop disease without appreciable exposure to emotional stressors, whereas others remain healthy in the face of severe and prolonged stressor exposure. The formula also highlights the difficulties involved in determining the precise role of stress in the development of any disease. In spite of these unknowns and difficulties, however, it is clear that many illnesses—perhaps most—are to some extent stress-related.

Causes of disease

Clearly the etiology of disease is multifaceted. However, it is possible to specify a combination of three characteristics or conditions that determine the likely presence or absence of disease. These three elements are the individual's susceptibility to the disease, the disease producing agent or agents, and the environment which the individual and the agent share.

The individual's susceptibility to disease is determined by a number of possible factors, including heredity, nutrition, personality factors, current health state, and attitudes toward disease itself. Individual susceptibility and resistance to disease play a more critical part in chronic stress-related diseases than in infectious ones.

The disease-producing agent is also a determining factor in the presence of the disease. The variations in strength of viral organisms help to account for varying infectious disease incidence. In the case of chronic diseases, the strength of a stressor, or its duration, may play a critical role in the onset of the illness.

Finally, environmental conditions may vary. Quality of public drinking water can be an environmental condition relevant to the onset of an infectious disease. Organizational structure or management style can be relevant environmental conditions in the case of some chronic disease.

The bottom line here is this: whether we are talking about a disease brought about by a microorganism or one whose etiology includes organizational stressors, the nature of the person, and the environment—along with the agent itself—is important. No disease has been proved, in the scientific and medical sense, to be caused by stress. It is possible, however, to differentiate disease on the basis of the three-factor conceptual schema just discussed. The results of such a process lead to an important distinction between infectious and chronic diseases as far as stress is concerned. It also facilitates the development of a disease continuum which provides an interesting perspective on the stress and disease link with which we are concerned here.

The disease continuum[1]

A useful, though somewhat arbitrary, dichotomy is the distinction between infectious and chronic diseases. An infectious disease is any disease caused by a specific, identifiable (but possibly unidentified) pathogen or microorganism. Dysentery, measles, and typhoid fever are three examples. A chronic disease is characterized by an extended duration, usually does not involve a microorganism, and is not communicable. Examples include ulcers and heart disease. It is our position that the chronic disease category is inextricably bound to stress. More specifically, we suggest that within the chronic disease category, stressors—with varying degrees of importance—play a role as causative agents.

It is theoretically possible to array the diseases currently known to man on the basis of the extent to which they are germ-produced versus being stress-produced. The notion of such a continuum is perfectly consistent with what we know about disease etiology and has already been proposed by Dodge and Martin (1970). A graphic representation of such a continuum may be found in Figure 4–2. It is important to note that the placement of specific illnesses along the continuum is primarily for illustrative purposes. While each illness's location is, we believe, consistent with authoritative medical opinion, our position is somewhat speculative and would not be universally accepted. There is little argument, however, that such a continuum is not representative of reality.

Very prevalent among the diseases that fall toward the right end of the continuum are the so-called twentieth-century diseases, that is, those afflictions which have become prevalent in recent years. These tend to be afflictions of the more advanced technological societies. One of the ironies of our industrialized age is that the progress that has contributed to the control and elimination of infectious diseases is responsible for contributing to the increase in stress-related diseases. Dodge and Martin (1970) posit a very interesting relationship between the incidence of a

---

[1] The basis for most of the material discussed in this section may be found in *Social Stress and Chronic Illness* by D. L. Dodge and W. T. Martin (University of Notre Dame Press, 1970). The notion of a disease continuum is very cogently advanced by these authors in their chapters III and IV.

FIGURE 4–2   The Disease Continuum

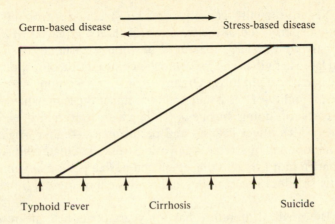

Germ-based disease ⟶ ⟵ Stress-based disease

Typhoid Fever   Cirrhosis   Suicide

disease and the prevalence of stress in society. Not surprisingly, they suggest a high positive correlation between stress levels and the stress-based diseases. But, they also suggest a high negative correlation between the level of stress in a society and the diseases at the left end of the continuum. However, this can be explained by the fact that the germ diseases tend to be prevalent in less-developed countries, which have escaped the additional stressors created by the level and pace of technological sophistication enjoyed in this country.

What the disease continuum, coupled with the kind of mortality rates cited earlier, suggests is that from a health standpoint there is both good news and bad news. The good news (and not really news) is that dramatic strides have been made in controlling infectious diseases. The bad news is that in some way our current environment is fostering the further development of stress-related chronic illnesses. It is our belief—and we believe the available data are strongly suggestive—that stress is a significant contributor to ill health. Furthermore, much of the stress experienced by people today comes about as the result of direct or indirect exposure to stressors associated with their roles as members of goal-directed work organizations. We hasten to add that it is our position only that this *is* the case, not that it should or even has to be true. Indeed, by identifying specific sources of organizational stress (particularly in Chapters 5 and 6), we hope to provide the means by which individuals, managers, and organizations can minimize the dysfunctional consequences of stress.

Stress, work, and disease outcomes

Negative health consequences of stress are probably more frequently experienced in the work world than anyplace else. This is due in part to the large amounts of time we spend in job and career-related activities and in part to the combination of responsibility accepted and effort put forth. Organizations are becoming increasingly sensitive to quality-of-life issues and the impact these may have on the human costs of doing business. It is clear that many employee difficulties which affect health—and performance—either originate in or are compounded by stressors at work. Stress can create a situation in which some minor precipitating event can push a person beyond his or her ability to adapt successfully, and a physical or mental breakdown occurs.

The medical literature has for years contained the results of studies that have offered evidence that many of the negative health consequences experienced by working men and women are associated with factors in their job or work environment. When it is reported, for example, that work-originated stress associated with job responsibility preceded heart attacks in 91 percent of heart disease patients, while only 20 percent of a normal control group reported such stress (Russek, 1965), it is difficult to ignore the potential role stress plays in our general health.

Obviously not everyone in all organizations experiences high levels of stress. Also, many individuals endure great amounts of stress without any corresponding health or performance decrements. Just as people differ in their pain thresholds, they also differ in their ability to tolerate stress. Because of these individual differences, one employee may be seriously affected by stress levels which would be hardly noticed by another employee. Indeed, in some cases, identical levels of stress may facilitate performance in one individual and severely hamper it in another.

We do not suggest that ill health is the only dysfunctional consequence of stress. High turnover and absenteeism, increased waste, accidents, poor labor-management relations, and a host of other factors are even more prevalent stress consequences than ill health and disease. But disease is a real outcome of stress and a very dramatic one at that. To the extent that the link between job stress and disease can be demonstrated, it should become easier to accept less severe, less drastic stress consequences which are even more costly from an organizational standpoint.

DISEASES OF ADAPTATION

We have made repeated references in this chapter to stress diseases and disease consequences of stress. We have made a distinction between infectious disease and chronic disease and suggested a strong relationship between the latter and stress. We have also referred to some specific afflictions as stress-related, such as heart disease and ulcers. Specifically, what we have discussed are what Selye, in a variety of previously cited writings, has termed the *diseases of adaptation*.

To understand the concept of diseases of adaptation it is helpful to return to some concepts introduced earlier. In Chapter One the role of the General Adaptation Syndrome (G.A.S.) in stress was cited. The G.A.S. is a series of responses made by our bodies—frequently without our being consciously aware of it—which are designed to help us deal effectively with a threat. It is very closely associated with the fight-or-flight response also discussed earlier. The biochemical and neuroendocrinological changes that take place during the activation of the G.A.S. are the body's attempt to adapt to the stressor and to keep it confined to the smallest area possible. In an ideal situation, the G.A.S. performs perfectly and the stressor is rendered impotent as far as causing negative consequences is concerned. In reality, however, we do not have a perfect G.A.S., and frequently the degree of imperfection is such that disease is a by-product. The *stress diseases,* or *diseases of adaptation,* are not the direct result of some external agent (such as an infection); they are the consequence of our body's imperfect attempt to meet the threat posed by one or more external agents.

As we saw in an earlier example, when we place our hand on a hot stove, one immediate result is a burn. That is, there is direct tissue damage caused by an external agent. While the heat may legitimately be thought of as a stressor, the negative effects we experienced were not a function of an imperfect adaptation. In contrast, if we are exposed to pollen (an external agent) and suffer the response of repeated sneezing and itching eyes, our problems are not a direct result of the pollen. Rather, they result from our body's attempt to adapt to the presence of the pollen. Similarly, diseases of adaptation are not a direct consequence of an external agent but are associated with less than perfect adaptive reactions to stressors we encounter in our lives. Our adaptive responses are aimed at restoring or maintaining homeostasis, so it is ironic that some of our attempts to maintain internal equilibrium are the cause of subsequent disruptions of that equilibrium.

What, specifically, are the diseases of adaptation? While there is far from universal agreement, Selye (1976) includes in this category high blood pressure, diseases of the heart and of the blood vessels, diseases of the kidney, rheumatic and rheumatoid arthritis, inflammatory diseases of the skin and eyes, allergic and hypersensitivity diseases, nervous and mental diseases, some sexual dysfunctions, various digestive diseases, metabolic diseases, possibly cancer, and diseases of resistance in general.

The next question might be how these diseases are associated with stress. While it is not our intent to provide a medical rationale for the etiology of the diseases referred to in the preceeding paragraph, it may be instructive to present a brief snapshot of the possible relationship between stress and some of the specific afflictions within these categories:

1. *Hypertension* is a blood vessel disease in which the blood flows through arteries at elevated pressure. One of the body's responses to stressors is to constrict artery walls, thus increasing pressure. When the alarm passes, pressure should drop back to normal, but if the stress is prolonged, even unconsciously, pressure may stay at abnormally high levels.

2. *Ulcers* are inflammatory lesions in the lining of the stomach or intestine. One known cause is a variation in cortisone levels. The manufacture of cortisones is greatly increased during periods of stress. Prolonged stress can easily create a perfect internal environment for the creation of lesions.

3. *Diabetes* is a serious disease involving insulin deficiencies which render its victims unable to absorb enough blood sugar. Stress increases the blood sugar level necessitating increases in insulin secretion. If the stress is persistent, the pancreas may weaken, resulting in a permanent insulin deficiency.

4. *Headaches* are frequently the result of muscular tension. Muscle tension is increased as we are exposed to stressors, triggering the onset of a headache after a sustained period of stress. Frequently, the headache itself is a stressor leading to increased muscle tension, which in turn increases the severity and duration of the headache.

5. *Cancer* is one of the more controversial entries in the adaptation category. One current cancer theory is that mutant (cancer) cells are continuously being produced in our bodies but are usually destroyed by the immune system before they can multiply and grow. Responses to stressors have been shown to bring about small biochemical alterations in the immune system.

The changes are thought by some to be enough to allow reproduction of small quantities of these mutant cells which in turn become malignant tumors.

Other examples are possible. Our objective is not to be exhaustive, however, but to provide a basis for furthering the reader's understanding that physiological damage can grow at least partially from a process which began psychologically. There is absolutely no suggestion intended that the diseases of adaptation are uniquely stress-induced or even that they are primarily stress-based. Few medical or behavioral science researchers would attempt to build such a case. As the disease continuum suggests, however (Figure 4–2), stress may play a greater or lesser role, depending on the specific disease. There is an element of adaptation in every disease. In some, this element plays a central role; in others, it is virtually insignificant. The more prominent a role adaptation plays, the more stressors the employee is subjected to, and the more predisposed he or she is to over or underadapting to stressors, the more likely that negative health consequences will result.

THE SPECIAL CASE OF CORONARY HEART DISEASE

Most dictionaries define an epidemic as something "affecting many people at once" or being "excessively prevalent." By these or any other definitions, coronary heart disease has become an epidemic in this country. In 1978 over one million people died from some form of cardiovascular disease, representing 53 percent of all deaths in the United States. Each year approximately one million Americans have a heart attack, and about 650,000 of them die (American Heart Association, 1978).

Heart disease by itself accounts for 52 million lost workdays annually, which represents almost 15 billion dollars in wages lost to this growing problem. Simply the cost of recruiting replacements for executives lost to heart disease costs about $700 million annually. The total bill, just in terms of dollars, is estimated to be close to 30 billion dollars per year in lost productivity, retraining costs, medical care and premature retirement. At current incident rates, one out of five American men will have a heart attack *before* he retires. In some categories based on age, occupation, medical and family history, diet, and other factors, that chance increases to one out of two.

Figure 4–3, in the form of a worksheet, is a slightly modified version of the formula used by the American Heart Association to compute one kind of organizational cost associated with heart disease, replacement costs. As an example, consider a company employing four thousand people. On the average it will have approximately one thousand male employees between the ages of forty-five and sixty-five (line 2). In an average year six will die from heart-related illnesses (line 3). Three will be lost to heart-related premature retirement (line 4). The company's annual personnel losses on line 5 due to heart disorders is nine. Annual replacement cost, based on average replacement cost figures, will be over $38,000 (line 6). Line 7 indicates that eventually two thousand employees will die of heart disease, assuming no further increase in incident rates. A company with ten thousand employees would be looking at an annual replacement bill of just under $100,000. Keep in mind that these are just replacement costs and do not include medical costs, performance decrements, and the like. U.S. government figures indicate that a coronary suffered by a federal employee costs the taxpayers an average of $10,000, *excluding* replacement costs.

FIGURE 4–3 The Price the Company Pays

1. Number of Employees   _____

2. Men in Age Range 45–65 (¼ of line 1)   _____

3. Estimated Heart Deaths per Year—6 of 1000 (.006 × line 2)   _____

4. Estimated Premature Retirement Due to Heart Problems per Year—3 of 1000 (.003 × line 2)   _____

5. Company's Annual Personnel Losses Due to Heart Disorders (sum of lines 3 and 4)   _____

6. Annual Replacement Cost (line 5 × $4,300), The Average Cost of Hiring and Training Replacements for Experienced Employees   _____

7. Number of Employees Who Will Eventually Die of Heart Diseases If Present Rates Are Allowed to Continue (½ of line 1)   _____

What makes the epidemic proportions of the coronary heart disease phenomenon particularly significant is that the current incidence levels reflect enormous increases in recent years. As recently as 1920, heart disease as a mortality cause was extremely rare. More so than in any of the other diseases mentioned thus far, we have what is clearly a twentieth-century phenomenon.

The role of stress

As is true with all the other diseases of adaptation, stress has been implicated in the etiology of coronary heart disease. To understand the possible mechanisms involved in the stress-heart disease link it is important to be aware that virtually all heart disease is preceded by coronary artery disease, and arteriosclerosis is the primary artery disease. Arteriosclerosis is an accumulation in the arteries of cholesterol deposits that eventually cause the arteries to harden and narrow as the cholesterol builds up in the artery wall. Eventually, the blood flow through the diseased artery is severely restricted and in extreme danger of clotting. Blood clots in diseased arteries are the major direct cause of heart attacks and cerebral strokes.

An individual with arteriosclerosis, is predisposed to heart disease. Add stress to this condition, and the danger of heart attack increases. This is true because stress tends to increase the frequency of the heart beat. The faster the heart rate, the greater the heart requirements of oxygenated blood, which it is unable to obtain due to the restricted blood flow through the diseased artery. With time the heart muscle, which is supplied by the arteriosclerotic artery, becomes paralyzed and stops working. When this happens, the heart muscle may die, resulting in a heart attack.

There is a theory about another possible role that stress may play in heart disease. It is somewhat speculative, and there is far from universal agreement within the medical community. However, it has a number of respected adherents and should be mentioned for that reason. It was originally advanced by Friedman and Rosenman (1974), two cardiologists interested in the role of personality characteristics in the incidence of heart disease. (Their approach to this individual difference factor will be examined in some detail in Chapter Ten).

Recall that virtually all heart disease is preceded by coronary artery disease in the form of arteriosclerosis. Arteriosclerosis is brought about by the build-up of fatty (cholesterol) deposits in the artery walls.

The stress response in humans is responsible for increasing the amount of cholesterol in the blood and may also increase the amount of time the blood needs to rid itself of cholesterol. Thus, during stress, blood fat levels increase and our ability to process blood fats decreases. Consequently, it is hypothesized, the linings of the coronary arteries are exposed to greater amounts of cholesterol for longer periods of time than would be true in the absence of stress. When stress is chronic over a period of years—perhaps decades—the resulting artery disease *may* be in large part a function of that stress.

Heart disease and job stress

In Greek mythology the King of Corinth was an unfortunate fellow named Sisyphus. Zeus, angered by Sisyphus' disrespect for him, sent him to Hades, where he was forever condemned to push a large, heavy rock up a steep hill, never quite getting it to the top. The heart disease candidate is often, like Sisyphus, an individual who works hard, puts out extra effort to meet a challenge, but who is able to take little satisfaction from those efforts. How many people in today's organizations fit this description? While it may be difficult to assess job stress and tension, evidence keeps mounting that these factors play a significant role in coronary artery and heart disease.

Related to the Sisyphus phenomenon, job satisfaction—or more correctly dissatisfaction—has been implicated in heart disease. Numerous studies in this country and abroad have found that persons with coronary heart disease report higher levels of dissatisfaction with aspects of their work such as lack of recognition, boredom, and poor relations with others on the job. All of these are potential stressors (For an excellent review of much of this research see Jenkins, 1976). Large-scale occupational studies have found relationships between people in occupations with high average rates of dissatisfaction and high mortality rates from heart disease. The obtained dissatisfaction-heart disease associations are even higher if the focus is upon *intrinsic* satisfaction (Sales and House, 1971).

Stressors such as high levels of work load, responsibility, time pressures, and conflict and ambiguity in job roles have also been implicated. The classic study in this regard was done by Friedman, Rosenman, and Carroll (1957). In studying tax accountants, they found marked increases in blood cholesterol levels as the April 15 tax filing deadline drew near. This corresponded with an increase in work load and pressure to complete assignments on time. Once the deadline passed, cholesterol levels did not immediately return to previous readings, but decreased over a two-month period before returning to normal. Other studies conducted at NASA and elsewhere are consistent with the results obtained in the accountant research.

It should be pointed out that not all of the evidence showing a relationship between stress and heart disease involves negative or bad events. The body may respond with a stress reaction to stressors that are positive. An example of this is the fan who suffers a heart attack as he cheers his hometown football team to victory. A more organizationally oriented example would be the effect of a promotion at work. Here there are data which indicate that men who have recently received a promotion suffered more heart attacks than a set of controls matched by age and occupation (Jenkins, Rosenman, and Friedman, 1966). Of course it may very well be the case that the most direct link was not the positive event of the promotion itself but the increased responsibility, work load or self-imposed pressure to excel that resulted from the promotion. Even if this is the case, however, these factors were stressors which arose as consequence of the promotion.

It can be argued that there are many risk factors in coronary heart disease that explain the rapid increase in the incidence of this disease as well or better than an explanation based upon increasing levels of job stress. It can be shown, for example, that people smoke more today than fifty years ago and that they exercise less and are more overweight than was once true. There is no question that these factors have contributed to the current epidemic. But there is also little question that the increased stress of modern life—both in and out of organizations—has had its impact. In fact, it is probable that some of these other risk factors are themselves affected by stress. Thus, the higher incidence of smoking may be a result of increased tension and increased obesity may be a consequence of work schedules that do not permit individuals to eat properly or get enough exercise. The factors contributing to heart disease are many, varied, and imperfectly understood. The evidence is increasing, however, that stress—particularly job stress—has a role.

STRESS AND MENTAL HEALTH

Thus far, our attention has focused on the physical health consequences of stress. It is true that this is the focus currently popular from a research standpoint, and significant strides have been made in recent years in improving our understanding of the stress-physical illness link. Nonetheless, the fact remains that far more employees suffer mental discomfort from stress than physical discomfort. The mental health dysfunctions are—more so than the physical ones—a direct and obvious result of stress. When 6 percent of the population are alcoholics; another estimated 10 percent are problem drinkers, and when 6 billion doses of prescription tranquilizers and 9 billion doses of amphetamines and barbiturates are consumed annually, there is strong evidence that people are experiencing high levels of tension, anxiety, and stress. And a recent New York State Narcotic Addiction Control Commission report that 36 percent of regular tranquilizer users used the drug at work is additional evidence that stressors in the work environment play a significant role.

What are the direct psychological consequences of stress? They can include depression, anxiety, nervous exhaustion, disorientation, feelings of inadequacy, loss of self-esteem, lowered tolerance for ambiguity, apathy, loss of achievement motivation and increased irritability. The really deadly aspect of these outcomes is that they can form a closed loop of increasing stress levels. Chester Comer, to whom we were introduced at the beginning of this chapter, is an example. The more stress Chester experienced, the more irritable he became. The more irritable he became, the more his interpersonal relationships suffered. The more his relationships suffered, the more stress he experienced, which increased his irritability, and so on. The stressor-stress reaction process can become a vicious circle, escalating with each completed revolution.

The extent of mental health problems that have grown out of job-related stress is very difficult to estimate. The $17 billion dollar annual decrease in productive efficiency as a result of stress, cited in Chapter One, is only a very rough estimate and provides no information on the number of employees affected. The British government recently reported that in the last fifteen years in Britain work days lost as a result of physical illnesses have risen 22 percent. For that same time period, the number of work days lost due to mental health problems rose by 152 percent in men and 302 percent in women. There is no reason to suggest that on a relative basis United States figures would differ substantially from the British ones.

The research literature abounds with studies suggesting relationships between mental health and job stressors. Mental health problems have been linked to lack of job satisfaction, work overload, deadline pressure, leadership style, job insecurity, underutilization of abilities, and involvement in repetitive, machine-paced work, to mention only a few (Kasl, 1973). While there are exceptions, most of the work done in this area is strongly supportive of at least statistical associations between the presence of stressors in the work environment and mental health problems.

As is true with physical problems, some mental health difficulties are more severe than others. Some are prolonged enough and/or disabling enough that the individual is required to seek the assistance of mental health professionals. Some occupational differences in the incidence rates of mental health disorders have been found by examining the occupational classification of individuals seeking professional assistance. In one such study Colligan, Smith, and Hurrell (1977) examined the admission records in community mental health centers throughout Tennessee. One hundred thirty occupations were examined, and after controlling for the distribution of the occupation in the general population, health technologists, waiters and waitresses, and nurses led the list based on admission rates per thousand. It is also of interest that while women comprised only 39 percent of the employed population in this study, they accounted for 53 percent of the admissions. This may reflect the fact that women are entering the work force now in unprecedented numbers, and many are encountering job stressors the first time.

Whether the outcome of being stressed is physical, mental, or both, the disease consequences of stress are significant in terms of individual welfare and organizational efficiency.

THE QUESTION OF CAUSATION

In any field of endeavor one hesitates before making the leap from correlation or association to cause. Most people recognize that evidence that events A and B occur together and/or do not occur singly does not necessarily mean that one causes the other to occur.

We may be able to show among a population sample, for example, that stress and blood pressure co-vary. That is, as the stress experienced by our sample increases, their blood pressure increases; as their stress drops, their blood pressure drops. Have we established that stress causes changes in blood pressure? Not really. It could be that changes in blood pressure bring about changes in stress. While that is not an intuitively attractive explanation, it is nonetheless theoretically possible. Another possibility is, of course, that changes in both variables are a function of some unidentified third variable.

Even if causation in the stress-disease link were established, Cook and Campbell (1979) point out that there are different kinds or degrees of causation. To return to our previous example, stress may be both necessary and sufficient to cause increases in blood pressure. That is, blood pressure may always go up in the presence of stress and never in its absence. The second level of causation occurs when stress is necessary but not sufficient for blood pressure increases. In other words, blood pressure will not rise in the absence of stress, but it may not rise in its presence either. The final degree of causation is when stress is sufficient, but not necessary, to elevate blood pressure. That is, if stress is present, blood pressure may rise but it may also rise in its absence.

The reason we have taken the time to develop this discussion is to emphasize that *there is no rigorous proof in the strict scientific sense that stress causes any of the diseases of adaptation discussed in this chapter. In no way, however, does this negate or diminish any aspect of the stress-disease relationship we have been examining.* At the present time there is no rigorous proof in the strict scientific sense that smoking causes lung cancer. Yet few responsible medical authorities would deny that cigarettes are a potentially dangerous health hazard. Just as it does not require proof of causation for decreases in smoking rates to have a positive effect on the public health, reduced stress levels among employees do not require proof of causation to result in improved health and effectiveness.

REFERENCES

American Heart Association. *Heart Facts.* American Heart Association Communication Division, 1978.

Colligan, M. J., Smith, M. J., and J. J. Hurrell. "Occupational incidence rates of mental health disorders." *Journal of Human Stress* 3(1977): 34–39.

Cook, T. D. and D. Campbell. *Quasi-Experimentation: Design and Analysis Issues for Field Settings.* Chicago: Rand McNally and Company, 1979.

Dodge, D. L. and W. T. Martin. *Social Stress and Chronic Illness.* Notre Dame: University of Notre Dame Press, 1970.

Evans, J. "Causation and disease: A chronological journal." *Journal of Epidemiology* 108(1978): 249–257.

Friedman, M. and R. Rosenman. *Type A Behavior and Your Heart*. New York: Alfred A. Knopf, Inc., 1974.

Friedman, M., Rosenman, R. and V. Carroll. "Changes in the serum cholesterol and blood clotting time of men subject to cyclic variation of occupational stress." *Circulation* 17(1957): 852–861.

Jenkins, C. D. "Recent evidence supporting psychologic and social risk factors for coronary disease." *New England Journal of Medicine* 294(1976): 1033–1038.

Jenkins, C. D., Rosenman, R., and M. Friedman. "Components of the coronary-prone behavior pattern: Their relation to silent myocardial infarction and blood lipids." *Journal of Chronic Diseases* 19(1966): 599–609.

Kasl, S. V. "Mental health and the work environment: An examination of the evidence." *Journal of Occupational Medicine* 15(1973): 509–518.

Kavanagh, T. and R. J. Shephard. "The immediate antecedents of myocardial infarction in active men." *Canadian Medical Association Journal* 109(1973): 19–22.

Lagerlof, H. "Psychophysiological reactions during emotional stress: Medical implications." In *Emotional stress*. L. Levi, ed. New York: S. Karger, 1967.

Levene, D. L. "Psychological factors in the genesis of myocardial infarction." *Canadian Medical Association Journal* 111(1974): 499–501.

Russek, H. "Stress, tobacco, and coronary heart disease in North America professional groups." *Journal of the American Medical Association,* 192(1965): 189–94.

Sales, S. and J. House. "Job dissatisfaction as a possible risk factor in coronary heart disease." *Journal of Chronic Diseases* 23(1971): 861–873.

Schwab, R. S. and J. S. Pritchard. "Situational stresses and extrapyramidal disease in different personalities." *Life Stress and Disease*. Proceedings of the Association for Research in Nervous and Mental Disease XXIX. Baltimore: The Williams and Wilkins Co., 1950.

Selye, H. *The Stress of Life*. rev. ed. New York: McGraw-Hill, Inc., 1976.

Wolf, S. and E. M. Shepard. "An appraisal of factors that evoke and modify the hypertensive reaction pattern." In *Life Stress and Bodily Disease*. H. G. Wolf, S. Wolf, and C. C. Hare, eds. Baltimore: The Williams and Wilkins Co., 1950.

FOR FURTHER READING

Dodge, D. C. and W. T. Martin. *Social Stress and Chronic Illness.* Notre
    Dame: University of Notre Dame Press, 1970.
Pelletier, K. R. *Mind as Healer, Mind as Slayer.* New York: Delacorte
    Press, 1977.
Selye, H. *The Stress of Life.* rev. ed. New York: McGraw-Hill, Inc., 1976.

Physical Environment and Individual Level Stressors

5

THE ONE-EYED DOE

A Doe that had lost an eye used to graze near the sea; and that she might be the more secure from harm, she kept her blind side towards the water, from whence she had no apprehension of danger, and with the other surveyed the country as she fed. By this vigilance and precaution, she thought herself in the utmost security; but a sly fellow, with two poaching companions, who had watched her several days to no purpose, at last took a boat, and came gently down upon her, and shot her. The Doe, in the agonies of death, breathed out this doleful complaint: O hard fate, that I should receive my death's wound from the side whence I expected no ill, and be safe in that quarter where I looked for the most danger.

Managerial Application • Some aspects of the work environment may unexpectedly prove to be stressors; nonetheless we ought to use foresight to guard in the best way we can against those stressors we can identify.

101

Thus far in our exploration of stress and work, we have examined the nature of stress, considered a framework for viewing work-related stress, studied a number of approaches to stress measurement, and surveyed the relationship between stress and dysfunctional health consequences. In this chapter we will deal with two types of stressors in the work environment: *physical environment stressors* and *individual level stressors*. Chapter 6 looks at *group* and *organization level stressors,* while Chapter 7 examines the role played by *extraorganizational stressors.*

Physical stressors in the environment are different in kind, but not necessarily in degree, from the other stressor conditions we have discussed. The physical stressors are environmental conditions or phenomena which produce stress emotions: extremes in temperature, light, and noise; excessive motion; and atmospheric pollution. While these are physical rather than psychosocial stressors, the underlying difficulty is the same—when such conditions are encountered they require an adaptation on our part. And because they create physical discomfort, we may react to them emotionally, increasing further the potential for stress.

Individual level stressors are due primarily to the organizational role played by an individual. Questions such as whether or not responsibilities are understood, employees are overloaded, deadlines are realistic, and whether differing expectations on the part of different people create conflict are related to stress at what we are calling the individual level. But before proceeding with specific environmental and individual level stressors, let us examine the nature of stressors more fully.

What are stressors?

Virtually any event, situation, or person that we encounter in our external environment can be a stressor. The two key words here are *can be*. While potential stressors abound, actual stressors are, fortunately, far less numerous.

The stress response is our body's effort to adapt to change, or more accurately, to maintain homeostasis. We experience stress when we are unable to keep or regain this personal balance. If there is no perceived external threat, there is no need to go into an adaptive posture, and there can be no stress. Recall from Chapter 1 that stress is an internal response to a disruptive external agent. That external agent is the stressor—the stimulus which elicits the stress response. Since under the right conditions virtually anything can produce a stress response, it follows that virtually anything *can* become a stressor. For this reason it is impossible to draw up a finite list of stressors and say "avoid these and you will lead a stress-free life." Practically speaking, however, some external conditions are far more likely to operate as stressors than others. This chapter and the two that follow are devoted to an examination of those common stressors.

While managers generally understand that physical or mental health problems affect employee productivity, it has been more difficult for them to accept that work can have an adverse effect on physical or mental health. It can have this effect when stressors in the work environment provoke stress responses in employees. But not all stressors provoke a stress response in all employees, nor will the same stressor always provoke a response in the same employee. And if a stressor does bring forth a response in several employees, the value of that response and its degree of disruptiveness may differ in as many ways as there are employees affected by it. To understand why and how that can be true, it is necessary to examine how stressors interact with other variables.

Consider for a moment two employees, Jack and Jill. Both are about to begin their annual performance appraisal session with the same boss. Both have achieved approximately the same level of performance for the year. In fact, just about every aspect of their upcoming performance reviews is the same, except that Jack is experiencing a great deal of tension, anxiety, and distress, and Jill is looking forward to it. Clearly, the performance review session is serving as a stressor stimulus for Jack and not for Jill. Why is this?

To understand why, it is important to realize that at least two other variables help determine the extent to which any stressor elicits a stress response: the environment in which the stressor occurs and the personal characteristics of the individual. McLean (1976) has labeled these two factors *context* and *vulnerability*. *Context* refers to the social and physical environment of the stressor. It may be something as broad as the national economy or as specific as the management style of the person you report to. *Vulnerability* refers to individual characteristics such as age, sex, personality traits, and emotional predispositions.

So our situation with Jack and Jill may not seem as similar when the environment and personal characteristics are taken into account. Perhaps, for example, Jill is skilled in an area that currently has a far greater demand than supply. She knows her skills are badly needed by the organization and that her boss is likely to let that influence her ratings. On the other hand, Jack's area of expertise is experiencing a declining demand at the same time many more people with his skills are entering the labor market. Jack knows he could be quickly and inexpensively replaced and that, unless his performance is exceedingly good, that might well happen to him. So here we have an environmental or context factor—supply and demand conditions for particular skills—influencing the degree to which the potential stressor of a performance review provokes a stress response.

Even more likely than environmental factors to effect this situation, however, are the personal characteristics of the two people involved, that is, their degrees of vulnerability to the stressor. If Jill is self-confident and enjoys high levels of self-esteem, and Jack lacks those attributes, Jill is far less likely to perceive the upcoming review as stressful. Jack is more likely to be stressed if he has a lower tolerance for ambiguity than Jill and is unclear as to just how his performance is perceived by the boss. Jack may also be more susceptible now simply because he is coping with a number of stressors in other areas of his life, leaving him more vulnerable to job stressors than he would be otherwise.

Much of the impact of a stressor is contingent upon an individual's perceptions. In a very important sense, it does not matter whether or not objectively Jack is likely to encounter anything during his performance review which will be threatening, damaging, or in any other way negative. All that is required is for Jack to feel concerned that something might go wrong for the stressor stimulus to evoke the stress response. There is a great deal of truth to the statement that we ourselves are the cause of much of our distress. We shall examine in more detail in Chapter 8 these individual characteristics which predispose us to experiencing stress.

PHYSICAL ENVIRONMENT STRESSORS

In a sense, all stressors are environmental in that they are part of the external milieu. An examination of the model in Chapter 2 will demonstrate this. All of the antecedents (stressors) in the first column of the model are part of the physical environment or are manifestations of environmental events, such as role ambiguity, overload, lack of group cohesiveness, management style, and others. Further, as was pointed out in the preceding section environmental conditions affect whether or not a particular stressor will evoke a stress response. Clearly then, all stressors are environmental in origin, and it is not our intent to suggest otherwise. There are, however, many aspects of the environment or many ways of classifying environmental stimuli. Some aspects of the environment are physical; some are psychological; others are anthropological; others still are sociological. Stress is a psychophysical response to these various environmental stimuli.

If we were to categorize most stressors, we would say that the majority of them are part of the psychological or sociological environment. Another examination of the research model in Chapter 2 will demonstrate this. The individual, group, organizational, and extraorganizational levels are comprised overwhelmingly of what we might call psychosocial stressors. One category of stressors doesn't fit this description very well, however. These are physical environmental stressors. In this context *environmental* refers to physical conditions in the environment which require that an employee adapt in order to maintain homeostasis. Extremes of temperature, for example, may be a physical environment stressor. Too much or too little light is another example. In short, environmental stressors in this sense are physical aspects of the environment, usually, but not always, perceived through one or more of the five senses.

Physical environment stressors are what Poulton (1978) refers to as *blue-collar stressors* because they are concentrated in blue-collar occupations more than in any others. (Although as modern life brings us with increasing frequency Love Canals, Three-Mile Islands and related events, exposure to enviromental stressors is increasing for all segments of the population.)

Being aspects of our physical environment is not the only way these stressors differ from the other categories. They may result in *direct* physical trauma as well. While heart disease may be an indirect consequence of too much stress, deafness is a direct consequence of overexposure to high noise levels. While it is not the direct physical trauma resulting from these stressors that we are primarily concerned with here, such consequences should not be overlooked. Our primary interests, however, are the performance and indirect health decrements which may result from exposure to these stressors.

While the list of potential physical environment stressors could be quite lengthy, we have chosen to focus on five which provide a fairly comprehensive sweep of this category: light, noise, temperature, vibration and motion, and polluted air.

Light

As we have all experienced on many occasions, improper lighting for the task at hand can cause problems. It may make the task more difficult, even impossible to complete, and it may result in the uncomfortable sensation of tired eyes or produce headaches. It can also increase our frustration level and our tension as we struggle to complete a task under less than ideal conditions. Most general office and assembly tasks require approximately twenty to forty footcandles of light (one footcandle equals the amount of light reaching one square foot of area, one foot away from a candle with a one-inch flame). Some severe tasks with minute detail, however, require six to ten times that level of light intensity. Insufficient light results in lowered performance, increased time requirements to complete tasks, and increased frustration.

Too much light or glare can also be the source of difficulties. Glare provides a good example of the differences between objective and subjective reports of stress. For example, a worker may complain of glare (subjective measure) that is too small to have a measurable effect (objective measure) on his or her work. Levels of glare that cause discomfort (subjective) may in fact provide optimum visibility (objective). Thus it is possible for a level of lighting intensity which is visually optimal to be a precursor to stress, particularly if the exposure is prolonged.

Aside from the objective questions of optimal intensities, minimal glare, and so on, good lighting is perceived as cheerful and stimulating, and thus, relaxing. In those few instances where there is a conflict between perceived comfort and optimal lighting, there may be good reasons to opt for illumination levels in the comfort range. Unless there is a large difference (which is most unlikely), comfortable levels of lighting are less likely to act as stressors than uncomfortable, but objectively optimal levels.

Noise

Prolonged exposure to excessive noise (approximately eighty decibels, roughly equivalent to traffic noise on a busy street) can produce deafness. From a stress standpoint, however, noise is a stressor primarily when it distracts. Excessive and/or intermittent noise interferes with our concentration and is a source of frustration that may lead to anger and tension. It overcomes the internal speech that we use in thinking and monitoring what we are doing.

Various studies have shown that successful noise adaptation is possible in a wide range of conditions. Even so, such adaptation is a stress response and, like all stress responses, it requires energy. Prolonged exposure, then, may lead to fatigue and consequent performance decrements. Not only can physical fatigue result, but as Glass, Singer, and Friedman (1969) have shown, there may be psychological costs involved in adapting to noise, including lowered tolerance for frustration.

Adaptation is possible, of course, even to the point that the absence of an originally disturbing noise can become a stressor, much like in the old story about the fellow who kept waking up in the middle of the night because his house was next to the railroad tracks and the 3:00 A.M. freight *stopped* coming through. Noise, in fact, seems to operate less as a stressor in situations where it is excessive but expected, than in those where it is unexpected, or at least unpredictable. The change in noise levels, more than the absolute levels themselves, appears to be the irritant. This, of course, is simply another way of saying that noise, like any stressor, causes stress when it forces us to adapt to change.

Temperature

In the majority of work environments today, temperature extremes are avoided through careful controls. Nonetheless, there are still individuals who work outside or in manufacturing operations such as steel mills, where temperatures cannot as a practical matter be controlled. Additionally, geographic regions where temperature extremes are commonplace are seeing more and more industrialization (e.g., the Alaskan pipeline and mining operations in the Arctic, where average temperatures are 50° below zero). The energy crisis is having its effect as well, with mandatory thermostat settings in many public buildings of 78° during the summer months.

Excessive heat is a potential stressor likely to generate both physiological and psychological costs, particularly to those engaged in heavy physical activities. Physiologically, heat stress results in increased blood flow and heart rate, higher oxygen demands, and fatigue. Psychologically, it can disrupt normal affective functioning and greatly increase irritability. It is more than coincidental that violent crimes increase during periods of high temperature and decrease when temperatures drop.

Extremes of cold also influence individuals psychologically, affecting energy levels and possibly decreasing motivation. From a performance standpoint, extreme cold affects the hands and feet and causes performance decrements among individuals performing tasks requiring the use of those limbs.

Once again, we see an environmental condition, temperature, acting as a stressor when it requires a great deal of adaptive effort from the individual. Even successful adaptation has its negative consequences in the form of the physical and psychic energy expended in order to maintain the adaptation.

Vibration and motion

Unlike heat and cold, vibration and motion do not ordinarily occur naturally in the environment. Vibration is usually experienced as a consequence of operating a tool such as a pneumatic drill or driving a vehicle which transmits engine vibration to the driver's seat. The to-and-fro motion of a ship or the roll of an aircraft, and, less frequently, the sway of a motor vehicle are the most common motion stressors. Physiologically, motion stress is precipitated by rotary accelerations of the head which are registered in the semicircular canals of the inner ear.

Vibration is a greater potential stressor than motion. The amount of vibration an individual can experience without eliciting a stress response depends upon the vibration's size of acceleration and its amplitude, as well as personal characteristics of the individual. Most of the consequences are physical in nature: blurred vision, headaches, shaking (particularly in the hand), and muscle tension (although very low frequencies, such as those found in massage units, may have a relaxing effect on the muscles). Long-term effects may include Reynaud's disease, where hands become swollen and pained.

Psychologically, the results of these stressors are more likely to be reactions to the physiological outcomes than to the stressors themselves. It is the blurred vision, the tensed muscles, the shaky hands, or the appearance of a long-term effect such as Reynaud's disease which serve as precipitators of psychological stress reactions.

Polluted air

As we are all aware, air pollution has become an increasing problem in recent years, as is indicated by a growing labyrinth of local, state, and federal regulations seeking to control the amount of noxious emissions from everything from automobiles to giant refineries. As serious as this problem is, this is not the air pollution with which we are concerned. There is no question that this type of atmospheric condition is a stressor posing both physical and psychological problems. However, our concern is with the quality of air in the workplace, a condition only very indirectly related to the more general problem of atmospheric pollution.

Many industrial operations produce by-products that pollute the air in the vicinity of the producing installation. Aside from during respiration, many substances may also enter the body through the skin. In quarrying operations the air may contain quartz dust, which, when breathed for an extended period of time, can produce fibrosis of the lungs. Asbestos dust and coal dust leading to "black lung" disease can be fibrosis producers, and recent evidence has linked the inhalation of asbestos to cancer. Metal work involves the heating and cleaning of metals, which produce potentially dangerous fumes and vapors. Sulphur dioxide is a toxic waste produced from a variety of manufacturing processes. One of the most common pollutants in the air is carbon monoxide, a special menace for individuals working in garages, traffic tunnels, and many segments of the transportation industry.

Various types of radiation are potentially dangerous. The use of radioactive materials is becoming more commonplace today. The use of X rays is also quite widespread, particularly in inspection and quality control functions. Ultraviolet radiation is a part of many processes, such as welding. Many types of electrical equipment change the ionization of the air, a condition which has been linked to performance decrements (Wofford, 1966).

An additional aspect of working in polluted environments should be mentioned. As our knowledge of the possible effects of exposure to these pollutants increases, we become more aware of the possible price we may have to pay for this exposure. This knowledge becomes a significant stressor for some. The worker may experience stress each day because of the knowledge that the asbestos he or she is exposed to may appreciably reduce the chance of living a healthy, normal life span.

INDIVIDUAL LEVEL STRESSORS

When we began our discussion of environmental stressors, we indicated that in one sense all stressors were environmental. In the same way, all stressors are individual. That is, how the stressor affects us as individuals is of critical importance.

As organization members we are exposed to a wide range of people, events, and situations which are potential stressors. One way of sorting these out to make them more manageable and amenable to discussion is to use the four organizational categories of the model presented in Chapter 2. Our interest at this point is in the individual level stressors. By that we mean stressors that are directly associated with the role we play or the tasks we have to accomplish in the organization. While in one way or another all work stressors are linked to the job we perform, the key here is the directness of the connection. Individual level stressors arise as a result of the job functions we perform.

Stressors at the individual level have been studied more than any other category, and there is more agreement about what constitutes a stressor at this level than at the other levels. It may also be true that individual level stressors account for more of the stress in organizations than any other level. At present, however, that must remain a speculative statement and may simply reflect the disproportionate amount of research directed at this level.

We will consider five major individual level stressors: role conflict, role ambiguity, work overload, responsibility for people, and career development stressors. Numerous other aspects of our organizational environments could quite properly be classified as individual stressors: time pressures and relationships with subordinates, peers, and superiors, for example. The five we shall treat in some detail, however, represent those upon which there is general agreement and which account for the bulk of the available research evidence.

Role conflict

How an individual employee behaves in a given position depends upon many factors. Some of these stem from the employee; others from the organization. A combination of the expectations and demands an employee places upon him or herself and those of other members of the organization results in a set of forces which may be termed *role pressures*. When a situation arises in which two or more role pressures are in conflict with one another, a condition of *role conflict* exists. Role conflict is present whenever compliance with one set of pressures makes compliance with another set difficult, objectionable, or impossible.

Some role conflict may be called objective. That is, it exists because two or more people are sending contradictory requests to the employee. One person asks the employee to do something that is forbidden by another person to whom the individual is responsible. Other role conflict is more subjective in nature and results from conflict between the formal requirements of the role and the individual's own desires, goals, or values. Thus, the salesperson directed to sell a product even if the customer doesn't need it may feel that this is a morally indefensible position and experience subjective role conflict.

It is apparent that the presence of virtually any type of conflict situation is a stressor. It is also true that much role conflict, particularly objective conflict, results from dysfunctional organization practices. Regardless of the source, the consequences tend to be disruptive of the achievement of organizational goals and injurious to the individual. Probably the best-documented consequence of role conflict is a decrease in job satisfaction. Kahn and his associates (1964) found not only that conflict produced job dissatisfaction and anxiety, but also that the more authority possessed by the individual or individuals sending the employee the conflicting message, the greater the resulting job dissatisfaction.

Other research has linked role conflict to heart disease incidence, high blood pressure, elevated cholesterol counts, and obesity. Thus, as a stressor, role conflict undermines job satisfaction (with all the negative outcomes so frequently found to be associated with that) and is associated with physiological changes that have both personal and organizational costs. Other difficulties, such as decreased quality of decisions made and reduction of creativity are very likely to result from the tension and anxiety associated with conflict.

While the data are sketchy, role conflict may be associated with absenteeism and turnover, as well. This is not surprising when you recall that the stress response is essentially one of fighting or fleeing, and both absenteeism and turnover may be attempts to flee.

Role ambiguity

Role ambiguity is a lack of clarity about one's role, job objectives, and the scope of the responsibilities of one's job. Almost everyone experiences some degree of role ambiguity. The first job, a promotion or transfer, a new boss, the first supervisory responsibility, a new company, or a change in the structure of the existing organization— all of these events, and others, may serve to create a temporary state of role ambiguity. While the effects of such transient ambiguity are not positive, neither are they particularly debilitating for most of us. They are expected in the situation, and while we may prefer it to be otherwise, we generally are able to deal with the ambiguity effectively and reach a state of clarity with minimal or no adverse consequences.

Role ambiguity does not have to be a long-term condition to function as a stressor. Nonetheless, the temporary conditions cited above do not usually cause a dysfunctional stress response. Except for those very few among us who are unable to cope with any lack of clarity, no matter how short the duration, it is the condition of chronic ambiguity which poses the greatest threat to our adaptive mechanisms.

Studies by Kahn and associates (1964) and French and Caplan (1970) have addressed the question of role ambiguity. Kahn found that men who experienced ongoing role ambiguity reported more job dissatisfaction, more job-related tension, and lower levels of self-confidence than men who did not report appreciable amounts of ambiguity. French and Caplan (1970) found ambiguity to be associated with indicators of physical and mental health such as elevated blood pressure.

More recently ambiguity has been linked to depressed moods, lowered self-esteem, decreased life satisfaction (in addition to decreased job satisfaction), lower levels of work motivation, and expressed intention to leave the job (Margolis, Kroes, and Quinn, 1974). Similar research has linked ambiguity to anxiety, depression, and feelings of resentment (Caplan and Jones, 1975).

Once again an incomplete, but growing, array of evidence indicates that a factor in organizational life—ambiguity—elicits a stress response that can be negative and maladaptive in nature. We view it as maladaptive because none of the outcomes—lowered satisfaction, decreased motivation, increased blood pressure, etc.—reduce the ambiguity experienced. No organization can be structured or managed in a manner that will eliminate this problem. But a variety of steps can be taken to minimize ambiguity. Uncertainty is largely responsible for feelings of anxiety and uncertainty results from a lack of information. Consequently, anything designed to increase information flow, such as additional communication channels, increased use of existing channels, updating of job descriptions, and improved orientation procedures, will have the effect of reducing anxiety.

Work overload

We have all experienced work overload at one time or another. Like ambiguity, it is not so much the transient condition which is a problem, but chronic overload, where for an extended period the individual feels overloaded much or all of the time.

An electrical system that is unable to handle all of the electricity introduced to it is overloaded. In most instances a fuse blows or a circuit breaker is tripped, stopping the input and preventing damage to the system. When an individual is unable to handle all the work input, that person may become overloaded. Unfortunately, unlike the electrical system, people do not have an automatic safety device, and the overload condition can lead to physical, mental, and job performance problems.

Overload may be of two different types: quantitative or qualitative. When employees perceive that they have too much work to do, too many different things to do, or insufficient time to complete assigned work, a condition of *quantitative* overload exists. *Qualitative* overload, on the other hand, occurs when employees feel they lack the ability to complete their jobs or that performance standards are too high, regardless of how much time they have. An engineer asked to design a containment system for a new nuclear power plant within three months may feel that, given the other projects he or she is already responsible for, three months is insufficient time. This is quantitative overload. The same assignment, given to a nonengineer, may cause qualitative overload since the individual may lack the necessary skills to complete the project.

From a health standpoint, research as far back as 1958 (Friedman, Rosenman, and Carroll) established that quantitative overload may cause biochemical changes, specifically, elevations in blood cholesterol levels. In an extremely well-designed study Sales (1969) also related cholesterol elevations to overload conditions. In addition to finding that role overload can exert marked negative effects on health, Sales suggested that overload is most harmful among those individuals who experience the lowest job satisfaction. Numerous medical studies have found relationships between coronary heart disease and heart attacks and conditions which at least indirectly suggest overload: working more than sixty hours a week, working two jobs, and foregoing vacations. Overload has also been linked to escapist drinking behavior, which in turn is linked to both health *and* performance difficulties.

Job performance may be affected by overload conditions in a variety of ways. The study by Margolis, et al. (1974) found overload to be associated with lowered confidence, decreased work motivation, increased absenteeism, and sharply reduced numbers of suggestions contributed by overloaded employees. Overload may also be indirectly responsible for decreases in decision-making quality, deteriorating interpersonal relations, and even accident rates.

Overload results from an interaction of the person with the environment. The absolute level of work needed to be done (what might be termed objective overload) is mediated by characteristics of the individual to determine subjective or perceived overload. What is too much for one person may be perceived as perfectly reasonable by another. Other stressors may also contribute to this one. Thus an employee who is experiencing role ambiguity—not knowing what is expected—may attempt to make certain that whatever *is* expected is getting done. Overload may well be a consequence of this strategy.

Occasional overload seems inevitable. Some, however, can be avoided or minimized through better scheduling, better assessment of resource needs, and more attention being paid to the fit or match between the individual's expertise and the requirements of the job. French and Caplan (1973) indicate that overloading may produce at least nine different unwanted outcomes: job dissatisfaction, excessive job tension, low self-esteem, threat, embarrassment, high cholesterol levels, increased heart rate, skin resistance, and increased cigarette consumption. These are outcomes which neither individuals nor organizations need.

Responsibility for people

Any type of responsibility can be a burden upon an individual, but for some, responsibility is much less likely to be a stressor than for others. Individual differences play a significant role. We probably all know someone who, after moving into a management or similar position, returned to the previous one because of a dislike for the increased responsibilities involved in the new job.

Different types of responsibility apparently function differently as stressors. One way of categorizing this variable is in terms of responsibility for people versus responsibility for things. While the distinction is somewhat artificial, the latter refers to primary responsibilty for equipment, budgets, and the like, while the former primarily involves responsibility for the activities of people. The available evidence supports the conclusion that responsibility for people is a much more potent stressor than responsibility for things. In one of the earliest studies which bears on this question, Wardwell and his associates (1964) found that individuals who had significant levels of responsibility for people were more likely to suffer from heart disease than individuals who had "thing" responsibilities. This could be partially explained by the fact that "people responsibilities" frequently mean more meetings that contribute to work overload and deadline pressures.

In a study conducted at NASA's Goddard Space Flight Center, French and Caplan (1970) found strong support for the hypothesis that responsibility for people contributes to job-related stress—at least for clerical, managerial, and technical/professional employees. The more people responsibilty the employee had, the more likely he or she was to smoke heavily and have high blood pressure and elevated cholesterol counts. Conversely, the more responsibility for things the employee had, the lower those indicators would be.

Part of the reason responsibility for people acts as a stressor undoubtedly results from the specific nature of the responsibility, particularly as it relates to the need to make unpleasant interpersonal decisions. Another part of the reason, as alluded to above, is that people responsibility positions lend themselves to overload, and perhaps role conflict and ambiguity as well. With this stressor, eliminating the condition is not a solution; some organizational members must have responsibility for people. But more careful attention to the fit between the individual and the job can result in the selection of those individuals who are less likely to be stressed. Additionally, as we shall see, there are ways of dealing with stress if it is not possible to prevent its occurrence in the first place.

Career development stressors

Career development stressors is the name we have chosen for those aspects of the individual's interaction with the organizational environment which influence that person's perception of the quality of his or her career progress. Career variables may serve as stressors when they become sources of concern, anxiety, or frustration to the individual. This can happen if an employee feels a lack of job security, is concerned about real or imagined obsolescence, feels that promotion progress is inadequate, and/or is generally dissatisfied with the match between career aspirations and the current level of attainment.

These stressors, while clearly having the potential to affect anyone at anytime, seem to be a problem most frequently for individuals in midcareer, from ages forty to fifty. It is during this period that many individuals experience doubts about the quality of their past accomplishments and the likelihood of significant future contributions. Frequently, the cause of stress is a discrepancy between actual accomplishments and expected ones. Erikson and his associates (1972) found that the highest levels of job satisfaction were reported by individuals whose promotion rate matched or exceeded their expectations. As advancement rates did not keep pace with expectations, dissatisfaction increased. The least successful men in the sample reported the greatest amount of stress in their lives.

More so than with the other stressors thus far discussed, career problems may be aggravated by factors unrelated to work. Concern over lack of career progress, for example, may be an extension of concern and confusion about the meaning of life. Particularly for men, middle age frequently becomes a period for soul-searching and self-doubt. Career progress then becomes a convenient focal point for many of these feelings.

Stress brought about by this category of stressors often manifests itself in the form of job dissatisfaction. In the extreme it may involve changing careers or even dropping out. More often it shows up in a variety of ways, all of which tend to be dysfunctional for both the individual and the organization. Blau (1978) has identified a number of negative consequences. Among them are reduction in the quality and/or quantity of the work produced, increase in accident frequencies, alcoholism and/or drug abuse, declining interpersonal relations on the job, and unwillingness by the individual to perform certain tasks, coupled with an increased tendency to question or challenge previously accepted management decisions.

Because these stressors may be precipitated by extraorganizational conditions, dealing with them effectively is difficult. In some cases it may be a relatively simple matter of helping an individual align expectations with realistic opportunities. Sometimes, however, because of the seriousness of the problem and the fact that it is extraorganizational in scope, resources for dealing with it are available only in the professional community. The alert manager will keep a sharp lookout—in himself or herself as well as others—for indications of behavior change that may be related to career stressors.

STRESSORS AND THE MANAGER

We will deal with the topic of stress management in Chapter 10. Nonetheless, a few words about this topic seem appropriate. It could be argued that a manager has very little control over the kind and degree of stress experienced by organizational members. Stress is, after all, an internal, idiosyncratic response which is difficult or impossible for the individual experiencing it to control, much less an outsider. Let us not lose sight of the fact, however, that this internal response is elicited by an external factor over which the manager may have quite a bit of control.

The first step in stress management is recognition of potential stressors. We have discussed two broad categories in this chapter, physical environment and individual level organizational stressors. Further categories will be pursued in the two subsequent chapters. Our purpose has been to increase awareness of what factors may serve as precipitators of stress, why they may be stressors, and what health and performance dysfunctions they may cause.

The second step in stress control is to alter either the environment, or the individual, or both with the objective of minimizing stressors. In a general way this involves creating an organizational climate in which communications are encouraged. While not a catch-all solution by any means, open communications are almost always a prerequisite to effective stress management.

By alteration in the individual we mean essentially two things. First is performance and job counseling with the aim of helping the individual clarify his or her job role, rearranging schedules and priorities to help alleviate quantitative work overload, improving understanding of alternative methods of meeting career objectives, and similar considerations. Changing individual behavior and, in many cases, beliefs and values, is a sensitive process. If a manager feels uncomfortable in entering that kind of a process with an employee, it had better be left to someone more adept, such as the career counselors who are increasingly being added to the staffs of large organizations.

The other approach to alteration in the individual is training and development. The usual objective here is to provide the individual with new or updated skills, knowledge, and expertise to allow that person to perform better in his or her job and consequently minimize the likelihood of some stressors' (such as career development) posing or continuing to pose a problem.

Organizational alterations of the environment involve a number of variables. In general the kinds of changes that may be appropriate here include the already mentioned need for increased communication, restructuring of work flows or job assignments, clarification of reporting relationships, and similar strategies. In the case of the environmental stressors the changes focus on improvement of physical conditions: better temperature control, changes in lighting, elimination or masking of noise, installation of air purification systems, and the like. What organizations and individual managers can do to reduce stress levels among employees is limited only by the amount of effort and creativity which are brought to bear on the problem.

APPENDIX

Stress Diagnostic Survey©

The following questionnaire is designed to provide you with an indication of the extent to which various individual level stressors are sources of stress to you. For each item you should indicate the frequency with which the condition described is a source of stress. Next to each item write the appropriate number (1–7) which best describes how frequently the condition described is a source of stress.

> Write *1* if the condition described is *never* a source of stress
> Write *2* if it is *rarely* a source of stress
> Write *3* if it is *occasionally* a source of stress
> Write *4* if it is *sometimes* a source of stress
> Write *5* if it is *often* a source of stress
> Write *6* if it is *usually* a source of stress
> Write *7* if it is *always* a source of stress

1. My job duties and work objectives are unclear to me.
2. I work on unnecessary tasks or projects.
3. I have to take work home in the evenings or on weekends to stay caught up.
4. The demands for work quality made upon me are unreasonable.
5. I lack the proper opportunities to advance in this organization.
6. I am held accountable for the development of other employees.
7. I am unclear about whom I report to and/or who reports to me.
8. I get caught in the middle between my supervisors and my subordinates.
9. I spend too much time in unimportant meetings that take me away from my work.
10. My assigned tasks are sometimes too difficult and/or complex.
11. If I want to get promoted I have to look for a job with another organization.

12. I am responsible for counseling with my subordinates and/or helping them solve their problems.

13. I lack the authority to carry out my job responsibilities.

14. The formal chain of command is not adhered to.

15. I am responsible for an almost unmanageable number of projects or assignments at the same time.

16. Tasks seem to be getting more and more complex.

17. I am hurting my career progress by staying with this organization.

18. I take action or make decisions that affect the safety or well-being of others.

19. I do not fully understand what is expected of me.

20. I do things on the job that are accepted by one person and not by others.

21. I simply have more work to do than can be done in an ordinary day.

22. The organization expects more of me than my skills and/or abilities provide.

23. I have few opportunities to grow and learn new knowledge and skills in my job.

24. My responsibilities in this organization are more for *people* than for *things*.

25. I do not understand the part my job plays in meeting overall organizational objectives.

26. I receive conflicting requests from two or more people.

27. I feel that I just don't have time to take an occasional break.

28. I have insufficient training and/or experience to discharge my duties properly.

29. I feel that I am at a standstill in my career.

30. I have responsibility for the future (careers) of others.

Scoring

Each item is associated with a specific individual level stressor. The item numbers and the appropriate categories are listed below. Add your responses for each item within each category to arrive at a total category score.

Role Ambiguity: 1, 7, 13, 19, 25

Role Conflict: 2, 8, 14, 20, 26

Role Overload—Quantitative: 3, 9, 15, 21, 27

Role Overload—Qualitative: 4, 10, 16, 22, 28

Career Development: 5, 11, 17, 23, 29

Responsibility for People: 6, 12, 18, 24, 30

The significance of the total score in each of the stressor categories will, of course, vary from individual to individual. In general, however, the following guidelines may be used to provide a perspective for each total score:

Total scores of less than 10 are indicators of low stress levels.

Total scores between 10 and 24 are indicative of moderate stress levels.

Total scores of 25 and greater are indicative of high stress levels.

REFERENCES

Blau, B. "Understanding mid-career stress." *Management Review* 67 (1978): 57–62.

Canstandse, W. J. "A neglected personnel problem." *Personnel Journal* 51 (1972): 129–133.

Caplan, R. D. and K. W. Jones. "Effects of work load, role ambiguity, and type A personality on anxiety, depression, and heart rate." *Journal of Applied Psychology* 60 (1975): 713–719.

Erikson, J., Pugh, W. M., and E. K. Gunderson. "Status incongruency as a predictor of job satisfaction and life stress." *Journal of Applied Psychology* 56 (1972): 523–525.

French, J. R. P. and R. D. Caplan. "Psycho-social factors in coronary heart disease." *Industrial Medicine* 39 (1970): 383–397.

French, J. R. P. and R. D. Caplan. "Organizational stress and individual stress." In *The Failure of Success.* A. J. Marrow, ed. New York: AMACOM, 1973, pp. 30–36.

Friedman, M., Rosenman, R. H., and V. Carroll. "Changes in serum cholesterol and blood clotting time in men subjected to cyclic variations of occupational stress." *Circulation* 17 (1969): 852–861.

Glass, D. C., Singer, J. E., and L. N. Friedman. "Psychic costs of adaptation to an environmental stressor." *Journal of Personality and Social Psychology* 12 (1969): 200–210.

Kahn, R. L. et al. *Organizational Stress.* New York: John Wiley and Sons, 1964.

Margolis, B. L., Kroes, W. M., and R. P. Quinn. "Job stress: an unlisted occupational hazard." *Journal of Occupational Medicine* 16 (1974): 659–661.

McLean, A. A. "Job stress and the psycho-social pressures of change." *Personnel* 53 (1976): 40–49.

Poulton, E. C. "Blue collar stressors." In *Stress at Work.* C. L. Cooper and R. Payne, eds. New York: John Wiley and Sons, 1978.

Sales, S. M. "Organizational role as a risk factor in coronary disease." *Administrative Science Quarterly* 14 (1969): 325–336.

Wardwell, W. I., Hyman, M., and C. B. Bahnson. "Stress and coronary heart disease in three field studies." *Journal of Chronic Disease* 17 (1964): 73–84.

Wofford, J. C. "Negative ionization: An investigation of behavioral effects." *Journal of Experimental Psychology* 71 (1966): 608–611.

FOR FURTHER READING

Kahn, R. L. et al. *Organizational Stress.* New York: John Wiley and Sons, 1964.

Kornhauser, A. *Mental Health of the Industrial Worker.* New York: John Wiley and Sons, 1965.

Marcson, S. *Automation, Alienation and Anomie.* New York: Harper and Row, Publishers, Inc., 1970.

Shepard, J. M. *Automation and Alienation.* Cambridge, Mass.: The MIT Press, 1971.

Groups and Organizational Stressors

6

THE OLD MAN AND HIS SONS

The old Man had several Sons, who were constantly quarrelling with each other, notwithstanding he used every means in his power to persuade them to cease their contentions, and to live in amity together. At last he had recourse to the following expedient:—He ordered his Sons to be called before him, and a bundle of sticks to be brought, and then commanded them to try if, with all their strength, any of them could break it. They all tried, but without effect: for the sticks being closely and compactly bound together, it was impossible for the force of man to break them. After this, the Father ordered the bundle to be untied, and gave a single stick to each of his Sons, at the same time bidding them to break it. This they did with ease, and soon snapped every stick asunder. The father then addressed them to this effect: O, my Sons, behold the power of unity! For if you, in like manner, would but keep yourselves strictly conjoined in the bands of friendship, it would not be in the power of any mortal to hurt you; but when you are divided by quarrels and animosities, you fall a prey to the weakest enemies.

Managerial Application • Intragroup conflicts can disrupt the effectiveness of groups and result in long-term stress. A group in conflict can bring a whole organization down to its knees.

122

Organizations have been the object of scrutiny, debate, and controversy among researchers and managers throughout this century. Organizational systems have been analyzed from numerous perspectives. A result of this scrutiny has been increased attention to a particular set of organizational characteristics to the exclusion of other features. For example, one group of researchers has paid particular attention to individuals and how they behave within organizations. Other researchers have examined the dynamics of interactions within work groups. Still another set of researchers uses a total organizational approach. Each of these different perspectives offers insight into the forms of behavior and performance in organizations.

Despite the considerable variation in how organizations are analyzed, there are some common viewpoints. In the behavioral sciences there is now an effort to employ three levels of analysis when examining organizational phenomena. The levels studied are the *individual, group, and organization*. In this chapter, stressors at two levels of organizational dimensions will be examined. First, the *group* and how it affects individuals will be discussed. Then, a total *organizational* perspective will be employed. In the previous chapter, individual level stressors were the focal point. Recall that in our integrative model displayed in Figure 2–4 five sets of stressors were considered important—physical, environmental, individual, group, organizational, and extraorganizational.

The organizational milieu

Before analyzing group and organizational stressors, it is necessary to clarify the composition of work organizations. Finding precise meanings for the term *organization* is like searching for a needle in a haystack; everyone has a different definition. Most definitions state that organizations are composed of individuals and groups who work together to achieve goals and objectives. They do not clarify, however, what kinds of individuals make up organizations, what kinds of goals exist, or whether excessive stress originates within the organization.

Groups are an important element in the composition of any organization. A *group* consists of two or more people who interact and share some values and norms. Some groups are established by the organization in order to accomplish specific goals. These are referred to as *formal* groups. Management creates the group and can dissolve it. It is also worth noting that any person can be a member of two or more formal groups simultaneously. In some cases, multiple-group memberships contribute to role conflict and role ambiguity. Organizations are also composed of *informal groups*. *Informal groups* exist when people interact together, on and off the job, and members derive satisfaction from such membership. Again, as with formal groups, an employee often belongs to several informal groups.

There is no precise description of how, when, and why behavior is affected by the structure or policies of an organization. However, there is some opinion that a more organic, nonbureaucratic structure is most effective for individuals with high achievement and autonomy needs, when the technology of the organization is changing and nonroutine, and when the environment is dynamic (Porter, Lawler, and Hackman, 1975). Whether the organization's structure is a stressor and is linked to behavioral and physiological outcomes is still a fuzzy issue. Identifying the role of group and organizational stressors requires the identification of specific stressors, since discussing the group or the total organization in broad terms won't provide managers with the information needed to attack specific stress-producing factors.

GROUP STRESSORS

The effectiveness of the organization is influenced by the nature of the relations among group members. The most widely known study of groups was performed at the Hawthorne plant of the Western Electric Company (Roethlisberger and Dickson, 1939). This study was originally designed to assess the impact of working conditions (e.g., lighting, rest breaks, etc.) on employees' productivity. It was determined that working conditions influenced the behavior of individual workers significantly less than various psychological and social conditions. Of particular importance was the emergence of a group "identity" on the part of study participants.

The Tavistock studies of coal miners (Trist and Bamforth, 1951) generated data on the results of breaking up work groups. Coal miners initially worked together in small, tightly knit work groups. Because of the dangers of working deep in the mines, there was a great deal of personal warmth among group members. A technological change (a shift from a "shortwall" digging method of coal extraction to a "longwall" automated method) was introduced. The old, small groups were replaced by a large, rather impersonal group arrangement. Productivity deteriorated after the change of procedures, and the miners expressed negative attitudes about the job and working conditions. The lower performance and morale is thought to have developed as a result of the emotional difficulties encountered by the miners after their small, tight-knit groups were disbanded.

The Hawthorne, Tavistock, and other group studies clearly suggest that work groups influence individual members. The group influence produces compliance among group members, shapes beliefs, alters perceptions, preferences, attitudes, and values, increases psychological arousal, and increases job knowledge. But group influence can also create stress within an individual. The stress may be created by the lack of cohesiveness within a group, by intragroup conflict, or by a lack of overall group support for its members.

There are many group characteristics that can be classified as stressors. We have selected four factors as representative of what we call *group stressors:* the lack of group cohesiveness, inadequate group support, intragroup conflict, and intergroup conflict.

Lack of group cohesiveness

The closeness among members of a group, their tendency to stick together, is referred to as *cohesiveness*. To some individuals being a part of a cohesive group is extremely important, for example, to the coal miners in the Tavistock study. The reaction to the disbanding of their cohesive groups was a decrease in personal job performance efforts.

The cohesiveness in a group can be a positive or negative stressor. If cohesiveness is a valued characteristic, a lack of it could cause low morale, poor performance, and physiological changes such as increased blood pressure. The role of cohesiveness as a stressor has yet to be adequately researched. If organizationally based solutions to coping with work stress are to be forthcoming, group cohesiveness will need to be assessed. Different levels of cohesiveness and individual need for cohesiveness are two areas requiring scrutiny. The lack of group cohesiveness may be meaningless to some employees; on the other hand, the lack of group cohesiveness may explain various physiological and behavioral outcomes in an employee desiring such stick-togetherness.

The assessment of cohesiveness can proceed along two paths. Self-report surveys, observation, and discussions with employees can give a picture of the degree of cohesiveness in a group and its importance among members. A second path is to monitor the performance of the group. Suppose for example that it is determined that a group of six employees has produced on a weekly basis the following:

	Units Per Week
Joe	20
Ralph	18
Barbara	19
Chris	20
Marc	19
Willie	18
Group average = 19	114

This has been the group rate of production for the past nine months. A second group over the same period of time has produced the following output:

	Units Per Week
Jesse	10
Randy	28
Mary	20
Beth	31
Sam	18
Marion	7
Group average = 19	114

The average production of the two groups is nineteen each. Note, however, that everyone in the first group is producing approximately the group average, while those in the second group are producing at many different levels. This data may signal higher levels of cohesiveness among the first group's members. Of course, the abilities and job experience of the members would have to be more closely examined before the first group could be considered more cohesive. In any event, through improved awareness of this characteristic, managers could initiate programs of action (see Chapter 10).

Inadequate group support

The effects of stressor stimuli on the employee are reduced when others share the stress. This, of course, is a broad statement that must be qualified. The statement is basically correct if group optimism about its success is high, individuals know each other, and if potential solutions exist to relieve the stress. Thus, *group support* designates a condition in which there is sharing among stressed members.

Schacter (1959) proposes that individuals need others for evaluation of their own emotional reactions and that other persons in the same emotional state provide them with information about appropriate responses. Simply being with others and being able to observe their behavior in times of stress is a form of group support.

Group support can be viewed as a resource to be allocated to an individual confronted with stress (Kahn and Quinn, 1970). The lack of the resource is itself a stressor for some individuals. Not all employees prefer or value group support, however. Some people do not experience a sense of decreased stress from the emotional support provided by co-workers. On the other hand, for those employees with a need for emotional aid, the group's support may be a potential stress reliever. From a managerial perspective the issues of cohesiveness and support overlap. Thus, cohesiveness is a goal of managerial action.

Intra- and intergroup conflict

Conflict is any antagonistic action between two or more people. Some observers contend that a group is like an arena in that it is a place where conflict boils over—group experience *is* conflict. Conflict and stress are common when individuals and small groups are brought together (Gibson, Ivancevich, & Donnelly, 1979). In fact, conflict is a part of the fabric of organizational life, and an organization without conflict is like a person without stress, lifeless.

One of the facts of organizational life is that no group has sufficient resources to fulfill all internal needs and meet all external requests. There is a scarcity of freedom, authority, and resources. To organize, a group must coordinate actions within itself and with other groups, and in doing so, it must limit the freedom of some members. There are also some members who have more skill, prestige, and status, which results in authority differentials among group members and between groups. And further, groups reward and punish members differently, creating internal conflict.

Intragroup conflict has three categories: *role conflict, issue conflict,* and *interaction conflict* (Hamner and Organ, 1978). As explained in Chapter 5, role conflict exists when the expectations associated with two or more positions that a person occupies are incompatible with one another or when mutually incompatible expectations are associated with a single position. Studies have found that high levels of intragroup role conflict are related to low job satisfaction, high job stress, and high propensity to leave an organization (Lyons, 1971).

A second type of intragroup conflict is called *issue conflict.* The conflict involves disagreement between group members over how to solve a problem. The disagreement may be caused by different perceptions, levels of experience, personal values, or sources of information. For example, a team of project engineers may be searching for a nuclear waste disposal procedure. On the team are young and middle-aged engineers who have differing opinions about nuclear energy and the technology available to deal with waste disposal. These differences could result in intense disagreement, even though identical information about the problem is presented to each engineer.

Disagreement over issues can, however, be a healthy by-product of intragroup interaction. Irving Janis (1972) has written a highly provocative book that touches on intragroup suppression of disagreement. He analyzes the Kennedy administration's handling of the Bay of Pigs invasion of 1961. There was a concerted attempt among President Kennedy's close aides to suppress disagreement among themselves about the plan to invade Cuba. Janis describes how cohesiveness, conformity among group members, and suppression of disagreement resulted in the disastrous invasion decision.

The issue of whether disagreement is the same as conflict depends largely on the perceptions of the group members; *interactional conflict* exists when members perceive antagonism toward each other. When one party blames another party for an event or for draining needed resources there is interactional conflict.

Intergroup conflict is another inevitable aspect of organizations for a number of reasons. First, when groups depend on each other to complete tasks, there is a potential for conflict. For example, in one manufacturing plant the product must be assembled by one group before it is sent to another group to be painted. The output of the assembly group is the input for the painting group. If there is poor coordination of this output-input process there is a high potential for conflict. Furthermore, groups often have goals that cannot be achieved simultaneously. As groups become specialized, they often develop dissimilar or even contradictory goals. Limited resources, rewards, and time help create dissimilar goals and lead to antagonism between groups. The antagonisms between groups at different levels of the hierarchy are often based on struggles for these limited resources and rewards. March and Simon (1958) predict that as resources are reduced (e.g., during a business recession), intergroup conflict tends to increase.

Intra- and intergroup conflicts can create stress for employees resulting in behavioral and physiological reactions. Whether the stress level created by such conflict becomes organizationally dysfunctional is an issue for managerial scrutiny. The first managerial concern is to identify the type and degree of conflict that exists. For that there are self-report, observation, and interview procedures available. After reliable and valid identification of the problem, the manager must decide whether the conflict is functional or dysfunctional. Next, strategies of conflict resolution have to be chosen and implemented.

Conflict within and between groups can create an uncomfortable atmosphere for employees. The squabbles, harsh words, and nitpicking that accompany conflict make going to work a stressful activity. Most employees prefer to work in a harmonious setting that allows them to discuss personal and job issues with other people. Dysfunctional conflict cuts off free-flowing interaction and can result in felt stress. Although all types of conflict are inevitable, and at times positive, it is in the manager's best interest to examine conflict before behavioral and physiological outcomes become a problem.

ORGANIZATIONAL STRESSORS

A problem with studying organization level stressors is identifying the more important ones. Any organization is more than a social device made up of people and resources designed to accomplish goals. So we have chosen for discussion organization level stressors that capture more than what is covered in discussions of individual and group variables.

The organizational level stressors selected are typically discussed as macrophenomena. That is, they are associated with an overall perspective of work. They, like individual and group stressors, are inevitable within organizations and need to be understood by managers.

Organizational climate

Organizations differ not only in physical structure but also in the attitudes and behavior they elicit in employees (Hellriegel and Slocum, 1974). The interaction of people, structures, policies, and goals generates an *atmosphere* or *climate*. The term *climate* designates the characteristics that distinguish one organization from another (Gibson, Ivancevich, and Donnelly, 1979, p. 525). It is the "feel" or "character" of an organization.

There has been much debate in the organizational behavior literature over the meaningfulness of the climate construct (Gibson, Ivancevich, and Donnelly, 1979). The debate focuses primarily on measurement. Reliable and valid measurement of climate has been difficult. Although self-report survey questionnaires are readily available, there is skepticism about the psychometric quality of such behavioral science instruments. Unfortunately, the measurement controversy has dampened efforts to clarify what is meant by the term *climate*.

In our opinion, organizations have a *climate* that generates a "feel" or personality. This personality, like individual personalities, does not fall neatly into a particular category. The personality or climate appears to affect the behavior of individuals and groups and also how organizations interact with each other. But how to measure an organization's climate is as of now a partially unresolved problem.

To illustrate the pervasiveness of what is designated as climate consider the "feel" when entering or visiting an elegant hotel such as the St. Francis in San Francisco. In most cases the feel is distinctly different from that of a less elegant one. Similarly, a baseball game at Wrigley Field in Chicago or Fenway Park in Boston elicits a different feel from one at the newer, more comfortable stadium in Kansas City. The dedicated fan senses history, tradition, past heroes, and won and lost pennants in Chicago and Boston. The "feel" is different, and it affects fan watching the game.

An organization's climate may be conducive to a relaxed style of working, or it may generate a high-charged, crisis-oriented style. And the climate can affect people differently. One study has measured organizational climate through properties such as intimacy, production orientation, esprit, and aloofness. Nurses, hospital administrators, and diagnostic personnel were asked to record their perceptions of the eight climate properties and need satisfaction. The results indicated that nurses associated need satisfaction with a climate high in esprit, while administrators reported more satisfaction in a climate high in consideration (Ivancevich and Lyon, 1972). The important point of this study is that if climate can be measured, it might provide managers with clues about how employees respond to the "feel" of the organization. These clues could be used to track down potential stressors before they affect the behavior of subordinates. Unfortunately, the sampling design, measurement, and overall research design of this and most studies of organizational climate have lacked scientific rigor.

Organizational structure

Organizational structure and its impact on stress and behavior have rarely been studied. One study of trade sales persons has examined the relationship between tall (bureaucratic), medium, and flat (System 4) structures on job satisfaction and performance (Ivancevich and Donnelly, 1975). It determined that sales persons in the flatter structure received more job satisfaction, experienced less stress, and performed more effectively than sales persons in the medium and tall structures.

The effect of the individual's position in the organizational structure has also been examined in a few studies. Most findings suggest that, holding other organizational dimensions constant, higher levels of stress are reported for individuals in the hierarchy who have little to say or who exercise little control over their job. These features are typically associated with middle and low-level managers and operating-level workers such as laborers, painters, secretaries, waitresses, and medical technologists.

The impact on stress of the type of structure one is faced with and the level one works at depends upon individual and group needs. For some individuals the organization's structure is unimportant and he or she does not perceive it as a stressor (positive or negative). Again, managerial scrutiny of the influence of structure on subordinate's behavior and performance is a needed first step.

Organization territory

Organization territory is a term used to describe a person's personal space or arena of activities. It is the arena in which the person works, plays, jokes, and thinks. It is physical, personal, and meaningful to the employee. Many people develop a feeling of ownership of their personal space (department, office, desk, table) in the organization. French and Caplan (1973), in a study of the impact of organizational territory on engineers working in an administrative unit and, conversely, administrators working in an engineering unit, concluded that territoriality is a powerful stressor. They found that men working in alien territories experienced stress and concluded that "crossing an organizational boundary and working in an alien territory entails stress and strain and poses a threat to one's health."

An easy way for the reader to evaluate the importance of an individual's personal space is to conduct the following exercise. When someone is standing up talking to you, note the physical distance between you. Then move closer to the other person. At some point you will move into the person's *zone of space discomfort;* he or she will become uncomfortable and move farther away from you. An observer of this exercise would see the discomfort signal as the distance closed between the two people.

Organizational territoriality with accompanying possessiveness seems to develop around the parts of the organization that have become familiar. The department, office, desk, and work flow are considered home territory; outside of the home are alien territories. Thus, there frequently is increased stress when one leaves the home base to do business elsewhere. An exception is when individuals seek refuge in another area to escape temporary stressors in their home territory. The managerial implication of the territory stressor is that managerially initiated changes of familiar patterns can trigger off significant stress. And even if the person stays in his or her own territory, this stressor can be a factor when other groups enter the territory.

Task characteristics

In 1965, Turner and Lawrence published *Industrial Jobs and the Worker.* In it they hypothesized a set of task attributes that directly and indirectly influence the affective and behavioral responses of the employee to the job. The six attributes were variety (the number of different activities that can be prescribed for a job), autonomy (the amount of discretion an employee has to carry out the job), required interaction (the amount of necessary face-to-face communication needed to complete the tasks), optional interaction (the amount of voluntary face-to- face communication needed), knowledge and skill required (the amount of mental preparation or learning to do the job), and responsibility (the level of felt accountability required for task completion).

Turner and Lawrence (1965) created a job attitude survey that measured job satisfaction and task attributes among 470 job occupants. They also collected attendance data on the job occupants. They found that the task attributes (labeled the Requisite Task Attributes, or RTA) were positively related to levels of job satisfaction and attendance.

Hackman and Lawler (1971) extended the Turner and Lawrence work and studied six task attributes, which they labeled variety, autonomy, task identity (i.e., the extent to which employees do an entire piece of work and can identify their efforts), feedback (i.e., the employees' information about how well they are performing), dealing with others, and friendship opportunities. A study of these attributes in a telephone company indicated that the employee's perceptions of four of the task attributes—variety, autonomy, task identity, and feedback— plus one other—task significance—are positively associated with job satisfaction and performance.

The results of the Hackman and Lawler (1971) extension of the Turner and Lawrence (1965) work and other studies (Aldag and Brief, 1979) have identified two sets of task attributes that are potential sources of motivation. The two sets are referred to as *extrinsic* and *intrinsic*. Extrinsic motivation is derived from sources other than the job itself. Such sources include pay, promotion, or fringe benefits. In a state of intrinsic motivation, the employee attributes job behaviors to rewards that are derived from the job itself. Such sources include variety, autonomy, task identity, task significance, and feedback. If these intrinsic sources are important to an employee, they can result in positive behavioral outcomes and even reduced stress. Whether intrinsic motivation is related to physiological changes (positive or negative) has not been reported in the literature.

One means of increasing an employee's level of intrinsic motivation and possibly affect behavioral and physiological outcomes is to redesign task attributes. Managerial efforts to redesign a job and increase motivation require that it be restructured to include the task attributes that are preferred by the employee and that depend upon performance. In this way job redesign may increase both satisfaction and performance. Merely redesigning a job to incorporate intrinsic characteristics that are not contingent upon performance may result in increased job enjoyment without enhanced performance. Perhaps changes in task characteristics are powerful enough to positively influence blood pressure, heart rate variability, and other similar variables.

To date most of the research reported has measured task attributes subjectively by self-report surveys. In addition, most of the research has examined all-male or predominantly male samples. Objective and subjective measures of task characteristics as stressors need to be used in the future as well as all-female and mixed samples. Certainly, task attributes influence employee's perceptions of their jobs. In view of these differences, it is important to consider further the extent to which these attributes are stressors.

Technology

Woodward (1965) found in her classic studies that optimal organizational design is a function of technology. The technological limitations in an organization may increase the number of potential stressors while restricting the range of alternatives available to a manager to reduce stress. For example, technological requirements may force a manager to forego introducing greater job autonomy or variety. Thus, it is not surprising that technology influences the attitudes, behavior, and performance of employees. *Technology,* as it is used here, refers to the ways an organization transforms resources and other inputs into desirable outputs.

Thompson (1967) describes three types of organizational technology:

1. *Long-linked*—Tasks are performed according to a sequence, for instance on the assembly line in an automobile manufacturing plant.

2. *Meditating*—Inputs are sorted on the basis of a classification system. Each class is worked on by a particular process, as in a bank with various service units (classes).

3. *Intensive* or *custom*—Few standardized procedures with more of a problem-solving orientation, such as in a research and development unit.

The technological arrangement used in an organization creates different mixes of employees by occupation and skill levels, styles of managing, levels of employee independence and authority, and even combinations of task attributes. Rousseau (1977) investigated production processes and consequences in thirteen organizations. She found that perceived levels of variety, task identity, task significance, feedback, and personal interaction all varied as a function of the existing technology. For example, reported levels of positive task attributes were lower in assembly line organizations than in others.

An issue of interest involves the fit between technology, task attributes, and the organizational structure. Does an incongruence in this fit create stress that manifests itself in negative behavioral and physiological outcomes? Schuler (1977) suggests that incongruence in this type of fit would result in role conflict and role ambiguity, two individual-level stressors. He tested his proposition in an engineering division of a public utility and found role ambiguity to be lowest in the most congruent task-structure-technology situation. He also unexpectedly found role conflict to be lower in one of the incongruent situations.

Exactly what middle and low-level managers can do about technology is a debatable issue. However, they may be able to modify task attributes and organizations' structural arrangements to fit the technological type. In any event, it appears that for some individuals an organization's technology may be a stressor that affects their behaviors and physiology. Limited evidence indicates that it is important to consider the fit of individual differences, task attributes, structure, and technology.

Leadership influence

In any organizational setting, there is one agent of influence who often has a significant impact on work activities, the climate, and the group—the leader. He or she is likely to have more powerful influence than any other aspect of work. Such influence derives to some degree from the fact that a leader is in a position of authority and power. With respect to legitimate power of office and the rewards and sanctions available to them, all leaders are created equal (Katz and Kahn, 1978, p. 528). They do not, however, remain as equals in the organization. Some of them are more considerate and able to work with employees; some know the political system and how to use it to their advantage; some have technical knowledge that is valued and needed by others; some serve as stress heighteners, while others are stress reducers. French and Raven (1960) have identified five types of influence, which they refer to as power: *legitimate, reward, punishment, expert,* and *referent* (influence ability based on identifying with another person).

The manner in which a person applies various power bases can influence outcomes in an organizational setting. Student (1968) examined leaders' use of influence and performance in a study of forty-eight work groups in an appliance factory. He found that supervisors who were perceived as using referent and expert power were considered more effective in achieving performance goals. The findings did not suggest that legitimate, punishment, or reward power were not important. Instead, it was determined that referent and expert power in this study were associated more with good performance than the other power bases.

Which leadership influence package is best? Unfortunately, answers to this question have resulted in much confusion. Simply stated, there is no best leadership influence package for all situations. The behavioral sciences, led by the work of McGregor and Argyris, have emphasized the supportive aspects of leadership. An assumption made by these researchers has been that supportive leader behavior will increase performance and morale. However, the early research findings of Fielder (1964) indicate that the socially distant leader often has a more effectively performing group than the supportive leader.

Research work at Ohio State has indicated over the years that both supportive and task-oriented leadership behaviors are needed to achieve personal and organizational goals. The Ohio State leadership styles emphasize *consideration* (the extent to which a leader has respect for subordinate's ideas and has created mutual trust) and *initiating structure* (the extent to which the leader is likely to define and structure his/her role and those of subordinates).

Schriesheim and Murphy (1976) found that supervisors giving more directions had lower-performing subordinates when they showed little consideration but higher performing subordinates when they showed a great deal of consideration. In this study they also examined job stress and found that, when people have anxieties about the job situation, task direction correlated positively with performance. Where anxiety was low, task direction had a negative relationship to performance, and consideration had a positive relationship. In other words, in stressful jobs employees perform better when the leader takes more responsibility for directing the task.

The effects of leader influence and whether it is a significant stressor are two issues requiring more careful analysis. Contingency models, trait theories, and behavioral approaches to leader influence are available in the literature. What is lacking in the numerous explanations of leadership are guidelines concerning the linkage between leader behavior and stress. It seems reasonable to assume that a leader's influence and how it is applied can be viewed as a stressor by individuals at different times. Few employees have never experienced stress when interacting with their leader. Of course, the reverse is also true. Leaders are stressed in many cases by employee behaviors.

Shift-work policies

. . . the human adult is an animal whose body is tuned by evolution and training to go about its business during the hours of daylight and sleep during those of darkness. Ask it to work at night and sleep during the day and it does both rather badly (Wilkinson, 1971).

This provocative quote refers to an organization stressor shared by many blue-collar (operating employee level) occupations: shift work. Since the end of World War I, the prevalence of shift-work systems in the industrialized countries of the West has increased steadily. Estimates indicate that about 20% of all industrial workers in the United States and Europe are shift workers (Tasto and Colligan, 1977). Dividing the 24-hour day into three, or occasionally two, equal divisions of work time is attractive for different reasons. For service industries, such as police and fire departments, hospitals, public utilities, and transportation firms, twenty-four hour operation is not only economically effective but socially necessary. In other industries such as steel, petrochemical, or pulp and paper production, the nature of the technology requires continuous twenty-four hour operation.

Although economic efficiency, customer service, and technological requirements are important reasons for using shift-work procedures, there are problems associated with having people working on shifts. The root of the problems lies in the difficulty people have in adapting their physiological and psychological rhythms to a familiar sleep-wakefulness cycle.

Many of our bodily processes fluctuate according to a cyclical rhythm. Figure 6-1 presents body temperature fluctuations experienced by people. The twenty-four hour cyclical rhythm is called the *circadian rhythm* and is found in fluctuations in body temperature, urine flow, metabolism, heart rate, skin conductance, cortical and medullary production of adrenal hormones, the sleep cycle, and general mental and physical functioning. Shift work can come in conflict with these known circadian rhythms. The resulting negative effect on the individual, however, will depend on such factors as the social and psychological environments within which the shift work occurs.

Our society is daytime-oriented. We go to work, eat, shop, socialize, and relax during the day. To ask people to deviate by working a night (11 P.M.-7 A.M.) shift is asking them to cut themselves off from the normal avenues of social interaction. If employees work a shift schedule over a long time, there will be some physiological adaptation. Unfortunately, many organizations enforce a rotating shift pattern, which makes adaptation extremely difficult. With a changing shift schedule it takes several days for the average individual to readjust eating and sleeping habits.

Because of the interaction of individual and family adjustment problems, shift work may be one of the most potent stressors we have discussed. Although some individuals enjoy working shifts, a changing

FIGURE 6–1   Time of Day-Body Temperature Relationship

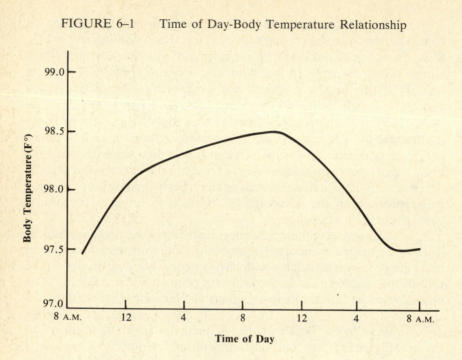

shift work schedule is damaging for many, both physiologically and psychologically.

An important managerial question should be whether the benefits associated with shift work are worth the physiological and psychological costs. These costs are inevitable. A report by the National Institute for Occupational Safety and Health (1977) spells out the potential costs in areas such as sleep, eating habits and digestion, general health, accidents, efficiency, social life, and family relations. Are the costs of shift work too great? Managers have to answer this question since they have some control over the shift work scheduling. Even a set schedule of afternoons (3 P.M.-11 P.M.) or nights (11 P.M.-7 A.M.) still involves adjustment. For five days the employee works a nonday shift and for two days he or she must return to a regular day schedule to fit in with the family and the rest of society. Indeed, shift work is often a hidden factor in the etiology of adjustment problems for many individuals. It can be a stressor that affects not only the behavior, performance, and physiology of workers, but also can affect their families.

Whenever attempts are made to discuss such broad topics as potential group stressors and organizational stressors, important factors

TABLE 6–1   Group and Organizational Stressors That May Be Candidates for Further Consideration by Those Studying Stress and Work

Potential Group Stressors	Potential Organizational Stressors
Group goal attainment ratio	Participation in decision making
Group maturity	Company size
Group pace of work	Communication flow
Group stability	Communication accuracy
Group status	Training and development opportunities
Group satisfaction	Pension plan
	Control procedures
	Counseling skills of supervisors
	Feedback skills of supervisors
	Image of fun in community
	Staffing practices
	Politics
	Loyalty
	Commitment

must be omitted. We have attempted to cover a representative sample of group and organizational stressors. The ones selected are important enough to be examined further by those interested in stress and work. However, a total picture is not emitted from the limited number of integrative model variables covered in this chapter.

Some of the omissions in our discussion of group and organizational stressors include variables such as those introduced in Table 6–1. These are likely candidates for comprehensive analysis. The variables included in future research will reflect in part other researchers' interests and judgments as to what group and organizational stressors are important. Value judgments and choices must be made by those conducting the study.

APPENDIX

Stress Diagnostic Survey©

For each item in the survey indicate how often the condition described is a current source of stress. Some of the items pertain to the

organization and some to your work group. For each item record the
number which best describes how often the condition described is a
current source of stress to you.

Record a *1* if the condition is *never* a source of stress.

Record a *2* if the condition is *rarely* a source of stress.

Record a *3* if the condition is *occasionally* a source of stress.

Record a *4* if the condition is *sometimes* a source of stress.

Record a *5* if the condition is *often* a source of stress.

Record a *6* if the condition is *usually* a source of stress.

Record a *7* if the condition is *always* a source of stress.

1. People do not understand the mission and goals of the organization.
2. The superior-subordinate reporting arrangements place pressure on me.
3. I am not able to control the activities in my work area.
4. The equipment available for completing work on time is poor.
5. My supervisor does not go to bat for me with the bosses.
6. My supervisor does not respect me.
7. I am not a part of a close-knit work group.
8. My work group does not support my personal goals.
9. My work group has no status or prestige in the organization.
10. The overall strategy of the organization is not well understood.
11. The overall policies initiated by management hinders good performance.
12. A person at my level has little control over the job.
13. My supervisor is not concerned about my personal welfare.
14. Technical knowledge is not available to remain competitive.
15. There are no rights to a private work area in this company.
16. The formal structure has too much red tape.
17. My supervisor does not trust me to do my job.
18. My work group is disorganized.
19. My work group provides me with no protection from unfair work demands made by bosses.

20. The organization lacks a direction and mission.
21. My work group pressures me too much.
22. I feel uncomfortable working with members of other work units.
23. My work group provides me with no technical help when needed.
24. The chain of command is not followed.
25. Technology to do significant work is not available.

Scoring Key

Stress Range

4–28	1, 10, 11, 20	=	Organizational Climate
4–28	2, 12, 16, 24	=	Organizational Structure
3–21	3, 15, 22	=	Organizational Territory
3–21	4, 14, 25	=	Technology
4–28	5, 6, 13, 17	=	Leader Influence
4–28	7, 9, 18, 21	=	Lack of Cohesiveness
3–21	8, 19, 23	=	Group Support

Since only a few variables in the organizational and group categories are presented, the significance of a total stress score is not important. Pilot testing research indicates that *mean* values for any stressor category above *4.00* indicates a moderate degree of stress. Mean values at the 4.00 level and above suggests that a closer, more detailed examination of the variable is warranted.

REFERENCES

Aldag, R. J. and A. P. Brief. *Task Design and Employee Motivation*. Glenview, Ill.: Scott, Foresman and Co., 1979.

Fielder, F. C. "A contingency model of leadership effectiveness." In *Advances in Experimental Social Psychology*, vol. 1. L. Berkowitz, ed. New York: Academic Press, 1964.

French, J. R. P., Jr. and R. D. Caplan. "Organizational stress and individual strain." In *The Failure of Success*. A. J. Morrow, ed. New York: AMACOM (American Management Association), 1973.

French, J. R. P., Jr. and B. H. Raven. "The bases of social power." In *Group Dynamics: Research and Theory*. D. Cartwright and A. Zander, eds. New York: Row, Peterson, 1960, 607–623.

Gibson, J. L., Ivancevich, J. M. and J. H. Donnelly, Jr. *Organizations: Behavior, Structure, Processes.* Dallas: Business Publications, Inc., 1979.

Hackman, J. R. and E. E. Lawler. "Employee reactions to job characteristics." *Journal of Applied Psychology* 55 (1971): 259–286.

Hamner, W. C. and D. W. Organ. *Organizational Behavior: An Applied Psychological Approach.* Dallas: Business Publications, Inc., 1978.

Hellriegel, D. and J. W. Slocum, Jr. "Organizational climate: measures, research, and contingencies." *Academy of Management Journal* 17 (1974): 255–280.

Ivancevich, J. M. and J. H. Donnelly, Jr. "Relation of organizational structure to job satisfaction, anxiety-stress, and performance." *Administrative Science Quarterly* 20 (1975): 272–280.

Ivancevich, J. M. and H. L. Lyon. *Organizational Climate, Job Satisfaction, Role Clarity, and Selected Emotional Reaction Variables in a Hospital Milieu.* Lexington, Ky.: Office of Business Development and Government Services, 1972.

Janis, I. L. *Victims of Groupthink.* Boston: Houghton, Mifflin Company, 1972.

Katz, D. and R. L. Kahn. *The Social Psychology of Organizations.* New York: John Wiley and Sons, Inc., 1978.

Kahn, R. L. and R. P. Quinn. "Role stress: A framework for analysis." In *Mental health and work organizations.* A. McLean, ed., Chicago: Rand McNally and Company, 1970.

Lyons, T. "Role clarity, need for clarity, satisfaction, tension, and withdrawal." *Organizational Behavior and Human Performance* 6 (1971): 99–110.

March, J. G. and H. A. Simon. *Organizations.* New York: John Wiley and Sons, Inc., 1958.

Porter, L. W., Hackman, J. R. and E. E. Lawler. *Behavior in Organizations.* New York: McGraw-Hill, Inc., 1975.

Roethlisberger, F. J. and W. J. Dickson. *Management and the Worker.* Cambridge, Mass.: Harvard University Press, 1939.

Rousseau, D. M. "Technological differences in job characteristics, employee satisfaction, and motivation: A synthesis of job design research and sociotechnical systems theory." *Organizational Behavior and Human Performance* 19 (1977): 18–42.

Schacter, S. *The Psychology of Affiliation.* Stanford, Calif.: Stanford University Press, 1959.

Schreisheim, G. A. and C. J. Murphy. "Relationships between leader behavior and subordinate satisfaction and performance: A test of some situational moderators." *Journal of Applied Psychology* 61 (1976): 634–641.

Schuler, R. S. "Role conflict and ambiguity as a function of the task-structure-technology interaction." *Organizational Behavior and Human Performance* 20 (1977): 60–74.

Student, K. R. "Supervisory influence and work-group performance." *Journal of Applied Psychology* 52 (1968): 188–194.

Tasto, D. L. and M. J. Colligan. *Shift Work Practices in the United States.* Washington, D. C.: National Institute for Occupational Safety and Health, 1977.

Thompson, J. D. *Organizations in Action.* New York: McGraw-Hill, Inc., 1967.

Trist, E. L. and K. W. Bamforth. "Some social and psychological consequences of the long-wall method of coal getting." *Human Relations* 4 (1951): 3–38.

Turner, A. N. and P. R. Lawrence. *Industrial Jobs and the Worker.* Cambridge, Mass: Harvard University Graduate School of Business Administration, 1965.

Wilkinson, R. "Hours of work and the twenty-four hour cycle of rest and activity." In *Psychology at Work.* P. Warr, ed. Middlesex: Penguin Books, 1971.

Woodward, J. *Industrial Organizations: Theory and Practice.* London: Oxford University Press, 1965.

FOR FURTHER READING

Cooper, C. L. and J. Marshall." Occupational sources of stress: A review of the literature relating to coronary heart disease and mental ill health." *Journal of Occupational Medicine* 49 (1976): 11–28.

Filley, A. C. *Interpersonal Conflict Resolution.* Glenview, Ill.: Scott, Foresman and Co., 1975.

Loftquist, L. H. and R. V. Dawis. *Adjustment to Work.* New York: Appleton-Century-Crofts, 1969.

Zaleznik, A. et al. "Stress reactions in organizations: syndromes, causes, and consequences." *Behavioral Science* 22 (1977): 151–161.

Extraorganizational Stressors 7

THE FATAL MARRIAGE

A Mouse being ambitious of marrying into a noble family, paid his addresses to a young lioness, and at length succeeded in entering into a treaty of marriage with her. When the day appointed for the nuptials arrived, the bridegroom set out in a transport of joy to meet his beloved bride; and coming up to her, passionately threw himself at her feet; but she, like a giddy thing as she was, not minding how she walked, accidentally set her foot upon her little spouse, and crushed him to death.

Managerial Application • Events outside of an organization can have a significant influence on behaviors inside the organization.

The focus of our discussion to this point has been on job and organizational stressors. We have, however, illustrated in our integrative model (Figure 2–4) what are referred to as extraorganizational stressors. These are actions, situations, or events outside the organization that may be stressful to people. Some managers view an organization as an insulated island with a set of policies, procedures, and people who perform jobs. People, however, like organizations, are inescapably bound up with the conditions existing in the outside world. So it is important to recognize that extraorganizational (outside) stressors exist and influence the on-the-job behavior of employees.

The everyday patterns of life of employees generally involve job, family, community, and social activities. Our daily roles as employee, parent, spouse, and community member do not occur in a vacuum. Therefore, this chapter examines some of the potential extraorganizational stressors that employees must deal with and learn to cope with daily.

For many people, extraorganizational stressors provoke stress more than any job, group, or organizational stressor. Some of the extraorganizational stressors we will discuss include societal change, the family, relocation, economic and financial conditions, race and class, and residential or community conditions (e.g., local taxes, public schools). In discussing these extraorganizational stressors it will once again become obvious that there has been little systematic study of this major category. Only a few of the behavioral theorists and researchers concerned with stress and work have elected to examine the impact of extraorganizational stressors on job behavior, performance, and stress.

The striking example of Roseto, Pennsylvania, which introduced Chapter 1, identified the significance of extraorganizational stressors. Recall that Rosetans derived support from each other and adhered to many of the values of a traditional peasant life-style. Since genetic and ethnic factors remained constant, this research suggests that the social homogeneity and life-style of the Rosetans had much to do with their superior health and ability to cope with stressors.

Life events

In Chapter 3 the life events theory and research of Holmes and Rahe were briefly introduced. These two researchers developed a method of correlating life events with illness and tested their views with more than five thousand patients. Previous research by Harold G. Wolff had indicated that stressful life events play an important role in the genesis of disease by evoking neurophysiological reactions (Wolff, 1950). Further studies reported that respiratory illness is about four times as likely to be preceded by acute life events stress (Meyer and Haggerty, 1962).

Initially, in retrospective studies, Holmes and colleagues (Holmes and Rahe, 1967) noted a strong correlation between the intensity of life changes and the onset of illness. Since these correlations were significant, the researchers attempted to determine whether life events could be used to *predict* the probability of disease onset in prospective studies.

Holmes and Rahe effectively pointed out the connection between life changes and lowered resistance to fight illness. This connection is illustrated by such information as that ten times as many widows and widowers die during the first year after the death of a spouse as nonwidowed individuals in a similar age group. The illness rate for divorced persons during the first year after the divorce is twelve times higher than for married persons (Forbes, 1979).

Whenever a predictive measure such as Holmes and Rahe's Social Readjustment Rating Scale (SRRS) is used (see Chapter 3), there is a possibility of influencing a person to become ill because he or she is informed that illness is highly probable. Of course, the SRRS is not intended to notify one of impending illness. Rather, its application should encourage preventive measures to reduce the probability of illness. Presently, most of the research dealing with life events focuses on determining the nature of the mind/body interaction which leads to the onset of disorders. It is still not known for certain whether stress overload merely predisposes a person to illness or actually precipitates it. But without a doubt, there is a link.

Work and outside-life work connections

The SRRS suggests that extraorganizational events are potential stressors. In fact, most of the SRRS events occur outside of the work setting. The home is considered to be a sanctuary in which we can be ourselves and relax. This unwinding and relaxation can help to reduce job-related stress. However, the home is also a place where job-based anger, hostility, and fatigue are dumped on friends and family, thereby creating new stress. The reverse is also true. That is, home-stimulated stress initiated by a spouse, children, or a problem with a neighbor can be dumped on co-workers or subordinates. The connection between work and outside-work stress is a vicious circle. Which comes first—the outside stress or the work stress—is not that relevant. A more pertinent question is how the stress build-up influences job performance and the quality of life outside the work place.

Those living or working close to us can usually pick up signs of stress even before we are aware of the build-up. Some warning signs include irritability about trivial matters, harping about the children's questions, inappropriate anger, a sudden increase in drinking or smoking habits, brooding, depression, insomnia, vague speech patterns, and increased use of antidepressants and tranquilizers. These and other signs are often too subtle for the stressed person to notice. Furthermore, most people display some of these symptoms occasionally. However, when they occur in groups and persist over time, there is probably too much work stress and/or extraorganizational stress on the person. This means that something must be done before major health and job problems occur.

An organizational perspective is also needed to understand better how extraorganizational events influence job behavior. An excellently designed quasi-experimental study clearly illustrates the connection between work and outside events. Stokols, et al. (1978) assessed the effects of exposure to traffic congestion (outside) on the mood, physiology, and task performance of automobile commuters. Traffic congestion was conceptualized as an environmental stressor. Participants were classified into three major traffic impedance groups: *low* (those who traveled less than 7.5 miles between work and home and spent less than 12.5 minutes on the road in either direction), *medium* (those who traveled between 10 and 14 miles and spent 17–20 minutes either way), and *high* (those traveling between 18 and 50 miles who spent from 30 to 75 minutes either way).

Participants had measures of blood pressure, heart rate, and mood taken regularly upon reporting to work. They also completed task performance tests regularly after reporting to work. As expected, subjective reports of traffic congestion and annoyance were greater among high and medium-impedance commuters than among low-impedance individuals. Also, commuting distance, commuting time, travel speed, and number of months as a commuter were significantly correlated with systolic and diastolic blood pressure. Task performance was also lower in high and medium-impedance participants. On the whole, the results indicate that exposure to traffic congestion is associated with significant differences in mood, physiology, and task performance of commuters.

The Stokols et al. (1978) results lend some support to the "vicious circle" proposition. The job, commuting, home, the community, the economy, and other events in a person's life are all potentially interacting stressors. Changes in any one of these areas can trigger stress provoking reactions in many other areas.

THE PHENOMENON OF CHANGE IN THE TWENTIETH CENTURY

At no time in the history of civilization have we experienced such rapid change in the world around us. Alvin Toffler in his highly popular book, *Future Shock* (1970), provides a clever, stimulating, and somewhat disturbing picture of modern life filled with continuous change. Toffler states: "There are discoverable limits to the amount of change that the human organism can absorb. . . . By endlessly accelerating change without first determining these limits, we may submit masses of men to demands they simply cannot tolerate."

Toffler offers a dramatic perspective on the rate of change experienced in American society. Dividing the past fifty thousand years of human history into lifetimes of about sixty-two years gives us about 800 human lifetimes. The first 650 of these lifetimes were spent living in caves. Writing has been available only for the past 70 lifetimes, making it possible to preserve information from one lifetime to the next. The wide use of print has developed within the last 6 lifetimes. We have only been able to measure time with precision for about 4 lifetimes. The electric motor is a creature of the last 2 lifetimes.

The accelerating rate of change around us inflicts a high level of physiological stress on people. The future shock of change itself can make people physically and psychologically ill. Toffler believes that if people are to deal effectively with future-change shock, ways must be found to adapt physically and to engineer our lives to create islands of stability.

The accelerating rate of change is illustrated by the technological events that have occurred in the last lifetime shown in Figure 7–1. Our lives are caught up in change and we have been literally forced to adapt to exponentially occurring changes. The American life-style is now one of mobility, urban crowding, consumption, noise, and rushed pace. What price has been and is now being paid for this lifestyle? As implied in Chapter 4 we have enjoyed a dramatic increase in health and a significant decrease in wellness. How much has change in factors outside of the

FIGURE 7-1   Technological Events Within the Lifetime

| 1900 | 05 | 10 | 15 | 20 | 1925 | 30 | 35 | 40 | 45 | 1950 | 55 | 60 | 65 | 70 | 1975 |

• Aircraft
• Electric Lighting
    • Synthetic Fabrics
        • Radio Broadcasting
            • Mass-production Techniques
            • Aircraft Carrier
            • Antibiotics
            • Electrification of Homes
            • Plastics
            • Frozen Foods
            • Injection Molding
            • Laser
            • Nuclear Power
            • SuperMarket
            • Video Recorder
            • Audio Cassette
            • Pocket Calculator
            • Miniature Computer
            • SST
            • Word Processing
                • LP Record
                • Motion Pictures
                • Rocket
                •Chemical Fertilizers
                • Food Preservatives
                • Jet Engine
                • Credit Card
                • Electron Microscope
                • ICBM
                • Life Support Machines
                • Mass-cargo Ship
                • Metal Extrusion
                • Skyscraper
                • Birth Control Pill
                    • Radar
                    • Television
                    • Xerox Process
                        • Microcircuit
                        • Atom Bomb
                        • Mass Transit
                        • Audio Tape Recorder
                            • Ball-point Pen
                            • Computer
                            • Phototypesetting
                            • Polaroid Camera
                            • Transistor
                            • Communication Satellite
                            • Jumbo Jet
                            • Moon Landing
                            • Organ Transplants
                            • Space Travel

workplace contributed to the decline in wellness? While a definite answer to this question is not possible, there is no doubt that changes and the rate at which they occur create a tangible biological arousal that makes people more vulnerable to other pressures in their lives.

In the next section we will move from the general category of environmental stressors to extraorganizational stressors that occur at the personal interface between life outside and life inside the organization. The manager, because of position and role expectations, is brought into many of the extraorganizational stressors. It is a complex web of stressors that most managers prefer to ignore or spend minimal time on. Unfortunately, avoidance strategies may lead to unpleasant performance decrements, unexplained behavior patterns, and alienation between manager and subordinates.

EXTRAORGANIZATIONAL STRESSORS

In this section we will discuss a representative sample of stressors in the extraorganizational category presented in our integrative model (Figure 2–4). We have included the extraorganizational stressors that managers and subordinates seem most concerned about. The extraorganizational stressors discussed here have rarely been included in research investigations of stress and work. Thus, the empirical basis for many propositions about the role of extraorganizational stressors on the job behavior of employees is somewhat lacking.

The family

Is the family a source of stress at work? Or is work a source of stress in family relationships? Again what emerges is a circular relationship. The job and family are interacting factors with which a person must cope on a regular basis.

The examination of the family as a source of stress is complicated by problems of the nature of the stressor variable itself. Stressors in the family vary greatly in severity and in degree of continuity. There are brief crises as well as long-term family contributors to stress. A particular family phenomenon may be a stress source, and it may also constitute a response to stress. Thus, the family stressor can be both an independent and dependent variable. It may also operate as a mediating variable.

Another kind of problem is that of measuring the family stressor. The complexities of measuring stress were delineated in Chapter 3, but some special problems occur when assessing family stressors. The specification of the differential degrees of stress is extremely difficult when measuring such family stressors as marital conflict, childrearing practices, family structure, or sibling rivalry. Measurement of family stressors is also complicated because hostilities that arise within the family may manifest themselves at work, in school, or in illness seemingly unrelated to family stress. The same type of displacement is true with regard to job stress manifesting itself at home.

The examination of stressors that may stem from the family inevitably leads to problems of the specific cause. Some family stressors can be traced to the job, the economy, or other factors outside the family. For example, causes of marital conflict may be difficulties that a spouse is experiencing on the job if this job stress is transferred to the home.

Although any stressor that seems based in the family can be traced to causes outside the family, it still seems important to examine the family more closely. Though the family may not itself be the source, it can be the unit within which stressors emerge, interact, and exert a significant impact on people.

One well-researched area of relevance is the broken home. The broken home can result from a death, divorce, separation, desertion, or minimal participation of key family members in their expected roles (e.g., illness of parent, absence of parent(s) because of work). In the broken home, family-based stressors tend to be multiple rather than single phenomena. In broken families where a specific event is responsible (e.g., death, divorce, not performing expected roles), numerous other kinds of stressor conditions may be found, including improper nutrition, illness, and sexual misconduct. These multiple conditions obscure the role of the broken family itself as a major stressor.

One particular study sheds light on the role of differing types of broken home situations as stressors (Langer, 1963). Langer examined the mental health status of respondents in relation to differing types of family history variables. It was found that levels of mental health risk relating to the broken home in childhood varied according to the cause of the breakup and according to the socioeconomic status of the respondent. The mental health risk associated with the death of a mother is particularly high among families of low socioeconomic status. Another finding was that respondents who came from a home marked by the stresses of divorce, separation, or desertion of a parent were themselves more likely to have broken marriages than respondents from stable homes. It should be noted that this systematic study relied primarily on retrospective data.

There has been research on family stressors that is more germane to the issue of stress and work than the Langer study. One such study that investigated career executives and how they coped with job and family matters was reported by Handy (1978). Based on a study of twenty-three husband-wife couples, Hardy developed a matrix of husband-wife congruence. Figure 7–2 presents his four-cell matrix. As part of a battery of tests the couples revealed differences between husband and wife on three attitude categories, dominance, achievement, and affiliation (similar to the three need categories of McClelland, 1962). *Affiliation,* a desire for association with someone, was linked to *nurturance,* a desire to support. The scores on the four categories were collapsed into two dimensions—achievement/dominance and affiliation/nurturance.

The titles for the four cells were developed by Handy and his colleagues to convey the flavor of the attitudes and values of those whose scores located them in each cell. Cell A contained *involved* individuals. These individuals had needs to achieve and dominate, but also had high social needs. Cell B subjects were designated *thrusting.* These were high achievers with a need for dominance who liked to act on their own. Most of the male executives fell into this cell. Cell C contained the *existentialists* or the loners. They had little desire to control others and were not particularly ambitious. Cell D was designated *caring* for the people who achieved satisfaction from looking after others. Many of the executive wives fell into this cell, but only two of the men.

The marriage patterns were arrived at by linking the individuals in each relationship so that you have A-A marriages (both in the same involved cell), A-B marriages and so forth, sixteen possible patterns in all. For convenience, Handy listed the male cell first, then the female. In the sample B-D was the most common, followed by B-B, A-D, and A-A.

The B-D pattern is the traditional family role stereotype. The husband works and the wife manages the home and children. The wife is operationally in charge of the home. The arena of family problems found in the B-D relationship involve money, children, and mobility. These couples run a regulated home with rules and ritual.

In the B-B pattern both husband and wife place a high value on achievement and dominance. They both want an arena in which to achieve something of value. If both husband and wife are working, the home base for these couples tends to be disorganized. Both husband and wife may find this irritating, and if the husband blames the wife, forcing her into a caring role, conflict may well develop. Since "thrusting" people

FIGURE 7–2   Husband-Wife Congruence Matrix

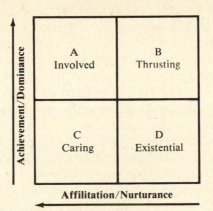

are aggressive under tension, the individuals in B-B relationships move against each other when they feel stress.

Similar descriptions are offered by Handy (1978) for other possible husband-wife patterns. It should be noted that Handy's sample is British and it remains to be seen whether it can be generalized to couples from other industrialized nations. The central lesson of the Handy research is that marriage patterns differ, and stress is dealt with differently in each type of marriage. Also, the nature of a marriage partner's job dictates certain family activity patterns. If job activities do not fit the marriage pattern, then either the job or the pattern must change if stress is to be minimized.

The conclusions of our discussion of the family are seemingly simplistic. The family can be a place of relief from job stress, a sanctuary for regenerating energy levels. It can be a source of strength for husband, wife, and children. Conversely, if the family patterns or family events are not right, they can affect work behavior, husband and wife relationships, and child rearing. Thus, the family can be a help in reducing stress or a contributor to a high stress build-up. The task ahead for researchers is to identify and measure stressors that originate in the family. On the other hand, managers need to be alert to the fact that family concerns are carried into the workplace.

Relocation

One extraorganizational stressor that is closely linked to job and organizational factors is associated with relocating a family after receiving a transfer or promotion. Moving families from one part of a city to another or across the country or ocean can be excessively stressful for all members of the family. Each year one of every five Americans changes address; the average home owner stays in a house for only about seven years. In addition, the average American switches jobs about every three years.

For the most part organizations do little to prepare family members for the potential stress associated with moving. Although an executive's identity and status are often enhanced by relocation, spouses often suffer because of the inability to transfer credentials. It is not unusual in the B-D marriage patterns (see Figure 7–2) for a wife's happiness to decrease as her husband's career status increases. Losing familiar friends and support often means that a woman must sacrifice her own needs and aspirations. Although the woman may not have professional status, she has often developed a name for herself socially in a community. Every relocation means that she is faced with reestablishing her identity from the bottom up.

Relocating also intensifies a couple's emotional dependence on each other. The loss of friends from the old community makes the husband and wife depend more on each other for human companionship. However, the organization requires the relocated person to spend more time learning the job, the new routine, and the new working relationships. Therefore, on the one hand relocating encourages more husband-wife dependence, while at the same time the new job steals the time needed for additional companionship.

Just as relocation increases family stress for the husband and wife, it also affects children. Certain age groups are more susceptible to relocation stress. Preschoolers experience feelings of loss and insecurity. They may even interpret a relocation as a form of punishment. A young child may revert to infantile behavior such as thumb-sucking and bed-wetting or they may experience more nightmares. Children in grade school may experience similar feelings of insecurity. Teenagers, for whom peer approval and relationships are so important, frequently have a particularly difficult time.

A new element in relocation involves female employees. In a growing number of cases, women that are promoted are asking husbands to change jobs and relocate. Some husbands welcome the move while others openly resist, and marital conflict increases. More managerial attention will have to be given to the relocation of working wives as more women move up the corporate ladder.

The unhappy, highly stressed, relocated employee is usually not a productive person. Managers who understand that relocation affects the family and that the family affects the relocated employee will be better prepared to deal with problems. Organizations can be very helpful in aiding families in understanding the reasons for relocation before moves are made. In addition, the spouse and children should be part of the relocation decision process. Organizations can provide workshops and counseling for families so that a rational approach to resolving differences of opinions and attitudes about relocation is used. Although organizations often pay for moving, housefinding trips, and the sale of homes, they fail to pay attention to the fears, insecurity, and disruption in the family resulting from relocation. By involving everyone in the relocation from the beginning, many of the fears and feelings of insecurity can be worked out. Relocation is extremely difficult in itself, and failing to consider the family needs, aspirations, and stresses is often a costly organizational mistake.

Economic and financial stressors

There is a story that Jim and Mary went grocery shopping one week for their family of five, spent ninety dollars and placed the groceries in the glove compartment of the family's subcompact automobile. Inflation, the cost of living and keeping up with the Joneses are worries of many individuals. The worry of having too few dollars to buy goods and services can be very stressful. The steep rises in price of food, clothing, medical care, services (e.g., utilities), and education have dampened the purchasing power of many people.

Although individual restraint and astute purchasing can relieve some of a person's financial difficulties, it is extremely difficult for an individual to cope with inflation. The individual seems helpless as hospital room costs jump 100% per year, hamburger prices increase 60% per year, and gasoline prices increase 40% per year. Digging deeper into an empty purse, savings account, or pocket doesn't mean that funds will be located. What the digging does is create stress about one's financial plight.

The perceived and/or actual inability to keep up financially has driven many people to seek second jobs. The extra work provides additional money but it also robs a person of leisure time and saps energy. These costs often result in increased irritability and stress. Hence, although initially financial problem stress is reduced, there may inevitably be an increase in fatigue stress. The net effect of moonlighting may be increased stress, more family problems, and reduced performance in a person's primary job.

Race and class

Race and class are sociopsychological sources of stress. Such things as job promotions and business opportunities are almost exclusively middle and upper-class stressors. Those at the bottom tend to exert more of their energy on surviving and finding a way to feed themselves. For example, insecurity is more likely to be found in low economic class black persons because the survival struggle taxes them physically and psychologically. For the most part the struggle of blacks has commanded increased attention in recent years among behavioral researchers. Other minorities have not been included in study samples as much.

In his review of the literature on race differences, Pettigrew (1964) presented evidence that there was a higher rate of physical illness and shorter life expectancy among blacks. Security is threatened more among blacks because of higher rates of divorce and separation, loss of employment, and by fewer opportunities to support a family. Blacks from low or middle economic classes have higher rates of premature and abnormal births than white counterparts. Research evidence seems to indicate that blacks are exposed to a higher number of these type of stressors than their class counterparts among whites.

Experimental evidence suggests that lower economic class individuals also suffer from a lack of self-confidence, especially blacks having to interact with whites (Katz and Benjamin, 1960). The white person represents a threat that leads to feelings of insecurity.

In summary, there is a growing realization among behavioral scientists of the need to investigate the stresses associated with race and class. We have, because of the limited research available, only briefly examined blacks' problems. It is not known at this point to what extent studies will be able to identify race and class stressors so that managers can learn to develop better interpersonal relations. However, we do know that being a member of a minority can generate stress that affects a person's quality of life both away from work and on the job.

Residential stressors

The residential area in which we live can be described in many different terms. The area's orderliness, natural beauty, cleanliness, safety, tax rate, transportation, and road conditions are features that are often used when describing one's community or neighborhood. These and other features can be stressors that influence the behavior of people.

Whether a residential feature is or becomes a stressor depends upon differing standards of comparison influencing people's perceptions. Previous residential experiences, different personality traits, and varying personal goals may influence their evaluations.

Research by Marens (1976) of community attributes that could be extraorganizational stressors focused on police protection, climate, streets and roads, public schools, garbage collection, parks and playgrounds, public transportation, police-community relations, and local taxes. Marens found that ethnic minorities are less satisfied with their community than are whites.

The Marens (1976) residential features and others such as condition of housing, convenience of services and shopping, neighborliness, and degree of noise, and air pollution are likely stressors. The degree of stress generated by such residential stressors is dependent on assessments of these attributes. It is important in studying potential residential stressors to examine personal characteristics such as race, education level, personality traits, experiences, class, population of community, and age. These characteristics may mediate the stressor-behavior linkage as they have been found to do in research on other extraorganizational stressors discussed in this chapter.

THE MANAGER AND EXTRAORGANIZATIONAL STRESSORS

By being aware and by listening carefully, the manager may reach the conclusion that extraorganizational stressors are the root of performance problems and interpersonal job difficulties. If this is the case the manager is faced with a dilemma. Entering an employee's extraorganizational arena is risky for any manager, since uninvited intrusion into an employee's private life is likely to create another set of unwelcome stressors. The dynamics of working relationships will in many cases, however, pull a manager into this arena. Subordinates may want to talk about this aspect of their lives, and managers are often brought into this arena through these discussions.

The organization's right to probe into extraorganizational stressors is a significant issue. Does a manager representing an organization have a right to probe into the family, financial, and residential activities that may be the cause of decreased performance? This is a difficult question to answer for many people. We believe that unless an employee allows the manager to enter into his or her private life, the manager should ordinarily stay out. The emphasis here is on the term *allow*. Employees generally allow some intrusion by managers, and only this part of their private lives should be probed by managers for answers to on-the-job behavior problems or stress warning signals.

If an employee wants no part of managerial intrusion into marriage, family, financial, or child rearing situations, then this preference must be accepted. What manager can accomplish anything positive if he or she is unwelcome?

Acceptance of the preference for privacy does not mean that managers can ignore extraorganizational stressors and how they affect other stressor categories. As stated above, many subordinates pull their managers into extraorganizational events to some extent. For these subordinates the manager will have some information about family, marital conflict, financial situation, and residential attributes. The manager must use this often incomplete information to construct a profile of job, organizational, and extraorganizational stress for subordinates.

The manager who appreciates and understands the dynamics of the interaction of the various stressor categories is better prepared to take some form of corrective action. Research has illustrated that family conflicts can affect job performance (Barilyn, 1970). Therefore, awareness of this home-work connection can help the manager interpret and understand why a person is not performing up to par. On the other hand, failing to accept the home-work phenomenon might result in hasty and incorrect decisions about the employee's performance.

In essence, managers can ignore the importance of extraorganizational stressors when information is available; they can use the available information that they have to develop strategies for helping their subordinates, or they can use the information to justify disciplining, reprimanding, or discharging subordinates. In our opinion, the choice is clear. Since managers are pulled into extraorganizational matters by many subordinates, they should attempt to help them. Help may be nothing more than lending an ear to the employee or referring the subordinate to professional experts, but it needs to be available. Thus, managerial awareness of extraorganizational stressors and the potential impact they can have on behavior is a necessary step from which all managers can derive some benefit.

APPENDIX

Stress Diagnostic Survey©

In this survey of extraorganizational conditions a number of events which you have experienced are presented. If you *have not experienced* the event listed *in the last 12 months,* place a NO next to the item. If you *have experienced* the event in the last 12 months simply report its occurrence by writing in a Distress Rating next to the event. You can use any number from 1 to 11, depending on how seriously the event troubled you.

For purposes of this survey distress may be defined as existing whenever you experience feelings of frustration, anxiety, tension, upset, or discomfort. Remember, your distress ratings should reflect how much frustration, anxiety, tension, upset, or discomfort the extraorganizational event caused you.

DISTRESS SCALE

Low Distress				Moderate Distress				Extreme Distress		
1	2	3	4	5	6	7	8	9	10	11

Marriage and personal relations

1. Engagement broken
2. Married
3. Divorced
4. Separated
5. Relationship with spouse or cohabitant changed for worse
6. Lack of satisfactory communications with spouse or cohabitant
7. Spouse or cohabitant began or stopped work outside the home
8. Sexual difficulties or dissatisfaction
9. Reunited with spouse or cohabitant after separation
10. Trouble with in-laws

11. Infidelity in relationship with spouse or cohabitant

12. Death of spouse or cohabitant

Children

13. Pregnancy in immediate household

14. Birth of child in immediate household

15. Miscarriage or stillbirth in immediate household

16. Found out unable to have children

17. Death of child

18. Serious disagreement with partner on child rearing practices

19. Child doing poorly in school

20. Child involved in illegal activities

21. Child a discipline problem

22. Child with severe personal problem (e.g., unwanted pregnancy, drug abuse, etc.)

23. Child negatively affecting relationship with partner

Family

24. New person moved into household

25. Person moved out of household

26. Someone stayed on in household after he/she was expected to leave

27. Serious family disagreement other than with spouse or cohabitant

28. Family member other than partner or child dies

29. All in all, how well would you say your marriage, children, family, and personal life have gone for you in the last 12 months? (Circle one answer.)

    1. The best ever

    2. Especially well

    3. Good

    4. Average

    5. Poor

    6. Really bad

    7. The worst ever

Residence

30. Moved to different residence in same city
31. Moved to different city or state
32. Unable to move after expecting to be able to move
33. Lost a home through fire, flood, or other disaster
34. Home was burglarized or vandalized
35. Difficulties with neighbors
36. Neighborhood not being properly maintained

Finances

37. Took out a mortgage
38. In arrears on mortgage or loan
39. Had mortgage or loan foreclosed
40. Received a cut in salary or wages
41. Suffered a financial loss or loss of property not related to work
42. Income failing to keep pace with expenses
43. Audited by Internal Revenue Service
44. Did not receive an expected wage or salary increase
45. Incurred an unexpected financial obligation
46. Experienced a substantial improvement in finances, such as major payraise, new sources of income, or an inheritance
47. All in all, how well would you say your housing, financial and legal matters have gone for you in the past 12 months? (Circle one answer.)
    1. The best ever
    2. Especially well
    3. Good
    4. Average
    5. Poor
    6. Really bad
    7. The worst ever

Scoring Key

There are a number of ways to score this extraorganizational stressor self-report survey. You can simply add up for each category marriage and personal relations, children, family, etc., the number of items you reported some amount of distress in. This will illustrate the stressor categories with the most frequent amount of stressors. A second scoring procedure is to total your distress scores for each item and category and determine which is causing the most problems. Any item score that is 6 or greater is an area that should be more closely examined. A total category score of 30 or more for marriage and personal relations (items 1–12), 27 or more for children (items 13–23), 18 or more for residence (items 30–36), and 25 or more for finances (items 37–46) warrants further review. Finally, examining your responses to items 29 (marriage, children, family, and personal life) and 47 (housing, financial, and legal matters) will provide you with a global picture of stress in some extraorganizational categories. This self-report survey is really more suited for having you consider extraorganizational events than it is for you to accurately measure stress levels or to compare your scores with those of other respondents.

REFERENCES

Barilyn, L. "Career and family orientations." *Human Relations* 23 (1970): 97–113.

Forbes, R. *Corporate Stress*. Garden City, New York: Doubleday and Co., Inc., 1979.

Handy, C. "The family: Help or hindrance?" In *Stress at Work*. C. L. Cooper and R. Payne, eds. New York: John Wiley and Sons, Inc., 1978, 107–123.

Holmes, T.H. and R.H. Rahe. "The social readjustment rating scale." *Journal of Psychosomatic Research* 11 (1967): 213–218.

Katz, I. and L. Benjamin. "Effects of white authoritarianism in biracial work groups." *Journal of Abnormal and Social Psychology* 61(1960): 448–456.

Langer, T.S. "Childhood broken homes." In *Life Stress and Mental Health*. T.S. Langer and S.T. Michael, eds. Glencoe, Ill.: The Free Press, 1963.

Marens, R. "The residential environment." In *The Quality of American Life*. A. Campbell, P.E. Converse and W.L. Rodgers, eds. New York: Russell Sage Foundation, 1976.

Meyer, R.J. and R.J. Haggerty. "Streptococcal infections in families." *Pediatrics* 29 (1962): 539–549.

Pettigrew, T.F. *A Profile of the Negro American*. Princeton, N.J.: Van Nostrand Reinhold Company, 1964.

Stokols, D. et al. "Traffic congestion, type A behavior, and stress." *Journal of Applied Psychology* 63 (1978): 467–480.

Toffler, A. *Future Shock*. New York: Random House, Inc., 1970.

Wolff, H.G. "Life stress and bodily disease—A formulation." In *Life Stress and Bodily Disease*. H.G. Wolff, S.G. Wolff, Jr., and C.C. Hare, eds. Baltimore: The Williams and Wilkins Company, 1059–1094.

FOR FURTHER READING

Antonovsky, A. *Health, Stress, and Coping*. San Francisco: Jossey-Bass, Inc., Publishers, 1979.

Brown, G.W. "Life events and psychiatric illness: Some thoughts on methodology and causality." *Journal of Psychosomatic Research* 16 (1972): 311–320.

Cassel, J. "The contribution of the social environment to host resistance." *American Journal of Epidemiology* 104 (1976): 107–123.

Hinkle, L.E., Jr. and W.C. Loring, eds. *The Effect of the Man-made Environment on Health and Behavior*. Atlanta: Center for Disease Control, Public Health Service, 1977.

Kinzer, N.S. *Stress and the American Woman*. Garden, New York: Doubleday and Co., Inc., 1979.

Lazarus, R.S. and J.B. Cohen. "Environmental stress." In *Human Behavior and Environment*. I. Altman and J.F. Wohlwill, eds. New York: Plenum Publishing Corporation, 1977.

Individual Differences 8

THE ASS EATING THISTLES

An Ass was loaded with provisions of several sorts, which he was carrying home for a grand entertainment. By the way, he met with a fine large Thistle, and being very hungry, immediately ate it up, which, while he was doing, he entered into this reflection: How many greedy epicures would think themselves happy amidst such a variety of delicate viands as I now carry! But to me, this bitter prickly Thistle is more savory and relishing than the most exquisite and sumptuous banquet.

Managerial Application • That which may be a profound source of stress for one employee may be the locus of significant satisfaction for another.

164

Who among us has not observed—and at different times both praised and cursed—the wide range of variation in behavior and abilities between people? One of the truisms in behavioral science is that in some ways we are like everyone else; in some ways we are like some others; and in some ways we are like no one else. The triteness of the observation does not reduce its validity. It would be difficult to make a more insightful and accurate statement than was made by the Vermont farmhand who observed that "people is mostly alike, but what differences they is can be powerful important."

The variations among individuals are a function of two broad classes of variables: heredity and environment. Let us briefly examine each before focusing on individual differences as moderators of stress. Heredity determines all the immutable characteristics we possess as a function of our choice of parents. Certain genetic qualities or predispositions are determined at the instant of conception. Except for identical twins (who are formed from the same ovum and sperm), we are all genetically unique, and therein lies a large measure of the individual variation with which we are concerned. As Dobzhansky (1956) observed of human genes, the number of possible combinations is "vastly greater than the number of atoms in the entire universe. . . . Every human being is, then . . . unique."

We still do not fully understand the scope of inherited trait characteristics. Of those that we know are at least partially genetically determined, some, like eye color, are not particularly important as stress moderators. Others, such as sex and certain disease predispositions, can be very important. Still others, such as differences in glandular secretions, may be of extreme importance.

For many individual differences the line of demarcation between hereditary and environmental determinants is somewhat obscure. This obscurity has led to the development and continuation of the so-called *nature or nurture controversy,* which is nothing more than arguments over whether heredity or the environment is the major determiner of some human characteristic. Nowhere is this ongoing debate better illustrated than in the case of intelligence. On one extreme are arguments that intelligence is fixed at conception; at the other is the position that intellectual ability is shaped wholly by the environment. As is usually the case, the truth is most likely somewhere in between.

The nature-nurture controversies notwithstanding, it is clear that much of what constitutes an individual's response repertoire is shaped by learning. How we interact with others, how we handle conflict, and how we attempt to cope with stressors are largely a function of our previous experiences. The patterns of our experiences *and* the meaning they have for us are as unique as our genetic makeup. The wonder is not that people are as different from each other as they are, but that they are as similar as they are.

From a managerial perspective, the importance of understanding individual differences does not lie in changing them. Whether it be employees' sex or their personality, there is little likelihood of meaningful change occurring as a result of managerial action. But it is crucial to gain an appreciation of the effects various stressors may have as a function of individual variation. We may not be able to change one person's poison and another's pleasure, but if we can distinguish between the two, we can contribute to individual and organizational effectiveness.

INDIVIDUAL DIFFERENCES, WORK, AND STRESS

One generally accepted principle among managers is that individual employees are an organization's most important resource and simultaneously the source of the most challenging problems that managers face. Individuals are the most important resource for the same reason that they frustrate managers: every individual is different in some manner from every other individual in terms of intelligence, skills, career aspirations, personality, needs, and of particular importance to us, in terms of reactions to organizational stressors.

In Chapter 2 we met Chester Comer. Chester, you recall, was faced with a series of relatively minor, yet nontrivial events that caused him discomfort, frustration, and anxiety. It was, in fact, his response to certain of the early events (for example, oversleeping) which set the stage for subsequent events to be stressful. Another person, with a different set of experiences, learned responses, temperament, priorities, and coping strategies, might well have experienced little or no stress in the events sequence which Chester found so debilitating. The question raised by the Chester Comer illustration is that of individual differences. It is a question of how and why some people respond to a situation with a negative stress reaction, some with little reaction at all, and others with a positive growth response.

These variations in response are what concerns us in this chapter. We will not be able to lay out as clear and definitive a picture of the role of individual differences as the reader may desire, but we will be able to provide a valuable perspective. We know beyond a reasonable doubt that cigarette smoking is associated with increased cancer rates. Yet many people smoke heavily all their lives and never develop cancer. There is growing evidence that the appearance of coronary heart disease is related to certain personality characteristics. Yet many people with these characteristics live long lives without the slightest sign of coronary problems. Nonetheless, we still caution against smoking and encourage people to modify certain personality facets. Similarly, none of the specific differences discussed in the remainder of this chapter bears a one-to-one relationship with stress. But there is evidence that all of them *may* be intermediate causes in the relationship between a stressor stimulus and a possible stress response.

INDIVIDUAL DIFFERENCES AS MODERATORS

The model presented in Figure 2–4 suggests that individual differences moderate the relationship between stressors and stress as well as that between perceived stress and various physiological and behavioral outcomes. As the name implies, a moderator is a condition, behavior, or characteristic that qualifies the relationship between two variables. The effect may be to intensify the relationship or to weaken it. The relationship between the number of gallons of gas used and total miles driven, for example, is affected by the variable of speed. Thus driving speed moderates or changes the nature of the relationship between gas consumed and distance traveled. Likewise, an individual's level of self-esteem may moderate or affect the extent to which that individual experiences stress as a consequence of being exposed to a stressor.

Consistent with the framework developed in Chapter 2, individual differences are categorized as either demographic/behavioral or cognitive/affective in nature. The distinction is not an arbitrary one. The potential effects of the moderators in the cognitive/affective grouping operate both between stressors and perceived stress *and* between perceived stress and outcomes. The differences in this category include need levels, locus of control, tolerance of ambiguity, self-esteem, and personality types. The demographic and behavioral differences are thought to moderate primarily the perceived stress and outcome relationship. These differences include age, sex, occupation, education, work schedule, and health status.

The differences included here should not be viewed as exhaustive. The range of variables that may serve a moderating function is virtually infinite. The choice of moderators to be included reflects first the current level of knowledge concerning stress and modifiers, and second our judgment of the degree to which individual, managerial, or organizational action may modify the moderator.

INDIVIDUAL DIFFERENCES: DEMOGRAPHICS/BEHAVIORS

Many of the differences among people are a function of their behaviors: what they do for a living, whether or not they take care of themselves, how much time they have devoted to their education, how hard they work, and many other similar kinds of behaviors or characteristics. Other differences relate most to what are traditionally referred to as demographic variables: age, sex, and similar attributes. In this section we will discuss some of these demographic and behavioral factors and examine their possible relationship to stress.

Age

Age and stress seem to be related in a couple of ways. The first has to do with a distinction between chronologic age and physiologic age (Selye, 1976). Chronologic age refers to time elapsed since birth. Physiologic, or true age, depends largely on the rate of wear and tear experienced by the body. The distinction between these two concepts of age clarifies why one person may be approaching both senility and the grave at age fifty, while another is in excellent mental and physical health at seventy. One of the factors that can account for the differences in these two people is the nature and duration of the stress they experience. Recall that the response to a stressor requires individual adaptation. It is this adaptation which produces some of the wear and tear associated with aging. Thus, one relationship between stress and age is that stress affects physiological age. Clearly one dysfunctional consequence of long periods of intense stress is a hastening of the aging process and the accompanying loss of performance frequently associated with aging.

But what we have just described is an example of how stress affects aging. Does age, correspondingly, affect stress? The answer is a qualified yes. The qualification is necessary because it is not necessarily age per se which relates to stress, but the experiences that tend to be associated with it.

One of the more significant of these experiences is embodied in the concept of *career stages*. This concept, which grew out of the work of Erikson (1950), postulates that an individual will pass through several stages in the development of his or her career. Miller and Form (1951), for example, hypothesize three stages: the *initial phase,* the *trial period,* and the *maintenance period.* Other writers have postulated other, but similar stages. These periods correspond to different age ranges into which most of the people at that stage would fall. Since each stage has a different set of objectives, with the individual attempting to meet different needs, different stressors tend to be prominent at each stage. A person in an advancement stage, for example, would find overload less stressful than someone in a maintenance stage. Likewise, lack of challenge would be much more of a potential stressor during the advancement stage than the trial stage. Age, consequently, as it is related to career stages, may moderate the potential effect of various stressors. What may be very stressful to a fifty-five-year-old employee contemplating no further major career advancement may not operate as a stressor at all in the case of the thirty-five-year-old comer.

Education

Education may moderate the stress relationship when educational differences are translated into differential stress reactions. How this happens is far from clear, but it almost certainly has to do with the fact that individuals at different education levels have also had other differences in life experiences, such as in social mobility and socioeconomic levels. That is to say, education, like age, may not be a direct moderator per se, but may moderate as a result of the other factors it influences in an individual's life.

One aspect of educational attainment which seems to operate directly is *educational discrepancy*. An individual may experience educational discrepancy when his or her educational level is considerably less than that of others in the same career or job. In a study of social and pyschological factors associated with illness, it was found that stress illness rates increased as individuals moved upward in social status above where their educational level would normally find them (Selye, 1975).

An interesting five-year prospective study carved out among 270,000 men employed at AT&T examined the relationship between education and one possible consequence of stress, coronary heart disease. For every part of the country, at every age, and in all departments of the organization, college men had lower incidences of heart disease than no-college men. Unfortunately, other stress reactions were not examined in this study, but it suggests that the level of education may moderate the stress relationship. As implied earlier, however, it is probably not education itself, but a constellation of factors associated with different educational backgrounds which is the true moderator (Hinkle, et al, 1968).

Occupation

In a very strict sense, occupational choice is more a product of individual differences than a difference itself. It is also true that the stressor conditions to which an individual is subjected vary as a function of occupation. Thus, part of the stress we may experience as we pursue our chosen field of endeavor is a function of variables associated with the occupation itself. Another part of the stress is brought about by how we respond to the stressor conditions we encounter at work but which are not unique to or more predominant in a particular occupation. Our primary interest in this section is with occupation as a moderator. Consequently, we will focus upon those fields where data indicate that the role occupant may be subjected to increased stress by virtue of the fact that he or she is in that occupation. From there we will look briefly at how occupational adjustment may moderate the stress relationship.

Stressful occupations

Since there is no standardized, universally acceptable method for assessing stress, it follows that there exists no totally applicable way to rank occupations by stress levels. A number of basic questions must be resolved before that will be possible. For example, what constitutes a high-stress occupation? If we know that individuals in that field are highly stressed, do we know they are stressed *because* of the occupation? Or, might they have been drawn to that field in some way by the fact they were already stressed? Until questions such as these can be answered, our attempts to rank occupations by stress level must remain highly tentative.

The above statements notwithstanding, there are data that suggest rankings of stress levels by occupation. Using coronary heart disease as an indicator, Guralnick (1963) distinguished between high-stress groups such as lawyers, judges, physicians, pharmacists, insurance agents, and real estate agents, and low-stress groups such as college presidents, college professors, and teachers. Colligan and his associates (1977) examined the admissions records of community mental health centers throughout one state to determine the rate of diagnosed mental health disorders for 130 major occupations. The results indicated a disproportionate incidence of mental health anomalies among the hospital and health care professions.

A few occupations have traditionally been considered so stressful that they have been subject to intense study by themselves. One of the most frequently studied, for example, is police work. Interestingly enough—and somewhat contrary to the TV-produced impression many people have of police work—life-threatening situations are not the primary stressor. Very seldom, in fact, is this aspect of police work cited as a source of stress. Rather, major stress stems from administrative issues and contacts with the court system (Kroes, et al., 1974).

The occupation that has been the most studied and theorized about when it comes to stress is that of air traffic controller. In spite of ideal physical working conditions, air traffic controllers experience considerable stress, presumably because of the long periods of intense concentration required and because of the life-and-death impact of their decisions. They suffer from incidences of ulcers, hypertension, alchohol-ism, divorce, and suicide many times the rates for the general population. The toll is so great that it is most unusual to find a controller who has been on the job for as long as fifteen years. In one comprehensive study, major negative physical and mental health changes occurred over time in a large sample of controllers (Rose, Jenkins, and Hurst, 1978).

By talking about certain occupations as being more stressful than others, we are saying that they contain more stressors and/or they intensify the stressor-stress relationship by virtue of what is involved in the occupation. As suggested earlier, there are a number of problems in rating occupations as stressful, not the least of which is the possibility that stress-prone individuals are drawn to certain occupations.

Occupational adjustment

Regardless of whether one is pursuing a high or low-stress occupation, the question of how well one adjusts to that field has implications for the extent of stress experienced. Occupational adjustment may be said to exist when there is a correspondence between the abilities, needs, and objectives of the individual and the requirements and the opportunities of his or her chosen occupation. When this correspondence is maximized, the stress potential of the occupation will be less than when there is little correspondence. Thus, occupation may moderate the stress relationship by providing (or failing to provide) a desirable fit between the individual and the occupational environment.

Individuals performing jobs to which they are not adjusted may find potential stressors more likely to produce stress responses. This can frequently be seen in the case of job promotions. Until the employee has adjusted to the new position, the potential for job-related stress is much higher. This is particularly true in the case of the individual promoted to the first level of supervision. In effect that person is entering a new occupation. Until the proper correspondence is achieved, that occupation can be expected to serve as an intensifier of the stress relationship. That is why any promotion should be accompanied by as much orientation and learning time as possible. The occupation need not be stressful for the lack of adjustment to produce unwanted stress outcomes.

Sex

All indications are that historically at least (and as we shall see, *historically* is a key qualification) women have neither experienced the stress levels encountered by men, nor have they shown the negative effects of stress nearly to the extent that men have. While mortality rates and life expectancies are affected by a multitude of interacting factors, they show differences between the sexes that a growing number of researchers attribute to the relatively larger amounts of stress experienced by males. Table 8–1 contrasts both the absolute difference in life expectancy between men and women and the increases each sex has experienced.

As can be seen, women started this century with a longer life expectancy than males, have increased that lead through today, and according to projections made by the National Center for Health Statistics, will increase the difference even further halfway through the next century.

In addition to the fact that as this book is written the average American man can expect to die eight years sooner than the average American woman, there are other related differences as well. At certain ages, compared to women, men are four times more likely to die of

TABLE 8–1   Life Expectancy at Birth (Years)

	1900	1970	Estimated 2050	Increase 1900–1970	Increase 1970–2050
Men	46.3	67.1	71.8	20.8	4.7
Women	48.3	74.8	81.0	26.5	6.2
Difference	2.0	7.7	9.2	5.7	1.5

coronary heart disease, four times as likely to die in an accident, five times more likely to die from alcohol-related disease, five times more likely to be murdered, and seven times more likely to kill themselves. In addition to these differences, the incidence rate for virtually every one of the diseases of adaptation discussed in Chapter 4 is significantly higher for men.

Why do these differences exist? There are two possible answers to that question. One is that there are differences between the sexes that biologically predispose men to disease and death (or conversely, protect women). This suggests that a genetic difference plays a role. The other possible explanation is that the differences are not true sex differences, but arise because of the differences in the roles played by members of the two sexes.

It seems unlikely that genetics has a great deal to do with it. It is improbable, for example, that genetics can explain the widening difference in life expectancy from 1900–1970. Genetic codes simply are not altered significantly in such a short time span. This is not to say there may not be some built-in differences. Women, for example, tend to react better physiologically than men while under stress. This may be due in part to the female hormonal system, which is not oriented toward triggering the body's stress reactions with the same degree of sensitivity as the male system.

The best explanation for the stress-related individual sex differences would seem to center primarily on role differences. While there are obviously many exceptions, throughout its history men and women have played different roles in our society. In the past, man was the breadwinner whose responsibility it was to provide the means for obtaining the necessities (and luxuries) of life for his family. He was the dominant figure in the family. He made the major decisions, he handled the family's financial dealings, and so on. The woman's role, that of wife and mother, was more passive and centered on providing a supporting home atmosphere for her husband. One thing which this role did not include was working outside the home and competing for jobs, salary, promotions, and corporate power. These were the exclusive domain of the men.

The price men have paid for this dubious honor of being the dominant sex (or at least thinking they were) has been very high. This price is reflected in mortality statistics, physical and mental health statistics, and what might be termed dysfunctional coping behavior. That is, men have higher incident rates of alcoholism, drug abuse and dependency, and violent behaviors. Thus, sex by virtue of its associated role differences may act as a moderator in the stress relationship. Examples would include the increased probability of a man's experiencing role overload as he seeks to promote and maintain his expected image as successful achiever and provider, increased intra-group conflict as he attempts to assert leadership and influence, and greater likelihood of career goal discrepancy as he fails to progress as rapidly as he must to fulfill his and others' expectations.

Two points need to be made. First, we have been describing some stereotyped male roles which drive many, but certainly not all, men. And we have described these roles in the extreme. There are far more examples of less extreme positions than there are of the aggressive, dominating drives described here. Nonetheless, even the more subtle examples are associated with increased stress reactions.

The second point is perhaps the most important. What we have been describing in terms of sexual role differences has been true historically. Today, however, there are growing indications everywhere that this is changing. Since the 1960s, in ever greater numbers, women have been casting off their old roles. One manifestation of this phenomenon is the movement on the part of women out of the home and into the work force. This has become so pronounced, that by 1979, for the first time in this country's history, more adult women were employed outside the home than not.

The significance of this movement into the work force is clear. From our standpoint, it means more and more women are playing organizational roles that they have not played in appreciable numbers in the past. Consequently, they are experiencing job, career, and organizational stressors in greater numbers and to a greater degree. While it is too soon to make any definitive judgments, indications are that as the distinction between male and female roles is shrinking, so also are the sex differences with regard to stress indications. For example, coronary disease among females below age forty-five, who have been long thought to have hormonal immunity to such problems, is increasing.

Incidence of peptic ulcers among females is increasing. While the overall male suicide rate is twice that of females, this relationship is reversed when only professional men and women are considered.

The upwardly mobile, career-oriented woman is subjected to stressors in addition to the ones associated with organizational life. In many cases she is a minority and experiences the added stress of being in that role. And since the married woman is much more likely than her husband to have disproportionate responsibilities for child and house care, it is not particularly surprising that stress-related consequences are increasing at almost epidemic rates among women.

There may well come a time when sex will cease to be a significant moderator of stress. But for the present and in the short-run future, differences in culturally imposed and accepted roles will continue to be important. Because of these differences, individuals will continue to respond differently to different stressors as a function of roles that have been determined partly on the basis of their gender.

Other demographic/behavioral differences

The list of potential individual differences that may be associated in some way with stressors, perceived stress, or negative stress outcomes and consequences is virtually unlimited. Family history, physical appearance, geographical area of residence, eating habits, religion, and a multitude of other demographic and behavioral factors may, for any particular individual, be of great importance. As representative examples of differences that have been shown to affect stress relationships, we will briefly examine the moderator role of health status, work schedule, and exercise.

Health status • By health status we mean the overall state of physical health. Some people always seem to feel good. They appear to be immune to the colds, flus, and digestive problems suffered by their colleagues. Others of us seem to suffer from a disproportionate share of physical complaints, particularly recurring difficulties such as allergies, asthma, anemia, and an assortment of other problems. Obviously a number of factors may be reponsible for these deficiencies, including heredity, previous medical history, and personal habits. It may be that many of these ailments are stress-induced initially. The point here, however, is that healthy people seem to be able to cope better with stressors than not-so-healthy people. Combating a physical ailment is an example of an attempt by the body to adapt. If, as Selye (1976) and others maintain, there is a finite amount of adaptive energy available, then directing some toward a physical problem leaves less for dealing with a psychological stressor. Possibly for this reason people with a positive health history seem better able to cope successfully with stress situations. Put another way, the employee with even mild chronic health problems is much more likely to experience negative stress reactions than a colleague.

Work schedules • Some people have been described as workaholics. They work inordinately long hours; they bring work home in the evenings and on weekends; and they never can quite find time to take a break or a vacation from their jobs. Excessive work hours and time commitment to the job have been associated with negative stress reactions (e.g., Buell and Breslow, 1960; Zohman, 1973). There seem to be three ways in which the work schedule can act as a stress moderator. First, differences in time spent on the job moderate exposure to job stressors. The eighty-hour-a-week individual has greater exposure to stressors than the individual who works forty hours a week.

Second, excessive work hours can use up physical and mental energy that would otherwise be available to help the individual cope with stressful situations. Third, and closely related to the second, an increase in the amount of time devoted to work usually entails a corresponding decrease in the time available for leisure and relaxation, during which adaptive energy reserves may be partially replenished.

Exercise • Physical exercise may be classified as an individual difference in the sense that people vary a great deal in the amount of exercise they get or provide for in their lives. It is a moderator of stress outcomes for many people since exercise can relieve tension, frustration, anxiety, and even depression. Exercise then is a moderator primarily insofar as it provides relief from the buildup of accumulated stress. More peripherally, it may also moderate by contributing to overall physical health, which in turn helps to mitigate negative stress outcomes.

INDIVIDUAL DIFFERENCES: COGNITIVE/AFFECTIVE

In one of the more enduring definitions, Allport (1961) defines personality as "the dynamic organization within the individual of those psycho-physical systems that determine his characteristic behavior and thought." Essentially then, what we referred to as cognitive/affective differences in Chapter 2 can be construed as aspects of personality. As was true in the case of demographic/behavioral differences, the number of potentially relevant cognitive/affective differences is legion. We have selected for further discussion five that are particularly relevant. The degree of stressfulness in any situation depends in part on perceptions of the individual that are influenced by one or more of these personality facets.

Need levels • Behavior is a function of needs. Everything we do is calculated—consciously or not—to satisfy some need, whether it is a basic need for food or a higher-order need for self-actualization. The astute manager is aware of this truism of human behavior and attempts to structure an environment in which behavior aimed at satisfying employees' individual needs contributes to organizational objectives as well.

The needs that are of greatest significance as moderators of stress in the framework of organizations are those related to the need for success and accomplishment. They are very closely akin to what McClelland (1961) refers to as the *need for achievement*. Individuals who display high levels of need for achievement attempt to excel, surpass others, attain high standards, make prolonged efforts to accomplish goals, and enjoy competition with others. Frequently these are people whose work is their central life interest. They are almost always people who devote a great deal of effort to whatever they are doing. Individuals with high achievement need levels tend to create conditions of work overload. Because of their orientation they may lack the ability to delegate, may create extraorganizational stressors as a result of their overattention to work concerns, and in general increase the likelihood of experiencing stress.

Lest we portray the workaholic as someone in search of stress overload, we should add that this is not the case at all. Corporate presidents do not arrive at that destination because of (or even in spite of) years of stress. The same characteristic that is likely to produce additional stressors for these individuals also reduces the likelihood of a negative stress response. For example, there is no question that high achievers foster conditions of role overload. At the same time, however, the intrinsic satisfaction and exhilirating sense of accomplishment they feel at getting a great many difficult tasks accomplished negate the potential negative effect of that stressor. Rather than feeling tension because of the work load, they experience satisfaction for their achievements. Thus these individuals can make a very positive organizational contribution in ways which they experience as very satisfying with less stress than many less effective organization members.

Self-esteem • The old maxim that people who feel good about themselves are happy people has a certain amount of validity. Possession of some minimal level of self-esteem is beneficial to effective functioning in any situation and is absolutely essential in extreme situations. Research suggests, for example, that the critical difference between those who survive a wartime prison camp experience and those who succumb to insanity and suicide is that the former group is able to muster forces to support their levels of self-esteem and consequently endure the stress of confinement (Bettelheim, 1958).

Higher levels of self-esteem are associated with greater confidence in one's ability to deal successfully with the environment. Conversely, low levels may enhance or facilitate the production of negative stress.

A direct indication that this is the case can be found in research conducted at the University of Michigan (Mueller, 1965). Negative relationships were found between qualitative role overload and self-esteem. That is, employees who reported being dissatisfied with themselves and their skills and abilities (low self-esteem) also reported high qualitative overload (lacking the necessary expertise to meet job demands). These same perceptions of overload were also related to negative psychological and physiological stress outcomes. Thus, self-esteem played a moderating role in the stressor-stress relationship.

Self-esteem has also been linked to stress-related health changes. Several studies have identified a negative relationship between self-esteem and coronary heart disease risk factors in occupational samples (see, for example, Kasl and Cobb, 1970; House, 1972). What seems clear is that self-esteem levels can play a role in either hindering or facilitating the stress response. In organizational settings effective use of both formal and informal reward systems may be able to alter at least the segment of an individual's self-esteem that is related to his or her activity in the organization. While we can only speculate on the effects of such action in reducing stress, certainly the potential positive effects of rewards and praise on job performance are well known to every manager.

Tolerance of ambiguity

Think back for a moment to a work situation where an impending decision was going to affect you in some way. Maybe it had something to do with your next assignment; maybe it dealt with relocating your office; or perhaps it was a possible change in company policy or procedures. Can you recall thinking to yourself, "I don't care what they decide to do; I just wish they would decide something so that I can get some work done"? If you are like most of us, you have found yourself in a similar situation—probably more than once. The underlying emotion you experienced was a need to know what was going to happen, or a need for more order and structure in the situation. Put another way, what you felt was a low tolerance for ambiguity.

Some people require a great deal of structure. They have a strong need to define all aspects of their work environment: exactly what they are to do, in what order they should proceed on various tasks, how the tasks should be accomplished, what management thinks of their work. These individuals are generally very reluctant to make decisions, preferring to have their superiors make them and then inform them of what to do. Other individuals, on the other hand, seem to have no trouble making these same kinds of decisions or operating without the detailed information required by the first group. The difference is that the first group has a low tolerance for ambiguity, while the second has a high tolerance.

It is likely that this personality facet of tolerance of ambiguity moderates the stress relationship. Individuals with a low tolerance for ambiguity who find themselves in job or organizational environments where there is little structure will very likely find that stressors are more likely to result in perceived stress and that perceived stress will produce more unwanted outcomes. Perhaps the clearest example of this is with role ambiguity. The individual with a low tolerance for ambiguity is going to find conditions of role ambiguity much more upsetting, anxiety producing, and stressful than someone with a higher tolerance.

While role ambiguity is perhaps the clearest example, it is certainly not the only one. All the individual level stressors are more likely to result in stress for someone with a low tolerance for ambiguity. The overload stressor, for example, poses problems of task priority. Group level stressors such as lack of cohesiveness and conflict present an ambiguous situation to those involved. And organizational stressors of climate, management style, and job and organizational design can intensify stress to the extent to which they detract from order, structure, and/or certainty.

A great deal more research needs to be done on the tolerance of ambiguity before we will know its precise nature as a moderator. In the meantime, however, it seems clear that placing individuals with a high need for structure in more structured environments will pay off in terms of reduced stress, increased levels of satisfaction, and quite possibly more effective performance.

Locus of control

Like tolerance of ambiguity, *locus of control* may serve to moderate some aspect of the stress relationship. Locus of control refers to individuals' perception of the extent to which control over external stimuli resides within them or is outside of them, beyond their influence. People who are *internals* perceive themselves as having more control over external happenings than people who are *externals*. More specifically with respect to stress, the locus of control concept relates to the perceived location of control over stressors. As Chan (1977) states:

> One psychological attribute which has been given extensive treatment . . . is the notion of an individual's amount of *perceived* control over an incoming stressful stimulus in specific, and over the environment in general. To the extent that an individual judges himself to have control or mastery in a situation, the probability is that he will be less likely to perceive the situation as threatening or stress-inducing and, in turn, less likely to manifest adverse reaction patterns.

Internals believe there is a relationship between their own behavior and the outcome of an event (stressor). Externals fail to see any relationship between their behavior and a stressor outcome. Using role conflict as an example, the employee who is an internal will perceive that he or she has at least some control over that condition and will act to reduce its potency as a stressor. This will generally be manifested in behavior designed to resolve or minimize the conflict. To the extent that these behaviors are successful, the stress potential in the situation has been reduced. Even if the behaviors do not meet with apparent success, the role conflict stressor is less likely to result in a stress reaction simply because the individual *believes* he or she can exercise some control in the situation.

Externals, on the other hand, see no relationship between their behavior and control of the stressor. In the extreme, they see themselves as helpless and unable to do anything. Consequently, not only is the existence of the stressor beyond their control, so is their response to that stressor.

Control locus is something which develops over a long period of time in individuals and is a cumulative function of the totality of prior experiences and their meanings. Consequently it is not something that is quickly or easily changed. There is reason to believe control locus is related to self-esteem, which is also resistant to change. Managers who play amateur psychologist will almost certainly find that their behavior modification attempts with respect to changing control locus are uniformly ineffective. It may be possible to contribute to an employee's self-esteem, which in turn may affect control locus. But practically speaking, this is an individual difference that isn't likely to be significantly altered by other people. Unfortunately, efforts to provide a better match between the individual and the environment (which may help in the case of low tolerance for ambiguity, for example) are not likely to be of much value either, short of eliminating all potential stressors.

Personality type: the coronary-prone behavior pattern

In the 1950s two coronary researchers associated with the Harold Brunn Institute for Cardiovascular Research began the development of an approach to predicting coronary disease, focusing on behavioral responses to environmental stimuli. Out of this research grew the well-known A and B Personality Types (see, for example, Friedman and Rosenman, 1974). The coronary prone behavior pattern, or Type A personality represents:

> . . . an action-emotion complex that can be observed in any person who is aggressively involved in a chronic, incessant struggle to achieve more and more in less and less time, and if required to do so, against the opposing efforts of other things or other persons (Friedman and Rosenman, 1974).

Major facets of Type A behavior include a chronic sense of time urgency, a hard-driving and competitive orientation that may include barely concealed hostility, a strong distaste for idleness, and chronic impatience with people and situations that are perceived as barriers to maintaining high levels of goal achievement. The factor composition of the Jenkins Activity Scale, a standardized measure designed to assess the presence of the Type A pattern, gives further insight into the behavior pattern. The three factors have been labeled *Speed and Impatience, Hard Driving,* and *Job Involvement* (Zyzanski and Jenkins, 1970).

Many writers have suggested that *stress* and *Type A behavior* are synonymous. That is, Type A individuals experience a great deal of stress, while their more relaxed, easygoing Type B counterparts seldom become upset or experience stress. Two aspects of this position are incorrect. The first is the assumption that Type Bs are easygoing, laid-back individuals. Type Bs may be every bit as goal-oriented as Type A; they may be as desirous of success and achievement. The difference is that the Type B person seeks satisfaction of those needs in a way that does not create the psychological and physical havoc that the Type A is subjected to.

The second incorrect aspect of this position is the equation of stress with "Aness" and lack of stress with "Bness." This is a gross oversimplification and is most likely wrong. There is no question, however, that there is a link between Type A behavior and negative stress consequences.

Western Collaborative Group Study • As in much of the stress literature, more work has been done on Type A and coronary heart disease than any other stress outcome or consequence. For one example (and there are dozens in the literature) let us look briefly at a study that highlights the relationship between Type A and stress-related coronary disease. The Western Collaborative Group Study (WCGS) was initiated in the early 1960s and assessed more than three thousand employees from eleven different corporations for the presence or absence of Type A behaviors. The study design used a double-blind procedure in which the researchers involved in the assessment of the behavior pattern had no knowledge of other risk factors and were not involved in any subsequent diagnosis. The diagnostic judgments, on the other hand, were made by cardiologists who were independent of the study and had knowledge neither of the behavior pattern classification nor other risk factors. The employees (all male) in the WCGS, ages thirty-nine to fifty-nine and free of coronary disease at the study's start, were measured annually for Type A behavior for eight to nine years. Additionally, data were gathered annually on socioeconomic factors, dietary and smoking habits, blood pressure, cholesterol, triglycerides, and lipoprotein levels.

The first follow-up data were reported after 2½ years (Rosenman, et al., 1966). Of the original sample, seventy participants had developed heart disease and 77% of these were Type As (compared with 50% for the entire sample). The behavior pattern was particularly predictive for the younger employees; in the thirty-nine to forty-nine year group, Type A men experienced 6½ times the incidence of heart disease that Type Bs did. Furthermore, the behavior pattern proved to be more predictive of heart disease than was blood pressure, cholesterol, or triglycerides.

Data after 4½ years of follow-up included 133 participants with heart disease (Rosenman et al., 1970). The predictive link between coronary problems and Type A behavior was still present with statistically significant higher incidences of disease in both age groups (thirty-nine to forty-nine, fifty to fifty-nine) among employees classified as Type A.

In 1975 the final follow-up report on the WCGS appeared (Rosenman et al., 1975). By this time 257 of the original sample had developed heart disease. After 8½ years Type A men had more than twice the rate of coronary disease among Type B men. Of approximately 1,500 employees classified as Type A, 178, or approximately 12%, developed heart disease.

Coronary-prone behavior and stress • There can be little doubt that Type A behavior is implicated in some way in heart disease. The precise role it plays, however, is less clear. We said earlier that it was incorrect to equate Type A behavior with stress. Yet the notion that there is some kind of relationship has been suggested by numerous medical and behavioral researchers. We feel there are at least two plausible explanations for the moderating effects of Type A behavior.

The first, and most commonly advanced notion, is that Type A individuals, by virtue of their characteristic behavior, increase the likelihood of exposure to certain stressors (such as overload) while decreasing their resistance to stress through refusal to relax, take vacations, slow down, etc. Thus, according to this school of thought, Type As create stress for themselves by constantly exposing themselves to stressors that their Type B counterparts avoid. Certainly the results of the WCGS cited earlier are consistent with this interpretation.

But another interpretation may also be consistent with the WCGS results. This interpretation, which we feel is conceptually sound and which we are investigating empirically, is strongly dependent on the notion that the individual's environment is important in eliciting particular behaviors. Simply stated, it may be that the behavior orientation of the employee is less important than the degree of fit between the employee's behavior orientation and the orientation of his work environment. Just as individuals may be Type A or B in their behavior, organizations may be A or B with respect to their environment, climate, or "personality." Figure 8–1 depicts the possible relationships between individual and organizational types.

According to this approach, the highest levels of stress will occur among the employee-organization combinations depicted in quadrants II and III. That is, stress would be more prevalent where the individual's and the organization's orientations don't fit. The more traditional approach,

FIGURE 8–1 · Combinations of Individual and Organizational Behavior Types

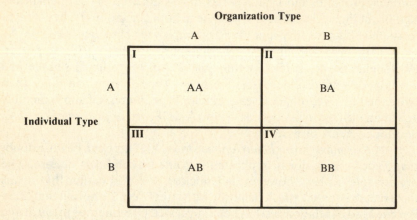

described earlier, would predict more stress in quadrants ı and ıı, that is, among Type As. Both approaches would see those in quadrant ıv as experiencing less stress.

Type A behavior is not difficult to identify in yourself as well as those with whom you have ongoing contact. Changing Type A behaviors is more difficult, but not impossible. While we are not convinced that changing Type A behavior is more desirable than seeking a match between individual and organizational orientations, moving toward the Type B end of the continuum probably will not hurt, and may well help. If nothing else, it gives the body a better chance to deal constructively with the adaptation demands placed upon it. Changing Type A behavior generally consists of reestablishing priorities, allowing more time for each activity, and diminishing the total number of activities.

Managers who identify Type A behavior in themselves and their subordinates and attempt to create a more congruent environment will have taken steps in the right direction. Beyond that, an examination of how effective current behavior patterns really are in achieving personal and organizational goals can further ameliorate the effects of Type A behavior. Whether one believes that Type A behavior per se increases the likelihood of stress outcomes or that the degree of person-environment fit is the moderator, it seems clear that this is one of the more potent moderators in task-oriented organizations.

IMPLICATIONS FOR THE MANAGER

The development of the individual from birth forward is, in a sense, the development of the individual's ability to deal with the environment and cope with its challenges. Because each of us develops differently we have idiosyncratic ways of responding to environmental stimuli. From that perspective, there are as many relevant individual differences in the study of stress as there are individuals.

From a more practical perspective, however, the major individual differences that appear to serve as moderators of the stress process are finite and relatively few in number. We have covered briefly some of the more significant differences. What can the manager do with this information? Certainly not change employees' ages. Or their sex. Nor is the manager likely to significantly alter most of the cognitive/affective differences we examined (indeed, management probably shouldn't attempt significant change in this area).

From a management point of view, knowing that these differences exist and using that knowledge in making decisions is the most fundamental and important implication. One does not have to be a psychologist to develop an awareness of key aspects of employees. All good managers know the strong and weak points of their subordinates. Most successful managers know the differences between employees with regard to what motivates them, what affects their job satisfaction and dissatisfaction, how they respond to new work assignments and dozens of other characteristics.

This, then, is what is important: knowledge of how these characteristics moderate stress, knowledge of individual employees with respect to these characteristics, and action based on these knowledges. It is probably true that most managers have not thought consciously about what a subordinate's tolerance of ambiguity is. But it is also true that most managers have that information and simply haven't thought about it. You know, for example, how much direction a particular employee needs, how much information he or she requires, how well that employee reacts to new and different work situations or departures from routine, how challenged or threatened he or she is by change. Knowing these things gives you a pretty good start on knowing something about the employee's tolerance of ambiguity.

The same is true for most of the other cognitive/affective differences. Much of the needed information is there; it simply has to be organized differently. Likewise, most managers are aware of the demographic/behavioral differences discussed. This chapter has attempted to provide some data relevant to how these differences moderate stress. All of this information can be used to structure the overall and individual work environments better in order to reduce employee distress. Examples include giving more attention to structuring work assignments for employees with a low tolerance for ambiguity, increased opportunities for receiving positive performance feedback for employees with low self-esteem, sensitivity to sex role differences in making job assignments and communicating with employees, giving special assistance in setting priorities for the workaholic, and keeping in mind that differences in age and corresponding differences in career stage may call for different behaviors on the manager's part.

In essence we are saying the same thing about individual differences as about the whole issue of the effective management of stress. The first step is *awareness*, awareness of differences and how they moderate the stressor-stress outcome-consequence chain. Also, awareness of where individual employees are with respect to these differences. The second step is *action*, in some limited cases, action to alter a particular difference. But primarily, action is intended to make maximum effective use of your awareness. That is, managerial decision making reduces the likelihood that these individual differences will contribute to employee distress.

APPENDIX

The Behavior Activity Profile©

The Behavior Activity Profile is designed to provide you with information regarding the extent to which you exhibit Type A or B behaviors. For each item you will be presented with two alternatives, *A* and *B*. You should indicate which alternative is most descriptive of you in the following manner:

> If A is totally descriptive of you and B is not at all descriptive, give yourself 5 points.
>
> If A is mostly descriptive of you and B is somewhat descriptive, give yourself 4 points.
>
> If A is slightly more descriptive of you than B is, give yourself 3 points.

Each of the above combinations can be reversed. Thus, if B is slightly more descriptive of you than A, give yourself 2 points; if B is mostly descriptive, give yourself 1 point; if B is totally descriptive, give yourself 0 points.

1. A. Even though the work standards I set for myself are very high, I still get very upset with myself when I fail to meet them.
   B. I try to maintain reasonable work standards that I can make without breaking my back. If I sometimes fail, I don't let it upset me.

2. A. Even when I'm sitting down I'm usually moving—tapping my foot, drumming my fingers, playing with a pencil, or some similar activity.
   B. I'm usually completely relaxed when I'm sitting, therefore I seldom move or change position.

3. A. In just about everything I do I tend to be hard-driving and competitive.
   B. I like to enjoy whatever it is I'm doing; the more relaxed and noncompetitive I can be, the more I can enjoy the activity.

4. A. I prefer being respected for the things that I accomplish.
   B. I prefer being liked for who I am.

5. A. Frankly, I frequently get upset or angry with people even though I may not show it.
   B. I rarely get upset with people; most things simply aren't worth getting angry about.

6. A. When I play a game or compete in an event, my enjoyment comes from winning.
   B. When I play a game or compete in an event, my enjoyment comes from participation and social interaction.

7. A. I frequently find myself in a hurry even when it isn't necessary.
   B. Frankly, I just don't like to rush, even when I know I'm running late.

8. A. My job provides me with my primary source of satisfaction; I don't find other activities nearly as gratifying.
   B. While I like my job, I regularly find satisfaction in numerous other pursuits such as spectator sports, hobbies, friends, and family.

9. A. I do my best work when I'm fighting a deadline.
   B. While deadlines may not bother me, I'd rather proceed at my rate without the hassle of meeting a deadline.

10. A. Having to wait makes me nervous.
    B. Waiting on someone or something is sometimes a good opportunity to relax.
11. A. I tend to wear myself out by trying to do too much.
    B. I like to get things done, but not at the expense of exhausting myself.
12. A. Meals tend to disrupt my schedule, and consequently I tend to eat very fast.
    B. I enjoy meals, and the more slowly and relaxed I eat, the more I enjoy them.

Scoring

Add up your total points. If the total is between:

  0–11 you exhibit strong Type B behaviors

12–23 you exhibit moderate Type B behaviors

24–36 your behaviors are a mixture of Type A and B and do not exhibit any clear pattern

37–48 you exhibit moderate Type A behaviors

49–60 you exhibit strong Type A behaviors

Refer to the text for a description of Type A and B behaviors and how they moderate stress.

REFERENCES

Allport, G. W. *Pattern and Growth in Personality*. New York: Holt, Rinehart and Winston, 1961.

Bettelheim, B. "Individual and mass behavior in extreme situations." In *Readings in Social Psychology*. E. E. Maccoby, ed. New York: Holt, Rinehart and Winston, 1958.

Buell, P. and L. Breslow. "Mortality from coronary heart disease in California men who work long hours." *Journal of Chronic Diseases* 11 (1960): 615–626.

Chan, K. B. "Individual differences in reactions to stress and their personality and situational determinants." *Social Science and Medicine* 11 (1977): 89–103.

Colligan, M. J., Smith, M., and J. Hurrell. "Occupational incidence rates of mental health disorders." *Journal of Human Stress* 3 (1977): 34–39.

Dobzhansky, T. *The Biological Basis of Human Freedom*. New York: Columbia University Press, 1956.

Erikson, E. *Childhood Society*. New York: W. W. Norton and Co., Inc., 1950.

Friedman, M. and R. Rosenman. *Type A Behavior and Your Heart*. New York: Alfred A. Knopf, Inc., 1974.

Guralnick, L. *Mortality by Occupation and Cause of Death*. USDHEW PHS. Vital Statistics, Vol. 53, 1963.

Hinkle, L. E. et al. "Occupation, education, and coronary heart disease." *Science* 161 (1968): 238–246.

House, J. *"The relationship of intrinsic and extrinsic work motivation to occupational stress and coronary heart disease risk."* Unpublished doctoral dissertation, University of Michigan, 1972.

Kasl, S. and S. Cobb. "Blood pressure changes in men undergoing job loss: A preliminary report." *Psychosomatic Medicine* 32 (1970): 19–38.

Kroes, W. H., Margolis, B. R. and J. Hurrell. "Job stress in policemen." *Journal of Police Science and Administration* 2 (1974): 145–155.

McClelland, D. C. *The Achieving Society*. Princeton, N.J.: Van Nostrand Reinhold Company, 1961.

Miller, D. and W. Form. *Industrial Sociology*. New York: Harper and Row, Publishers, Inc., 1951.

Mueller, E. F. *"Psychological and physiological correlates of work overload among university professors."* Ann Arbor: Unpublished doctoral dissertation, University of Michigan, 1965.

Rose, R. M., Jenkins, C. D., and M. W. Hurst. "Air Traffic Controller Health Change Study." U.S. Department of Transportation, Contract No. DOT–FA73WA–3211, August, 1978.

Rosenman, R., Brand, R., Jenkins, C., Friedman, M., Straus, R., and Wurm, M. "Coronary heart disease in the Western Collaborative Group Study: Final follow-up experience of 8½ years." *Journal of the American Medical Association* 233 (1975): 872–877.

Rosenman, R., Friedman, M., Straus, R., Jenkins, C., Zyzanski, S., and Wurm, M. "Coronary heart disease in the Western Collaborative Group Study: A follow-up experience of 4½ years." *Journal of Chronic Diseases* 23 (1970): 173–190.

Rosenman, R., Friedman, M., Straus, R., Wurm, M., Jenkins, C., & Messinger, H. "Coronary heart disease in the Western Collaborative Group Study: A follow-up experience of two years." *Journal of the American Medical Association* 195 (1966): 130–136.

Selye, H. *The Stress of Life*. New York: McGraw-Hill, Inc., 1976.

Syme, S. L. "Social and psychological risk factors in coronary heart disease." *Journal of American Heart Association* 44 (1975): 17–21.

Zohman, B. L. "Emotional factors in coronary disease." *Geriatrics* 28 (1973): 110–119.

Zyzanski, S. J. and C. D. Jenkins. "Basic dimensions within the coronary prone behavior pattern." *Journal of Chronic Diseases* 22 (1970): 781–795.

FOR FURTHER READING

Friedman, M. and R. Rosenman. *Type A Behavior and Your Heart*. New York: Alfred A. Knopf, Inc., 1974.

Godberg, H. *The Hazards of Being Male*. New York: Nash Publishing Corporation, 1976.

Kinzer, N. *Stress and the American Woman*. New York: Doubleday and Co., Inc., 1979.

London, H. and J. Exner. *Dimensions of Personality*. New York: John Wiley and Sons, Inc., 1978.

Stress and Performance

THE HARPER

A Man who used to play upon the harp, and sing to it, in little ale-houses, and made a shift in those narrow confined walls to please the dull sots who heard him, from hence entertained an ambition of shewing his parts in the public theatre, where he fancied he could not fail of raising a great reputation and fortune in a very short time. He was accordingly admitted upon trial; but the spaciousness of the place, and the throng of the people, so deadened and weakened both his voice and instrument, that scarcely either of them could be heard, and where they could, his performance sounded so poor, so low, and wretched, in the ears of his refined audience, that he was universally hissed off the stage.

Managerial Application • The measurement of performance involves some degree of subjective judgement on the part of an evaluator such as a manager. What a manager rates as performance is not always what the performer rates as performance.

Explanations of why some people perform well when others don't have filled volumes. The behaviorists view performance as a complex operant; differential psychologists attribute performance variance to individual differences; ergonomists believe that performance differentials are best explained by examining the interaction of a person and the work environment. One variable missing from most explanations of performance is stress. Some research indicates that no change in the performance of job tasks, enhancement, or degradation can be the result of *stress*. The nature of stress and its impact on performance depend largely on the interaction of task, environmental, and individual factors.

Some researchers claim that stress always produces performance degradation. However, this is a rather simplistic, overstated position. The effects of stress on performance can be very complex. Noise, for example, may be a stressor that at first enhances performance and then later impairs it. Our discussion in this chapter will point out that the impact of stress on job performance in organizational settings is still largely unresearched. However, the importance of the stress-performance linkage will be highlighted as our discussion is completed.

MOTIVATION AND ITS EFFECTS UPON PERFORMANCE

Most of the many theories of motivation can be placed in one of three major classifications. First, there are the *biological* and *physicalistic* viewpoints stemming from the work of Hull, Watson, and Spence. These psychologists focused on drives and instincts to explain arousal and direction of behavior. Second, there is the *cultural* tradition, which has emphasized feelings, needs, and motives. In the cultural view, learned experiences and the nature of the psychosocial environment explain the arousal and direction of behavior. Finally, there is a *philosophical-theological* view of motivation that emphasizes humanistic and personal growth factors. Whichever motivational theory is used, there is agreement that workers' action occurs as an effort to improve conditions that are not optimal. The action becomes more powerful, up to the limit of the person's capacity, as the departure from the optimum becomes greater, and diminishes as it lessens (Welford, 1973). Therefore, stress buildup occurs when motivating conditions on the job are not improved by the person's action (e.g., working harder and longer).

The notions of action, optimum conditions, individual capacity, and departure from optimum can be used to integrate the concepts of motivation and stress. However, several assumptions about these concepts need to be made. These assumptions are presented by Welford (1973) as follows:

1. Individual action may be triggered not only by departures from optimum, but also by signs or symbols of them. Effects often occur before the stressful situation occurs and may diminish when it comes.
2. The effort to change any departure from optimum seems to be inversely related to the difficulty or unpleasantness involved in correcting it.
3. In almost any real-life situation several motives operate simultaneously on different time scales to determine behavior.
4. People tend to avoid extremes of stimulation and seek moderate levels.

These four sets of assumptions suggest that moderate stimulation, conflict, and predictability tend to increase arousal. People appear to perform best under conditions of moderate demand (also referred to as stress). Performance problems in organizations may result from too much stress (demand) or too little stress (demand).

Another implication of the four sets of assumptions is that the specification of "optimum" should not only be conceived in physical capacity terms, but also in terms of information processing capability. In most work situations performance is constrained more by the time taken to reduce uncertainty or by the amount of information handled than by physical ability. Some of the most pressing demands facing employees arise from the uncertainty and complexity of decision making or the data sources that must be reviewed.

STRESS AND AROUSAL

Arousal motivation theory has been used to examine the stress-performance linkage. The logic of arousal motivation is captured in the following statements:

1. Physical stimulation that affects an organism contributes to its physiological and psychological arousal level;

2. The impact of a stimulus on the arousal level of the organism is a function of such variables as its intensity, meaningfulness, and complexity;
3. Having attained a state of normal arousal, the organism becomes more sensitive to other aspects of the environment and is more able to deal with them in an efficient manner.

The argument of the arousal theorist is that once optimum arousal (activation) is achieved, organisms are more receptive to the external stimuli in the environment at the time (Korman, 1974). Thus, if a person is faced with a job task situation that is making demands for a specific type of behavior, such as preparing a report or operating a machine, the prediction of the arousal framework is that there will be a U-shaped relationship between arousal and performance. Such a model displaying the U-shaped relationship is presented in Figure 9–1.

At the optimum arousal level performance is at its highest point. Before and after the optimum arousal point is reached, performance is not at the highest point. While the model is interesting, it does not provide managers with much information about when the optimum point is reached by subordinates. It also contains loose ends that most people fail to recognize as major issues that need to be considered in using arousal theory to understand performance.

Some issues involving arousal theory

Let us assume that you are driving in the morning traffic on a clogged metropolitan freeway with noise, traffic congestion, "fender bender" accidents, and flashing police lights all about. This trip involves a significant degree of physical stimulation, whatever measure of stimulation is used (e.g., variability, meaningfulness, or intensity). On the other hand, assume that a week later you are alone in Colorado climbing a mountain, where the only noises are the wind, animal hoots and whistles, and the crunch of your feet on the snow. The level of physical stimulation in the mountain seems less than that experienced on the freeway. If this is the case, the two environments should affect you differently.

How environments (freeway and mountain climbing) affect a person is an important question. Is it simply that the stimuli affect the neurons of the body in a different manner? If so, then all we have to do to affect a person's level of arousal is to focus on the physical stimuli

FIGURE 9–1   Inverted U-Shaped Relationship Between Arousal and
                 Performance

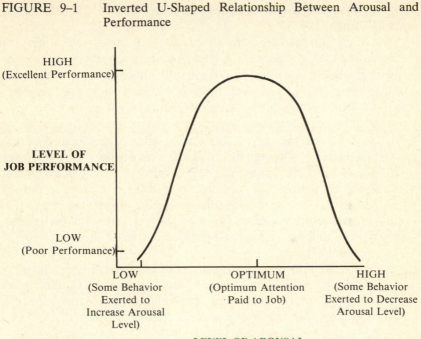

LEVEL OF AROUSAL

involved (Korman, 1974). Suppose, however, that the effects of physical
stimuli are a function also of the social and psychological characteristics of
the situation and of the individual differences of the person being
considered. In that case, attempts by a manager to develop an optimal
physical environment are considerably more difficult, since many factors
(e.g., social, psychological, personal) have to be weighed in addition to
physical stimulation.

        Korman (1974) raises a question involving the testing of the
U-shaped arousal hypothesis. He states that according to arousal theory,
predicting behavior at any time has to take into account two variables.
The first variable is the degree of arousal that the person is used to and is
predicted to desire. The second is the amount of arousal that the person is
subjected to at the moment. So, if a person's typical arousal level is say an
8 (assuming we can measure it), and the present environment arousal
level is a 5, increasing. behavior would be predicted. However, if a
person's typical arousal level is a 3, and the present environment arousal
level is 5, decreasing behavior would be predicted. In other words, for any
given level of arousal of each variable (person and environment),

opposing behaviors would be predicted, depending on the level of the other (Korman, 1974).

If arousal explanations of motivation are to be useful to managers attempting to regulate stress and performance, it is necessary to measure arousal. If one uses validity and reliability criteria to assess what is available to measure arousal, there is a mixed pattern of research evidence. The findings can be summarized as follows:

1. There are only moderate correlations between different measures of physiological arousal; this suggests that whatever each of these measures is measuring (e.g., electrocortical activity, vasomotor activity, respiratory activity, pupillary diameter, etc.), each one is measuring something separately from the others, in addition to the commonality that exists. These findings suggest the presence of more than one type of arousal.

2. A simple self-report measure of arousal, either estimated in a general subjective sense, or measured by a checklist, may correlate more highly with physiological measures than the physiological measures correlate with each other.

These measurement issues indicate that more work developing and testing psychological measures of arousal is warranted. Perhaps more concern about the psychological aspects of arousal will expand our understanding of individual arousal and how it operates in the performance of job tasks.

Available research on arousal

There is research on arousal that has some value for managers. Scott (1966) indicates that introducing variety into dull, repetitive environments can lead to increased task performance. This suggestion lends support to the low arousal portion of the inverted U-shaped curve. Research results from laboratory experiments have supported Scott's contention. However, a major problem with these laboratory studies is that the subjects' preferred arousal levels were not measured prior to any experimental intrusion.

Research is also available that indicates that individuals differ consistently in their preference for levels of stimulation. For example, there are data to support the conclusion that the stimulus-seeking scale measure (Zuckerman et al., 1964) predicts preferences for visual complexity, alcohol usage, and other preferences. Furthermore, the scores on the scale vary positively as a function of educational attainment, which seems to support the assumption that past exposures to stimuli affect stimulus-seeking behaviors.

These research findings have not provided enough information about the role individual differences play in arousal level. Managers need to know how subordinates' arousal levels differ and what stimulates individual arousal levels to the point where performance is optimized. Arousal theory and available research have not provided such guidelines. It has provided, however, a starting point that needs to be examined further in a more management-based context. McGrath (1976) has attempted to modify the inverted-U relationship so that managers can integrate the concepts of stress, arousal, and task in order to draw managerial implications.

McGrath's modification of the inverted-U hypothesis

McGrath (1970) examined the theoretical proposition that stress leads to arousal in a linear fashion and that the relationship of arousal to performance is curvilinear. In order to test his views about stress and performance McGrath used a Little League baseball setting. He studied all sixty players of four teams for the entire season of thirty-six games.

The time at bat was chosen as the unit of activity. For each time at bat, the following measures were obtained:

1. Arousal or experienced stress: pulse rate (PR), breathing rate (BR), and measure of behavioral activity while in the on deck circle
2. Batting performance: a rating of how well batter hit ball
3. Success of outcome: whether runners advanced, runs scored, and outs made
4. Situational demand (SC): index of the degree to which a favorable versus an unfavorable outcome of the time at bat would affect game
5. Game criticalness (GC): an index of the potential effect of the game on the team's season success

The results of the study led McGrath (1970) to the following conclusions. Differences in situational demand led to differences in arousal (pulse rate). This relationship was positive monotonic. The relationship also held in a specific situation (SC) and for game criticalness (GC).

Age, considered an index of experience (boys were ten to twelve years old), did not yield differences in arousal. Age did, however, have an effect on performance. The older boys performed better than younger ones. Furthermore, the findings indicated a positive linear relation between demand (SC or GC) and arousal (pulse and breathing rates). There was also an inverted-U relation between demand (SC or GC) and absolute level of performance.

But the hypothesis that arousal has a curvilinear relation with performance was not supported. At any level of demand, including very high demand, the higher the arousal the better the performance. This led the research team to conclude that differences in opponent task ability was important and represented task difficulty. With this in mind it was decided that performance increases monitonically with increasing demand and with increasing arousal. The inverted-U apparently arises when both arousal and task difficulty, with their opposite effects, operate simultaneously as mediators between demand and performance.

McGrath (1976) displayed the arousal-task difficulty mediators as shown in Figure 9–1. At low levels of demand, performance is relatively low because arousal is low. At high levels of demand, absolute performance is low, not because arousal is high, but in spite of it and because task difficulty is high.

The reformulated McGrath model of stress-performance indicates that performance demands of a situation have three separate and direct effects: 1) an increase in consequences; 2) an increase in perceived task difficulty; and 3) an increase in actual task difficulty. The effectiveness of task performance is a function of three factors: 1) difficulty of task; 2) ability of the person; and 3) arousal. Ability depends on experience and talent. Arousal depends on perceived consequences and uncertainty. Uncertainty depends on the closeness of perceived task difficulty and perceived ability.

The McGrath (1976) reformulated model has some significant managerial implications. If a manager wishes to increase task performance (e.g., the job an employee is doing) a number of procedures can be implemented—make the job easier, increase the employee's ability to do the job, or increase the employee's arousal level.

Making a job easier can be accomplished through redesigning the characteristics of the task. Job enrichment strategies may be appropriate

FIGURE 9–2   McGrath Views of Arousal and Task Difficulty Mediators

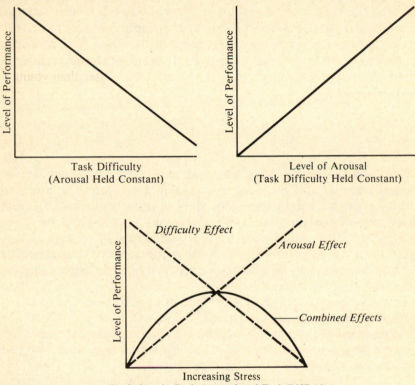

for this redesign work. Of course, not all jobs can be or should be redesigned. However, if an employee is overloaded (quantitatively or qualitatively), reducing task difficulty can improve performance. Training and development can increase an employee's task ability. Selecting and using powerful training and development approaches must be done cautiously. Increased arousal to perform based on training and development requires effective experiences for the employee, and as most managers know, not all training and development programs are effective.

Increasing arousal can be accomplished via a number of managerial strategies, such as creating a work atmosphere that enables the employee to receive preferred outcomes (rewards). If a manager is in a situation in which an employee's perceived ability is much higher than perceived difficulty, overconfidence will result in low arousal. The manager's job in this case would be to increase the employee's perceived difficulty or decrease the employee's perceived ability. This requires creative management tactics that involve convincing employees that the task is more difficult and they are less able than they think. This is difficult and requires effective, clear, and powerful communications to create the desired changes in perceptions.

JOB TASKS AND STRESS

An employee performing job tasks (e.g., typing, machine operation, operating on a patient, reading a blueprint, or flying an airplane) can be faced with various kinds of stress conditions. The task itself can be a source of stress. A secretary may be stressed because typing budgets is considered a stressful task (Condition 1). A task can be performed during periods in which other stressors are operating. The stressed secretary may have mental conflict that is also influencing her job performance (Condition 2).

In some cases tasks are performed to reduce or remove stress. This situation involves task performance as a coping process (Condition 3). For example, the secretary may have a request to prepare a purchase order before doing anything else. Thus, she would suspend working on the budget to type the purchase order.

A fourth situation (Condition 4) might involve task performance, or decrements in it, that a manager could view as an indicator of stress. In this condition the manager must be astute enough to pick up changes in performance. This means that there must be some criteria of performance that can be used as benchmarks of comparison for the manager.

Condition 1: task stress

The four conditions can be useful to a manager because they suggest possible differences in the relations between stress and performance. In Condition 1 an inverse or negative relation between task-based stress and task performance is suggested. Task stress can be caused by any of the stressors discussed when the job was our main focal point (Chapter 5). Such stressors as overload, responsibility for people, working conditions, ambiguity, conflict, and physical danger are all potential sources of stress. Proper management of these job or task-based stressors is needed to keep their strength at a minimum level. Chapter 10 discusses management strategies to deal with organizational and job stressors.

Condition 2: operation of other stressors

The interaction of many types of stressors has been identified throughout the book. We suggested in Chapter 7 for example that extraorganizational stressors can distract the employee from job performance tasks. For example, marital conflict or financial worries can be so powerful that task performance suffers. Condition 2 suggests that there may be a significant interdependence between task performance and various categories of stress. This view is somewhat different from the opinion that task performance depends on the level of stress.

Condition 3: a coping process

In Condition 3 the performance of a job task is a coping behavior intended to reduce or remove the effects of stressors (McGrath, 1976). In essence, the more successful a person is in performing a coping task, the less the stress experienced from the primary stress-provoking task. The actual task performance of the *primary* task when engaging in a coping task will be reduced. A coping process might include stopping performance of a primary task in order to focus on the coping activities or initiating a coping task for which higher performance results in quicker and greater reduction of stress.

We continually engage in coping tasks. For example, one of the possible effects of exercising during the work day (e.g., jogging at lunchtime) is to reduce the stress from primary job tasks. The exercise itself is a task that takes the person away from his or her primary job and causes a temporary reduction in the performance of the primary stress-producing task. It is assumed that the higher the level of performance of the exercise, the more or the sooner the reduction of stress.

Condition 4: indicator of stress

Observation of task performance can provide managers with an estimate of the amount of stress being experienced by an employee. Erratic performance by a consistently good performer may be a signal that stress is hindering performance. The key to using performance as an indicator of stress is valid and reliable measures of a person's typical performance. Of course, everyone has a bad day or even a bad week, and a number of sample points of job performance need to be taken before concluding that performance is down and perhaps that stress is high.

Even when performance decrements suggest high levels of stress, the manager must identify the stressors causing the problem. This is a difficult job that requires diagnosis and observation. More than subjective reports by employees are needed. Examination of previous performance, managerial observation of on-the-job activities, and careful listening to employee discussions and opinions are required steps in diagnosing performance decrements and pinpointing the causes of such changes.

SEARCHING FOR THE OPTIMUM STRESS POINT: A CHALLENGING MANAGERIAL JOB

Managers continually search for the optimum stress point. Theoretical discussions of locating points of optimum stress and performance are useful because they provide information that a) optimum stress points differ among individuals; b) optimum stress points are impossible to identify accurately for each subordinate; c) optimum stress points vary over time and in different situations; and d) optimum stress can be converted into productive energy.

The information provided by the theoretical discussion of optimum stress also suggests that successful people thrive on a certain amount of stress. Stress arouses individuals to action and can be positive when it stimulates motivation and achievement. An employee without some stress would not be challenged and excited enough to perform the job. Optimum stress prepares an employee for peak performance.

Forbes (1979) has developed an optimum stress-performance continuum that suggests behaviors which indicate when these levels are reached. She identifies behavioral activities at optimum stress-performance levels such as high energy, mental alertness, high motivation, calmness under pressure, thorough analysis of problems, improved memory and recall, sharp perception, and an optimistic outlook. A manager could use these categories as checkpoints in determining the stress-performance levels operating at a specific time.

Measuring Forbes' indicators of optimum stress-performance is difficult. She only offers a brief self-report checklist to determine the stress-performance mix. This type of measure is not acceptable to those who need a valid and reliable assessment, so much more work on developing measures is needed to provide managers with at least a rough approximation of the stress-performance level.

Progress in identifying optimum stress-performance levels depends largely on the quality of measurement used to assess behavior and whether warning signals of nonoptimum levels are taken seriously. As already emphasized in Chapter 3 and throughout this book, measurement is never perfect in any science. Even medical scientists, who rely primarily on physiological measures and use sophisticated instrumentation, have to deal with inaccuracies. Thus, measurement problems and issues will continue to exist and less than perfect indicators will be used to judge whether an employee is underloaded or overloaded with stress.

The warning signs of being underloaded, or not aroused sufficiently, include boredom, apathy, increased accidents, grievances, absenteeism, negative outlook, increased fatigue, insomnia, and change in appetite. These are also signs of being overloaded, or being aroused too much. In addition, being overloaded results in more errors, indecisiveness, and a loss of perspective. These are warning signs that a manager may be able to identify. Most of these signs are not accurately measured, but they can be roughly determined by observing the behavior of subordinates.

A final comment

The word *stress* has become a six-letter dirty word for many people. The conclusion that excessive stress leads to poor performance has become widely accepted. The inverted-U curve, however, indicates that a moderate amount of stress and a moderate amount of task difficulty have positive performance effects. If this viewpoint is reasonable (and we believe it is), the work outlined for managers involves finding the right mix of stress and task difficulty.

The message of this chapter is that stress, motivation, arousal, task difficulty, task performance, and their relations are all concepts that managers must deal with in carrying out their jobs. Perfect managerial plans to unravel the complex issues offered in the chapter simply do not exist. But there are individual and organizational techniques for managing stress. Some of the available techniques are the focus of the next chapter.

REFERENCES

Forbes, R. *Corporate Stress*. Garden City, New York: Doubleday and Co., Inc., 1979.

Korman, A. K. *The Psychology of Motivation*. Englewood Cliffs, N.J.: Prentice-Hall, Inc., 1974.

McGrath, J. E., ed. *Social and Psychological Factors in Stress*. New York: Holt, Rinehart and Winston, 1970.

McGrath, J. E. "Stress and behavior in organizations." *Handbook of Industrial and Organizational Psychology*. M. D. Dunnette, ed. Chicago: Rand McNally and Company, 1976, 1351–1395.

Scott, W. E. "Activation theory and task design." *Organizational Behavior and Human Performance* 1 (1966): 3–30.

Welford, A. T. "Stress and performance." *Ergonomics* 16 (1973): 567–580.

Zuckerman, M. et al. "Development of a sensation-seeking scale." *Journal of Consulting Psychology* 28 (1964): 477–482.

FOR FURTHER READING

Horn, J. "Peak performance—the factors that produce it." *Psychology Today* 11 (1978): 110.

Levine, S. "Stress and behavior." *Scientific American* 224 (1971): 26–31.

Welford, A. T. ed. *Man Under Stress*. New York: Halsted Press, 1974.

Managing Stress

10

THE FOX AND THE HEDGEHOG

A Fox, in swimming across a river, was forced down by the rapidity of the stream to a place where the bank was so steep and slippery, that he could not ascend it. While he was struggling in this situation, a swarm of flies settled on his head and eyes, and tormented him grievously. A Hedgehog, who saw and pitied his condition, offered to call in the assistance of the Swallow to drive them away. No, no, friend, replies the Fox, I thank you for your kind offer; but it is better to let the swarm alone, for they are already pretty well filled, and should they be driven away, a fresh and more hungry set would succeed them, and suck me until I should not have a drop left in my veins.

Managerial Application • If we are not careful and proceed without proper consideration, our attempts to reduce stress may serve only to increase it.

For most employed adults, work represents a time commitment exceeded by no other one single activity. Ideally, this time should be satisfying, should contribute to the individual's quality of life, should respect health, and leave the individual adequate time for rest and leisure pursuits. Unfortunately, this is not the case for many millions of workers. For them the work environment contains numerous sources of tension, anxiety, frustration, and conflict. Rather than providing satisfaction, it is often a source of dissatisfaction. Rather than contributing to growth, it inhibits it. Rather than respecting health, it often serves as a catalyst for physical and mental health problems. And rather than allowing the individual leisure time, it may become a central time commitment that detracts from the development of off-work pursuits.

It is for these reasons that the management of stress is of such crucial importance. Whether it is measured in terms of human health and happiness or in terms of organizational effectiveness and efficiency, stress is a major variable that organizations cannot afford to overlook. It has been estimated that by the mid-1970s, stress had become the nation's most pervasive health problem, exceeding the common cold in incidence rates. And unlike the common cold, the locus of much of this outbreak may be found in today's organizations. Because of increasing job complexity, rapid changes in technology, and the growing impermanence of organization structures, stress is a problem we will most likely see intensifying in the years ahead.

An effective manager never ignores a turnover or absenteeism problem, a decline in quality or quantity of output, or any other symptom that the organization's goals are not being met in the most efficacious and timely manner. The effective manager, in fact, views these occurrences as symptoms and looks beyond them to identify and correct the underlying contributory causes. Yet the manager is likely to recognize as underlying causes *only those things that he or she has been taught to recognize.* And chances are very good that stress is *not* on the list of possible suspects, so it goes undiagnosed and unprescribed for. Thus, the very first step in effective stress management is recognition, or as we have earlier emphasized, awareness that stress *may* be an underlying cause of individual and group work problems and recognition of its existence in those individuals who are experiencing stress.

From a managerial perspective, the starting place for stress awareness should be with the individual manager, i.e., self-awareness. To recognize stress in others, the first prerequisite is the ability to recognize it in yourself. Most of us have a low degree of personal awareness. For example, how many people know the answers to these questions:

1. What is your resting pulse rate?
2. What is your blood pressure?
3. When is your energy level at its peak during the day?
4. What are your biggest time wasters during the day?
5. What aspect is it of situations you find stressful which produces your stress reaction?

Most people know the accurate answer to only a few—if any—of these personal questions. A necessary step in managing stress is to learn about yourself and identify when you are stressed. For example, here are some signals that indicate job stress above the level which is good:

1. *Rapid pulse* or *pounding heart;*
2. *Increased perspiration* from hands, underarms, and forehead;
3. *Tightening of the forehead and jaw;*
4. *Inability to sit still* or keep your feet still while you're sitting;
5. *Tensing of shoulder and neck muscles.*

Other personal indicators of stress include tension headaches, insomnia, chronic fatigue, hyperventilation, indigestion, loss of appetite, increased impatience, and increases in alcohol intake or drug usage.

Anyone can pick up these stress warning signals if they do the necessary self-diagnosis work. These signals can be matched with job situations or events. You might find, for example, that one or more of these reactions occurs as a major deadline approaches or perhaps during counseling sessions with subordinates.

Just as there are indications of stress overload, there are indications that you are operating at an optimal stress level. When you are stimulated, feel good, are mentally alert, have sharp perception, and are realistic and calm under important, pressure-packed situations, you are probably experiencing what for you is the optimal amount of stress. These positive indicators provide just as important diagnostic information as the negative ones.

Whatever the indicator, strategies and techniques of stress management may be helpful—and even necessary—in dealing effectively with the stress. There are a number of ways to categorize these strategies and techniques. One way, for example, is to distinguish *preventors* and *relievers.* A *preventor* is something you do to eliminate a stressor or stop it from becoming a source of stress. A *reliever,* on the other hand, is something you do to help dissipate or overcome negative stress or distress. Another way to characterize approaches to stress management—the one we have chosen to use for the remainder of this chapter—is to focus on *organizational methods* and *individual methods*. Organizational methods include those actions taken by management to minimize potentially harmful stress in the work environment, such as might result from role conflict, work overload, or lack of cohesion. Individual methods, on the other hand, relate to actions and activities engaged in by the individual that may or may not take place within the organization. To some extent this distinction between individual and organizational methods is artificial, but we feel it provides a meaningful way of organizing a discussion of stress management.

ORGANIZATIONAL APPROACHES TO STRESS MANAGEMENT

Just as knowing yourself and being able to identify stress in yourself is a prerequisite to successful organizational stress management, it is also important for the manager to know his or her employees. A stress-overloaded employee will usually exhibit a change in personality, work habits, or general behavior. Only by being familiar with customary behavior patterns can the manager identify these changes, some of which may be very subtle. The following are some of the changes in employee behavior patterns that *may* indicate stress overload:

1. Working late more than usual or the opposite, increased tardiness or absenteeism;
2. Difficulty in making decisions;
3. Increases in the number of careless mistakes;
4. Missing deadlines or forgetting appointments;
5. Problems interacting and getting along with others;
6. Focusing on mistakes and personal failures.

Not every behavioral change is stress-related, of course, and even many that are, are consequences of highly transient, nonrecurring conditions or events. We all display some of the above behaviors some of the time. It is when they occur in bunches or with increased intensity that we have a signal to be concerned about. Some of these signs may be obvious; others may be so subtle that only the very alert manager can detect them. In either event, when an employee's good habits become poor or sloppy habits; when good performance becomes spotty or poor performance; or when friendliness changes to irritability and short temper, something is wrong that requires managerial awareness and action.

Preventive management

In medicine the treatment of problems has historically followed what is referred to as the *disease approach*. When you have an earache, you visit the physician for treatment. This disease approach involves treatment after an ailment has manifested itself and caused discomfort or pain. An emerging trend in medicine today involves *preventive practice*. The emphasis of preventive medicine is on identifying *potential* problems at early stages, thus enabling the physician to treat and/or prescribe in a manner that minimizes the likelihood that the problem will become pathological. In short, the emphasis is on keeping people healthy, not just on making them well. Similarly, a preventive management strategy that seeks to identify and correct environmental and job problems before they become organizationally and individually pathological is a sound investment. Improvement in the health and job effectiveness of employees is possible if prevention or proaction is the managerial focal point rather than a traditional reactive strategy. Dealing with a problem after it has become a problem, crisis management, is the managerial equivalent of the disease approach in medicine. It may cure the problem, but how much better off would the individual and the organization have been if the problem had been defused *before* it became a problem?

New, healthier, and more productive ways of working in organizations are possible though preventive stress management. The early diagnosis of stressors and stress constitutes the awareness part of preventive management and is a necessary, but not sufficient, step in the process. Action to eliminate or minimize stressors is the necessary second step. Redesigning jobs, altering reward systems, changing workflows and schedules, identifying career paths, clarifying roles, altering organizational structures, and providing development opportunities are some examples of potential courses of preventive management action. These and other managerial interventions can minimize the negative effects associated with job and organizational stressors. In the sections that follow, we will discuss in more detail some specific managerial strategies for preventing or relieving work-related stress.

Role analysis and clarification

In the framework for studying stress presented in Chapter 2, one of the important levels of intraorganizational stressors was the individual level. Most individual level stressors in organizations are based on how the employee sees his or her job. Is it clear? Does trying to do it cause conflict? Is it manageable? Is it consistent with his or her own expectations and career strategies?

Most of those questions depend for their answer on information that the role occupant requires about the nature, scope, and place of the job, and information the manager requires about employees' perceptions. If role problems are suspect as a source of stress in an organization, what better place to begin gathering information than from the role occupants themselves? Questions asked of subordinates that can be rich sources of stressor-reducing information include:

1. What do you think is expected of you?
2. What do you expect of me (your manager)?
3. What information do you need in order to do your job well?
4. What areas, if any, trouble you about the nature and scope of your job?

Answers to these questions may help to better inform the employee about the job, and aid in reducing conflict and ambiguity. Or, in some cases, changes may need to be made in job descriptions, divisions of labor, structural reporting relationships, or similar aspects of the job and its environment. A manager, for example, is responsible for establishing an unambiguous division of labor that is understood. You, as a manager, cannot be certain that it is understood unless you ask and observe.

Another vehicle for addressing role problems has to do with overload. In the vast majority of cases, the individual who is overloaded knows it better than anyone else. Employees may feel a natural reluctance to communicate that information, however, for fear of looking bad or being labeled a complainer. The kind of information exchange that is necessary to facilitate role analysis and clarification should also be helpful in creating an environment where there is less reluctance to discuss overload problems with managers. In fact, organizations can make it a standard operating procedure that, when a person is overloaded, he or she has both the right and responsibility to say no and work out an acceptable solution with management.

Ongoing role analysis can suggest strategies for maximizing the fit between a role occupant and the job or organizational environment. The idea of maximizing fit has grown out of the job stress research at the University of Michigan's Institute for Social Research (see, for example, French, 1973; Kahn and Quinn, 1970; Caplan, 1976). According to the Michigan researchers, fit can be maximized and stressors reduced through redefinition of the jobholder's role, reduction of overload conditions via a system for work reassignment, and institutionalizing procedures for reducing stress when it occurs (such as delegation of work during conditions of overload). Harrison (1976) makes an excellent point, however, when he emphasizes the need for organizational programs that treat employees as individuals. Attempts to reduce stress by treating everyone alike may be like the hedgehog's approach to the fox's distress—well intentioned, but likely to increase rather than decrease stress.

Before leaving this topic there is one approach to recasting roles that has generated sufficient interest in the last decade to warrant specific mention. We are talking about *job enrichment*. Job enrichment involves redefining and restructuring a job to make it more meaningful, challenging, and intrinsically rewarding to the jobholder. (Enrichment should not be confused with enlargement, where the emphasis is mainly upon adding task components.) In the context of job stress, the impact of job enrichment is on rewards, participation, utilization of skills, role overload, and time. The logic of enrichment holds that restructuring or "loading" a job can make it more intrinsically rewarding and challenging. Therefore, the jobholders will participate more in doing challenging things that utilize their skills, without being overloaded with trivia or routine activities.

It is necessary to keep in mind, however, that restructuring a job to make it more challenging may be very stressful to some people. Many employees are comfortable in their present jobs; they don't want to change. Once again, the manager must be aware of each employee's situation and *act* accordingly.

Altering organization climate

Like the weather, everyone is always talking about organization climate without doing anything about it. *Climate* is an ambiguous term that describes a set of properties in the work environment related to employees' perceptions of how the organization deals with them.

Everything from leadership styles to retirement policies have at one time or another been included under the climate heading. The rationale that alterations in climate may be an effective stress management strategy is based on the assumption that a "good" climate contributes to satisfaction and feelings of being in a supportive environment, both of which are probably associated with reduced levels of stress. As Newman and Beehr (1979) point out, however, the evidence bearing on relationships between climate factors and stress is speculative and needs to be empirically tested.

Chief contributors to the type of climate prevailing in an organization are the day-to-day practices and philosophies of its managers. Structural imperfections, too much red tape, not being able to participate in decision making, poor or inefficient communications, and impersonal relationships are examples of variables that contribute to climate and are a function of company management.

Let us look briefly at one climate variable that has received a fair amount of attention as a stress reducer: increased participation in decision making. Studies have shown that low participation for some is related to job dissatisfaction and job threat. The implication would seem to be that by altering climate through increased participation, positive results may be achieved. The key word there is *may*. Some possible problems should be kept in mind. Trying to encourage participation while remaining autocratic will result in confusion and increased stress. So will encouraging participation and then ignoring it. If you invite participation and then do nothing about it, feelings of distrust and manipulation will take over, leading to increased stress.

The meaningfulness of decisions employees are invited to participate in is another consideration. Most people are neither particularly interested in nor feel better from participating in decisions about where to locate the water cooler or how many waste baskets to purchase. The manager who attempts to alter climate through a program of increased participation should ask the following questions:

1. What benefits to the participators and organization are likely to result?

2. What areas can my subordinates be permitted to participate in?

3. How meaningful and relevant are the decisions?

4. Is this something that will be viewed positively across the board?

This last question raises another potential problem. Some people do not want increased participation. Every situation is different. Examine yourself, your employees, and the potential stressors that may be operating. From these data and your answers to the questions above, decide to either use participation or discard it as a possible stress reducer.

Management by Objectives

Management by Objectives (MBO) is perhaps one of the more widely used and discussed management techniques. Pioneered by Peter Drucker (1954), MBO is both a philosophy of management and a management process that focuses upon the setting of goals, action planning to achieve these goals, and periodic review of the degree of goal attainment obtained. It is worthy of discussion as a stress management strategy because it and similar goal-setting programs are designed to improve or correct many of the variables we have identified as organizational stressors. For example, by jointly determining a subordinate's area of responsibility and setting goals, managers and subordinates are supposed to improve their communications, role expectations, respect for each other, and so forth. Supposedly, everyone—the individual, the manager, and the organization—is in for some benefits. While the actual implementation of MBO is frequently not as problem-free as the theory, it can be an effective contributor to reduced stress.

We can minimize the chances of failure and increase the chance for success with good front-end diagnosis and work. From a stress management perspective, finding out what the stressors are and whether MBO can contribute to doing the job necessary to correct them is an important first step. Training employees and preparing them for things that are likely to happen (more paperwork, more meetings between supervisor and subordinates, more openness) are also necessary. MBO efforts that are successful in reducing stress meet a number of criteria:

1. They pay attention to the needs not only of the organization but also the people.
2. They involve an extensive training and preparation phase, preparing people with extensive communicating and question answering.

3. They are not designed as cure-alls for everything. (Zero in on the stressors that you're going after. All of them can't be eliminated or reduced by a single method.)

4. They don't bite off too much at the start.

This last point is an important one. One of the reasons why MBO itself becomes a stressor (and it frequently does) is that some programs involve covering too many objectives, too many manager-subordinate meetings, and a tremendous amount of paperwork. We have found the "lot of everything syndrome" to be very stressful. The employee experiences "MBO overload." Instead of attempting to solve everything at once, use a more gradual strategy. Suppose, for example, that role ambiguity, conflict, and overload are the major stressors with which you as the manager are concerned. The initial MBO effort should be directed at minimizing or reducing these stressors. Starting small will pay off in less confusion, more enthusiasm, and less stress.

The physical environment

There is an old story about the husband who unexpectedly returned home, much to the chagrin of his wife and her lover. The lover quickly hid in the closet but the husband eventually opens the door and discovers him. He yells, "What are you doing in my closet?!" The lover, standing shivering in his underwear, shrugs and says, "Everybody has to be somewhere."

The lover's retort is hard to argue with. We all are indeed somewhere. If that somewhere is work and if it is physically comfortable, the physical work environment is not likely to serve as a stressor source. In Chapter 5 we mentioned several environmental stressors: light, noise, temperature, vibration and motion, and pollution. Most of the time these variables are stressors when physical facilities are old or part of an operation, such as manufacturing, where noise or heat or other physical stimuli are abnormally intense.

There are basically only two ways to deal with physical environment stressors, and frequently neither is completely satisfactory. Either the environment must be altered (the noise lessened, the glare reduced, etc.) or the people in the environment must be protected from the stressors (by wearing ear plugs, using tinted glasses, etc.). In most environments, where applicable, the latter has been done because of management interest and union and government requirements. Frequently the former has also been accomplished to the extent that it is physically, economically, and/or technically feasible.

Short of modifying the environment or the people, management may be able to minimize the effects of negative stressors by judicious changes in usual operating policies. Thus, providing shorter but more frequent breaks, waiving customary dress requirements, changing work schedules, and providing a facility where the employee may temporarily escape the stressor are examples of ways in which physical environment stressor effects may be reduced, although certainly not eliminated.

One other aspect of the work environment that could be related to the production of stress should be noted. The actual physical layout of the work area may serve to either facilitate or hinder the accomplishment of work objectives and consequently may be a stressor. Inefficient work flow due to deficiencies in the physical arrangement of people and/or equipment may be a source of stress. Frequently those with the best inputs regarding what changes should be made are the individuals who are affected day in and day out. The smart manager will combine his or her own observation with the experience of those performing the tasks in question.

Providing employee facilities

A small, but growing, number of companies is providing employees with a variety of facilities that reduce stress. In a subsequent section of this chapter we will look at a number of individual methods of stress reduction including exercise, meditation, and biofeedback. Organizations may in effect encourage these individual strategies by providing time and/or facilities for them.

As an example, in 1978 U. S. firms spent $2.5 billion on fitness and recreational programs for employees. Companies like Xerox, Rockwell International, Weyerhaeuser, and Pepsi Cola are spending tens of thousands of dollars for gyms equipped with treadmills, exercycles, and jogging tracks—and full-time staff. One of the more impressive operations is Kimberly-Clark, where $2.5 million have been invested in a 7,000 square foot health testing facility and a 32,000 square foot physical fitness facility staffed by fifteen full-time health care personnel.

Some companies, like the Chicago headquarters of McDonald's Corp., are providing biofeedback facilities. At McDonalds, executives take relaxation breaks using biofeedback devices to lower respiration and heart rate. Equitable Life Insurance Company has a biofeedback facility used by employees when they feel tense. (The company has informally estimated that every $15 spent on treatment alleviates symptoms that would have cost three times that in lost productivity.) Other companies like Connecticut General Life Insurance and Sunny Dale Farms are encouraging (and providing time for) employees to meditate.

Organizational efforts do not have to be elaborate or involve large amounts of capital. They may involve nothing more than arranging for employee discounts at the YM/YWCA or the use of a nearby church gymnasium. What is important in all of these efforts is that the organization is facilitating improved health and stress reduction for its employees, something from which everyone gains.

Other organizational approaches

A variety of other managerial actions and strategies may be useful in stress reduction and control. In the career area, for example, a manager has the opportunity (if not the responsibility) to help subordinates examine their careers realistically. Subordinates may be encouraged to do some self-analysis about strengths and weaknesses. Some organizations are equipped to provide expert career counseling and career planning discussions, although this is a relatively sophisticated area that most managers are not trained to pursue in great detail.

Another organizational method that may be valuable in reducing stress is improved selection and placement. Some individuals are more susceptible than others to certain stressors. The traditional approach to selection and placement is to find the person with the skills and ability to handle the job. It seems reasonable to extend these criteria to include consideration of the person's tolerance for ambiguity, ability to handle role conflict, and other individual differences that moderate the stressor-stress outcome relationship.

Training is another area. Managers can benefit from training in the management of stress, and more and more companies view such training as a sound investment. Employees may profit from training in improving their self-awareness and in deciding on appropriate personal stress management strategies. In addition, it seems reasonable to conclude that *any* training that helped employees perform their jobs more efficiently, reduced conflict, improved communications, or improved subordinate and superior relations would have a positive effect on stress reduction.

No single method can be recommended for managing stress in all organizations. There are many approaches that could, if used wisely, reduce stress resulting from the stressors identified in the model in Chapter 2. If the employee's role or the organization's structure can't be changed, or if additional information or better placement isn't the answer, it may be best to adopt more individually oriented methods. Dealing with potential stressors requires time and patience on the part of the manager. It requires careful and judicious use of diagnosis, awareness, and action.

INDIVIDUAL APPROACHES TO STRESS MANAGEMENT

The topics discussed as organizational approaches relate primarily—but not exclusively—to actions initiated by organizations (management) rather than individual employees. Likewise, the techniques examined in this section for the most part must be individually initiated, although organizations may take steps to facilitate this initiation.

Many individual approaches to stress management are highly idiosyncratic, such as prayer, and thus are not amenable to discussion in a volume such as this. On the other hand, the last few years have seen several techniques for stress reduction and improved mental and physical health that merit mention. Foremost among these are meditation, biofeedback, and various forms of physical exercise. Managers familiar with these are in a position to provide subordinates—as well as themselves—with direction in possible approaches to stress reduction.

Meditation

Meditation of one variety or another is a virtually universal technique. Almost all of us take time now and then to contemplate our lives, and we all daydream occasionally. These may be considered possible forms of meditation. Prayer, listening to music, or watching a sunset are other examples. Anything that redirects our mental processes away from daily concerns may be thought of as a form of meditation. Obviously, then, many forms of meditation exist. The meditative forms that have achieved popularity in recent years are derivatives of Eastern philosophies. Foremost among these—at least in its popularity—is Transcendental Meditation, or TM as its adherents refer to it.

The Maharishi Mahesh Yogi, who has been described by the *Wall Street Journal* as a latter-day Dale Carnegie, is responsible for the introduction of TM to the United States around 1960. TM is one of the simpler meditative techniques, requiring no particular philosophic commitment, no special postures or positions, no unique diets, and no external trappings of any kind. Its simplicity may account in part for its popularity with the American public. Adherents claim it helps an individual be a more relaxed, productive person by reducing stress, relieving tension, and increasing efficiency, health, and creativity.

TM uses a *mantra,* a single word or sound that the meditator concentrates upon, to shut out other distractions. The actual meditation process is quite simple. Selecting a setting with a minimum of distractions, the meditator assumes a comfortable position, concentrates on his or her mantra, and enters a state wherein both physical and mental relaxation is at a peak. The choice of setting is very important. If at home, it should be out of range of telephone, television, and stereo. If at the office, it should be at a time when there is minimal likelihood of interruption. Ideally, phone calls and unscheduled visitors would both be put on hold. Frequency and duration of meditation sessions vary, but the standard recommendation is to practice TM twice daily for 15–30 minutes at a time.

Does it work? A variety of positive outcomes have been associated with the practice of meditation (transcendental and otherwise): reduced heart rate, lowered oxygen consumption, and decreased systolic and diastolic blood pressure (See, for example, Benson, 1975 and Gavin, 1977). Kuna (1975) reviewed the research literature on TM as a work-stress management technique. He found evidence that TM had a positive effect on work adjustment, work performance, job satisfaction, and lowering of anxiety. Kuna concluded that TM was an effective strategy for handling stress and that it fostered resistance to stress, thus serving as both a preventor and a reliever.

Another form of meditation which has grown increasingly popular is the Benson technique (Benson, 1975). The Benson technique is a simple form of meditation very similar to TM. It is designed to elicit the *relaxation response,* which Benson maintains is the opposite of the stress response. As with TM a mantra is employed to block extraneous thoughts from the meditator's mind. Benson reports (1970) that his technique elicits essentially the same physiological changes as TM.

Biofeedback

While a great deal of public interest in biofeedback has been triggered in recent years, very few people actually use biofeedback devices at home or in the office. In reality there is nothing new about biofeedback—it's been around as long as humans have. Every time you take your pulse, check your breathing rate, or place your hand on your forehead to see if you have a fever—that's biofeedback. What is relatively new is the instrumentation, the machines that monitor bodily processes and give us information about them. Conceptually, biofeedback training is based on three assumptions: first, that the neurophysiological functions can be monitored by electronic devices and fed back to the individual; second, that changes in physical state are accompanied by changes in emotional states and vice versa; third, that a state of relaxation is conducive to establishing voluntary control of various bodily functions.

The potential role of biofeedback as an individual stress management technique can be seen from the kinds of bodily functions or processes that can, to some degree, be brought under voluntary control. These include brain waves, heart rates, muscle tension, body temperature, stomach acidity, and blood pressure. Most of these processes are affected by stress. The potential of biofeedback, then, is its ability to help induce a state of relaxation and restore bodily functions to a nonstressed state. One advantage of biofeedback over nonfeedback techniques is that the information provided gives individuals precise data about body functions. Interpreting the feedback, the individual knows how high his or her blood pressure is, for example, and discovers through practice means of lowering it. When the individual is successful, the feedback provides instantaneous information to that effect.

While much further research is needed into both the potential and the benefits of biofeedback, there are sufficient data to conclude that it can be of value. The best results have come with specific stress-related problems. Numerous studies, for example, have shown biofeedback to be successful with reducing migraine and tension headaches. In one particularly well-designed study, individuals learned to regulate their blood pressure in a single session. They also learned to decrease their heart beat rate, and (in perhaps the most interesting aspect of all) these two things were independent of one another (Shapiro, Tursky and Schwartz, 1970). Another innovative application of biofeedback has been reported for dealing with gastrointestinal problems. Here, individuals were taught to regulate the production of stomach acid, which is associated with the occurrence of ulcers (Gorman and Kameya, 1972).

The application of biofeedback requires instrumentation. There is a great variety of feedback equipment available for purchase, much of it of questionable accuracy and reliability. Further complicating matters, there is a wide variation in the price of equipment, with little apparent association between price and quality, at least at the lower end of the price scale. Cost is a related drawback. While feedback trainers can be purchased at prices ranging from $25 to $25,000, much of the equipment below $500 is severely lacking in sensitivity and accuracy (the authors know of one company that sells a "biofeedback trainer" for $4 which is nothing more than a plastic mood ring). Individuals interested in biofeedback should proceed carefully in the selection of instrumentation.

Exercise

Various government reports on physical fitness have concluded that the physical state of the average American is far from what it could or should be. The implication this has for employee effectiveness, efficiency, and even longevity is not lost on corporations, who in 1979 averaged over a hundred calls of inquiry a week to the President's Council on Physical Fitness and Sports seeking advice and assistance in establishing their own programs.

Physical fitness experts have long argued that one of the easiest, most beneficial ways to bring about a favorable change in a person's life-style is to engage in some systematic exercise activity. Many physicians believe that the single most important indicator of health is cardiovascular endurance, and that is what regular exercise can develop, particularly activities such as jogging, bicycling, and swimming. The evidence is unequivocable that proper exercise, wisely engaged in, is a positive force in physical health and well being. But what of the mental benefits? What about stress reduction? Available evidence would support exercise as an effective stress management tool, as well as a contributor to physical health. Exercisers report feelings of reduced tension, heightened mental energy, and an improvement in feelings of self-worth.

Research tends to support these reports. In a study of the effects of exercise, middle-aged men were divided into two groups. Half participated in a nineteen-session exercise program consisting primarily of jogging; the other half did not exercise. Both groups were tested before and after, using an instrument that yielded scores on three stress emotions—anxiety, depression, and hostility. The exercisers showed significantly greater reductions in all three stress emotions as compared to the no-exercise control group (Lynch, Folkins, and Wilmore, 1973).

The psychological and physiological processes by which exercise results in stress reduction has been the subject of much speculation. It has been suggested, for example, that changes occur when an individual overcomes a challenge (such as a strenuous exercise program). The positive outcome provides a sense of accomplishment, which in turn allows for more adaptive responses to distressing situations. Ismail and Trachtman (1973) have suggested that the stress reduction benefits are the result of physiological and biochemical changes resulting from exercise. According to this viewpoint, increased circulation to the brain increases the availability of glucose, which results in improvement in oxygen transportation and consequently improved mental functions. Regardless of the explanation, the research on exercise and stress strongly supports exercise as a stress management strategy.

A word of caution is in order, however. Unlike the other approaches to stress management we have discussed, there is a potential element of risk involved with exercise. No one should just suddenly start a program of vigorous exercise, particularly the average, over-thirty-five, inactive adult. The first, absolutely essential step is to see a physician (ideally one who is in the practice of preventive medicine) and receive professional advice on a proper exercise program. Your physician should definitely be consulted before you take one step in any exercise program.

Other individual approaches to stress management

There are many approaches to stress management other than the ones thus far discussed. As an example of the range of possible techniques, we will briefly examine three additional approaches: the stress diary, muscle monitoring, and drugs.

Stress diary • Usually, the better the understanding a person has of a phenomenon, the better equipped that person is to deal effectively with it. This is the rationale underlying the use of a stress diary. The diary is a record or personal log of the events that precipitate a negative stress response in the person. There are two steps involved in the use of a diary as a stress management device: the *recording phase* and the *analysis phase*.

In the recording phase the individual keeps a running record of the events that caused stress. Whenever a situation is encountered that causes significant discomfort, tension, upset, frustration, and so on, a description of that event is recorded including, as specifically as possible, what it was that caused the upset and what kinds of feelings (e.g., anger, frustration, anxiety) were experienced as a result. The events should be recorded as objectively as possible, taking care to avoid evaluative or subjective statements. The length of time one should keep this record before entering the second phase will vary, but generally three to four weeks is a minimum.

The purpose of the analysis phase is to examine the accumulated events with the purpose of identifying common threads in the recorded incidents. For many people, the events in their lives that are sources of stress can be grouped into one or two or three categories. Knowledge of these categories can be used as the basis for reprogramming some behaviors. For example, you may discover that a common theme in many of the stressful events in your log is that stress was precipitated when people did not respond to you the way you felt they should. This knowledge, coupled with a decision not to take responsibility for other people's reactions to you, may lead to a significant reduction in the degree of stress experienced by you in those situations.

Muscle monitoring • Frequently we get very tense—that is, our muscles are tight, our jaw is set, or we may even be clenching our teeth—and we do not realize it. If we do become aware of it, we can usually relax—relax our jaws and facial muscles, our neck muscles, and any other parts of our body that may become tense. The key is to become aware of it. One effective way of doing that is to associate paying attention to your muscle state with some reoccurring event. For example, whenever you receive a phone call, or whenever you get up from your desk, take a few seconds to become aware of tension in your body and to relax. Eventually, you will develop the habit of doing it frequently, and most people find that after a while their muscles are relaxed more and more frequently. One female executive who was a very intense person found that she had a tendency to stiffen her neck muscles whenever she was deeply involved in something. By monitoring herself, she was able to change the habit and consequently prevent the headaches she had been experiencing.

Drugs • By drugs we are referring to legally obtained prescriptions. This means we are including neither illegal drugs, such as marijuana or cocaine, nor nonprescription products such as alcoholic beverages and cigarettes, which contain chemical substances and may act as stress reducers.

It has been estimated that from 20–50 percent of patient visits to a physician are stress-related. While 15 percent of American adults are treated with antianxiety drugs each year, that figure represents only 30 percent of the individuals who experience high levels of stress. There is no universally agreed upon classification of different types of prescription drugs. For the most part, however, drugs used to treat stress fall into three categories: barbiturates, antidepressants, and minor tranquilizers.

Barbiturates, or sedatives, are central nervous system depressants and include the familiar brand names Phenobarbital and Seconal. Antidepressants, not very widely prescribed as a group, include Elavil and Marplan. The minor tranquilizers comprise the most widely used group and include Librium, Valium, and Miltown, among the most frequently prescribed. Pharmacologic treatment is usually a short-term, immediately effective method of alleviating negative stress responses. Since drugs in effect mask symptoms, rather than deal with the primary causes of stress, they are not considered a long-term solution. Additional problems associated with long-term use include the very real possibility of psychological dependency and/or physical addiction. In recent years there has been a great deal of publicity concerning the misuse of these drugs—particularly the benzodiazepines in the minor tranquilizer group. While there is little doubt that some individuals have over-used the drugs or used them inappropriately, there is little doubt that they are effective in reducing stress.

SOME CONCLUDING THOUGHTS

Health has been defined by the World Health Organization, not simply as the absence of disease, but as a state of physical, mental, and social well-being. The advancement of health in this broadly defined way is a matter of legitimate interest for all institutions. Nowhere is this concept more important than in the work environment. And within the work sector it is important, not just because of its desirable social consequences, but because it is an inescapable part of the conditions that determine worker and organizational effectiveness and efficiency.

Organizational theorists and practicing managers have long been aware that a host of different factors may detract from optimal performance: dissatisfaction with the job, poor physical working conditions, bad interpersonal relationships, lack of job security, dissatisfaction with pay, insufficient challenge, too much work, not enough work, too much supervision, too little supervision, ineffective communications, lack of advancement opportunities, lack of interest in assigned tasks, leadership style problems, disagreements over policy, and on and on. The list is practically endless—or at least it seems that way much of the time. The one aspect these problems have in common is that all of them represent a deviation between what is and what should be, according to employee perceptions and expectations. Anytime we experience a deviation of this type, we expend effort to deal with it. In other words, when experienced by an employee, all of these situations or conditions require *an adaptive response, mediated by individual characteristics and/or psychological processes, that places special physical and or psychological demands upon a person.*

The reader will have noted that the preceding statement repeats the working definition of stress first presented in Chapter 1 of this book. In one sense then (and we realize it is in only one sense), the common denominator for all of these organizational problems is that they produce stress. Eliminate or reduce the stress associated with them and you have eliminated or reduced their capacity to produce dysfunctional organizational consequences. Viewed from this perspective, stress management becomes an essential requirement for achieving optimal organizational functioning. Ideally, stress management focuses on prevention—eliminating stressors and removing the conditions favoring stress responses. However, since total prevention is not practical (nor perhaps even desirable), stress management focusing on relieving stress must also play an integral role in the total program.

An important point here is that stress management is not a sudden new responsibility added to the myriad of other concerns a manager must be attentive to. We are *not* saying, "O.K., in addition to your other duties you have to control stress levels or conditions that may lead to stress among your employees." What we are saying is that many of the responsibilities a manager *already* has and many of the problems a manager *already* has to deal with can be effectively recast or redefined as stress management concerns. It has been said that genius is nothing more than the ability to look at old things in new ways. Stress management represents the application of a new perspective to old concerns.

Eustress

Stress is a neutral term. The fact that it is an adaptive response that places special demands upon an individual is neither good nor bad, harmful nor beneficial. It is simply descriptive of what takes place in terms of an individual's response. Very clearly, the thrust of this volume has been directed almost exclusively toward the negative features of stress, toward its disruptive and debilitating outcomes. The emphasis of this chapter has been on preventing and relieving stress responses. There is another side of stress management however—and indeed, another side of stress—that needs to be identified to insure a balanced perspective in viewing stress and work.

As we indicated in the first chapter, not all stress is bad. What *is* bad is *no* stress. Life is a series of adaptive responses to external situations. To live is to encounter stress. But while many stressors result in *dis*-stress, many may also produce *eu*-stress. *Eustress* is a word coined by Selye (from the Greek *eu*, meaning good, as in euphoria) and refers to stress that is good or produces a positive outcome. Working a crossword puzzle or completing a challenging work assignment involves stress; both require adaptive responses that make special demands on us. Both are stressful, but the stress is eustress. Rather than anxiety, we experience positive stimulation; we experience intrinsic satisfaction, perhaps even exhiliration, over having accomplished a challenging goal.

Eustress is necessary in our lives. In fact, some of the distress we experience is nothing more than an absence of eustress (lack of job challenge, for example). The same stimulus may result in distress in one person and eustress in another. Part of the task of effective stress management—and part of the manager's job—is to recognize individual differences in this regard and structure work environments accordingly. Just as effective stress management requires reducing distress, it also requires increasing eustress.

By providing opportunities for employees to achieve, to accomplish challenging and intrinsically interesting goals, to grow both professionally and personally, the manager is practicing effective stress management. To paraphrase the well-known prayer of Alcoholics Anonymous, the objective you should strive for is to minimize the opportunities for distress that can be minimized; maximize the opportunities for eustress that can be maximized; and develop sufficient awareness of your employees (and yourself) to know the difference.

APPENDIX

Stress reduction goal exercise

Objectives: 1. To *illustrate* that a goal-setting process can be applied to reducing self-identified job, life, and career stressors.

2. To *develop* an action plan that can serve as a program for stress reduction.

The notion of psychological stress refers to affective, behavior, and physiological responses to aversive stimuli in the environment. A number of environmental events are capable of producing stress responses. Stress responses occur if an event is seen as threatening, at which point a person typically mobilizes his/her resources in an effort to reduce or eliminate the stressors. Goal setting is an important action step in coping with the stressors. Therefore, this exercise asks the participant to focus on job, life, and career stressors. What *actions* can you take in the form of goals to reduce the impact of the stressors?

Exercise procedures

1. The first step is to list the three most obvious and powerful JOB, CAREER, and LIFE stressors you generally must cope with. The concept of stress being used is the unsatisfying or negative form. Those three stressors that have what you consider to be adverse consequences on you in each of the three areas should be your focus.

2. Now that you have clearly stated three categories or stressors, establish goals that, if achieved, could reduce or eliminate some or all of the stressors. In preparing your goals consider the following attributes:

1. CHALLENGE: Are the goals difficult but not too difficult?
2. COMMITMENT: Are the goals worthwhile and attractive enough?
3. CLARITY: Do I understand exactly what the goal means?
4. ACCURACY: Is the goal accurately stated?
5. TIMELINESS: Does the goal have a realistic time or deadline associated with it?

The goals should be used to reduce the stressors you identified in Step 1. They should be written in two sentences or less and should have some target dates attached to them. You should also have a plan for evaluating your progress—how you will determine whether the stressors have been reduced or eliminated. If your evaluation determines that you fell short of your goal, try to determine the cause and use that information in reformulating your goal. The goals should also be monitored three months after they were originally established.

REFERENCES

Benson, H. *The Relaxation Response.* New York: William Morrow and Co., Inc., 1975.

Caplan, R.D. "Occupational differences in job demands and strain." Paper presented at the meeting of the American Psychological Association, Washington, D.C., September, 1976.

Drucker, P. F. *The Practice of Management.* New York: Harper and Row, Publishers, Inc., 1954.

French, J. R. P. "Person role fit." *Occupational Mental Health* 3 (1973): 15–20.

Gavin, J. F. "Occupational mental health—forces and trends." *Personnel Journal* 1977: 198–201.

Gorman, P. and Kameya, J. "Voluntary control of stomach pH." Research note presented at the Biofeedback Society Meeting, Boston, November, 1972.

Harrison, R. V. "Job stress as person-environment fit." Paper presented at the meeting of the American Psychological Association, Washington, D.C., September 1976.

Ismail, A. H. and Trachtman, L. E. "Jogging the imagination." *Psychology Today* 6 (1973): 79–82.

Kahn, R. L. and Quinn, R. P. "Strategies for the management of role stress." In *Occupational Mental Health.* A. McLean, ed. New York: Rand McNally and Company, 1970.

Kuna, D. J. Meditation and work. *Vocational Guidance Quarterly* 23 (1975): 342–346.

Lynch, S., Folkins, C. H., and J. H. Wilmore. "Relationships between three mood variables and physical exercise." Unpublished data, February, 1973.

Newman, J. E. and T. A. Beehr. "Personal and organizational strategies for handling job stress: A review of research and opinion." *Personnel Psychology* 32 (1979): 1–44.

Shapiro, D. P., Tursky, B. and G. E. Schwartz. "Differentiation of heart rate and systolic blood pressure in man by operant conditioning." In *Biofeedback and Self-Control.* T. X. Barber et al., eds. Chicago: Aldine-Atherton, 1970.

FOR FURTHER READING

Barber, T. X., et al., eds. *Biofeedback and Self-Control*. Chicago: Aldine Publishing Company, 1976.

Benson, Herbert. *The Relaxation Response*. New York: Avon Books, 1975.

Bloomfield, Harold. *TM—Discovering Inner Energy and Overcoming Stress*. New York: Dell Publishing Co., Inc., 1975.

Cooper, Kenneth. *The Aerobics Way*. New York: M. Evans and Co., Inc., 1977.

Goldberg, Philip. *Executive Health*. New York: McGraw-Hill, Inc., 1978.

McQuade, Walter and Ann Aikman. *Stress*. New York: Bantam Books, Inc., 1974.

Pelletier, Kenneth R. *Mind as Healer, Mind as Slayer*. New York: Dell Publishing Co., Inc., 1977.

Epilogue

    An epilogue indicates a closing section to a book. This is the final section of this book, but hopefully it will not be interpreted as the final word about stress and work. We are only at the very infant stage of understanding the interrelatedness, consequences, and problems of stress and work. The tired request for more and better research doesn't indicate a closing but a beginning. The material presented in the book strongly suggests that behavioral and medical researchers and especially managers will continue to be challenged by stress and work issues.

    When a person suffers a coronary heart attack, the physician treating the patient attempts to determine the sociopsychological state of the victim. In particular the physician seeks signs of the patient's experienced stress. Physicians working with patients are not alone in their concern with stress. In this book we have spelled out behavioral science, managerial, and individual interests in stress. Indeed, stress is *the* topic of interest in industrialized societies.

    Besides conventional wisdom that too much stress is not good for a person's longevity or quality of life, we have identified other forms of evidence. Physicians and psychiatrists have used *clinical impressions* to trace stress. *Laboratory studies,* especially the work of Selye, have also been conducted to study the effects of stressful stimuli on organisms. *Epidemiological studies* that attempt to link stress to various disorders have been conducted. Despite these attempts to study stress, there are still major gaps in our knowledge about stress and work. Many of these gaps became obvious as we moved through the book. In actuality, the material presented in this book indicated that little rigorous research is available on stress and work. There is certainly some excellent research, but it is presented in a limited number of studies, and rarely has the managerial application value been highlighted by the researchers.

Filling the gaps—opportunities

Filling some of the gaps in applied managerial practices and in stress and work theory building and research may require following some very basic suggestions. The suggestions are pointed toward improving our understanding of stress at work, in the home, and in society and will require work by model builders, researchers, and managers.

First, although the construct *stress* has become a popular word, it remains to a large extent a vague and ambiguous concept. In too many cases, the general meaning of stress is assumed to be known. There are even writers and researchers who present detailed empirical findings without themselves explicitly defining the concept. It would be asking for too much to request a single definition that others could accept as reasonable and unambiguous. However, one suggestion that is feasible would be to have theorists, researchers, managers, and lay people examining stress specifically define their meaning of stress. This would help others in evaluating the work or ideas presented.

Second, research in which measures of the independent variable are not kept separate from the dependent variable are common. In some laboratory experiments the reader is not clearly informed about the variable mix, and often the researcher's model of presenting hypotheses is not presented. This problem may be the result of individuals from different backgrounds and disciplines studying stress. Each discipline varies somewhat in its methodologies and concern about explicitly presenting independent and dependent variables. Perhaps development of models that clearly display various types of variables could help some of this problem. We have proposed such a model in Figure 2–4. By adding clarity in definition and separation of variables, the domain of the researcher or practitioner can be charted for the reader or interested person. For example, if clarity and separation were practiced, the manager could determine from our model that five categories of stressors are of interest, that individual differences mediate the stress-outcome linkage, and that general adaption diseases are the potential outcomes of stress.

Third, research and integrative model building are needed to specify the physiological processes through which all forms of stress operate. In many ways the evidence linking stress to disease is similar to that linking cigarette smoking to coronary heart disease (House, 1974). In neither case do we know exactly how, physiologically, these factors produce disease. Continually searching and analyzing how physiology, disease, and stress are linked is a challenging task for the future. This search, in our opinion, can be more fruitful for society if the combined talents of medical and behavioral scientists are used.

The need to combine the skills of interdisciplinary teams to examine stress and work is made obvious when coronary heart disease is the focal point. After years of research by biomedical researchers and their careful development of traditional coronary risk factors such as blood pressure, serum cholesterol levels, and ECG abnormality, coronary heart disease is still a puzzle. Reports from the well-designed prospective Framingham study strongly indicate a high degree of predictive error. In a sixteen-year follow-up study on Framingham participants, only twenty-five percent of those forty-five to seventy-four years of age who were in the highest decile of coronary risk (high blood pressure, high cholesterol, smoking, low glucose tolerance, and ECG abnormalities) actually developed coronary disease.

The Framingham results and much of what we have discussed throughout this book strongly suggest, in our opinion, that the medical and behavioral science communities can each benefit from the other's expertise. The medical community is especially prepared to provide expertise in the theory and measurement of physiological factors, while the behavioral science community seems to be able to provide theory and measures of sociopsychological variables. Research results using the talents and measures offered by medical-behavioral teams should be more insightful than what is currently being published.

Fourth, most of the available research on stress and work has been retrospective. That is, the researcher has asked participants to look back at past events or circumstances that may have affected them. Certainly, retrospective research has predominated the life events research stimulated by the work of Holmes and Rahe (1967). We believe that much progress in understanding how life events affect future illness episodes has been gained from the retrospective research. However, many questions remained unanswered, and opportunities to conduct prospective studies exist. Predicting future illness and performance under various stress circumstances would be valuable information for developing preventive programs and/or altering management procedures. Hinkle (1974) reports on a study in which 838 men between the ages of forty and sixty-five have been followed prospectively. This study incorporates stratified random sampling, medical data, social and psychological data, a diary of daily activities, and psychological testing. This prospective study is being used to study and predict the occurrence of coronary heart disease. More of the Hinkle type of research is needed to establish preventive medical and corrective managerial programs to combat the ravages of job, organizational, and extraorganizational stressors.

Fifth, the majority of stress and work research derives from studies of workers in selected organizations. Most typically, the populations have been in professional occupations or what are assumed to logically be stress-filled occupations, such as air traffic controllers, police officers, or fire fighters. Do the findings from these populations and occupations generalize to other segments of society? Research on stress examining blacks versus whites, young versus old, working career women versus homemaking women, and career men versus career women is needed now more than ever. The external validity of stress research can only be increased if populations studied are representative of the population in general. To date the external validity issue has not been systematically examined by most individuals studying stress and work phenomena.

Sixth, research is needed to determine what kinds of individuals perform and function best at various stress levels. Are certain types of individuals, Type A or Type B, more likely to thrive or perform in work situations that are compatible with their behavior patterns? When do organizational stressors, job stressors, and extraorganizational stressors become dysfunctional for certain types of individuals? What kind of individual performs best at various arousal levels? How should work schedules, vacations, and rest periods be used to minimize stress build-up in individuals? Research assessment of these and similar questions seems warranted if the quality of work and life is to be improved.

Seventh, research is required to examine the impact, success, and failure of individual and organizational coping responses to deal with stress. Is meditation a scientifically validated coping process for certain individuals? What does exercise (e.g., jogging versus tennis or walking versus swimming) do for an individual under stress? What kind of individual selects various responses for coping with stress? How can organizations intervene optimally to reduce or eliminate stress? These kinds of questions can be researched by using rigorous experimental research designs.

Eighth, much of the early research on stress dealt with only two variables, a hypothetical stressor and a response variable. As the amount of research on stress has increased, factors mediating stress responses have been identified. Future research of stress should routinely take account of the type of individual differences suggested in Chapter 8. Sources of stress must be proposed and measured, responses to stress must be measured, and some individual or situational properties presumed to mediate the stress response must also be measured. If the complex interactions among stressors, moderators, and stress response are to be studied simultaneously, multivariate research designs will be needed. To date, too few studies have used such designs. Furthermore, the available multivariate research has usually been conducted in laboratory settings. We need multivariate studies in ongoing organizations to increase our understanding.

Ninth, there is currently a lot of guessing about the industry cost of organization-oriented stress. If the nature and magnitude of the full cost of stress is to be determined, standard procedures of accounting must be implemented. Accounting research that examines the cost of stress in absenteeism, training, recruitment, insurance, turnover, illness, and poor performance is sorely needed. The accountant has the expertise available to help management put into proper perspective the costs of stress. The effect of such accounting research might well be to immediately rethink various managerial practices or procedures that are contributing causes to the accumulation of costly stressors.

Tenth, much more research is needed on the measurement of stress. Continued laboratory and field empirical studies with more refined measurement instruments of pertinent stressors are needed. The majority of laboratory and field studies covered in this book have relied on one form of measurement. In the behavioral sciences the self-report test is popular, while in medical science physiological and personal history measures are widely used. What would be exciting and insightful would be to use a multitude of high-quality measures to examine the causal linkages and associations discussed in the book. Studies that use a number of measurement instruments such as behavior rating scales, psychological self-report inventories, personal diaries, biomedical measures of autonomic stress reactions, and interview responses are needed. Individual researchers and practitioners can and need to work more diligently at constructing valid and reliable measures of stress.

If more and better research on stress and work is to be forthcoming, much more work on validating, cross-validating, and refining measurement tools are needed. Unfortunately, at this date there are few systematic efforts of measurement refinement available to highlight as commendable examples. The continuing work of Holmes and others (Dohrenwend and Dohrenwend, 1974) on life events, Jenkins (1978) on assessing coronary prone behavior pattern, and Rose et al. (1978) in measuring hormone secretion under stress are examples of the few available commendable efforts to refine measures of stress, stressors, and mediating variables.

Finally, the call for more longitudinal research has been expressed in every behavioral and medical science discipline for years. It seems that this call is one of the most avoided requests found in the literature (Ivancevich and Matteson, 1978). Instead of more and better longitudinal research designs, one finds a growing list of cross-sectional research. Some of the cross-sectional research is good, insightful, and interesting. However, a gap in knowledge will always remain unless more longitudinal attention is paid to stress and work.

Kimberly (1978) cleverly points out that the difference between longitudinal and cross-sectional research is not unlike the difference between motion picture photography and still photography. In the case of still photography, the photographer is able to capture all of the components that are visible at a moment in time. The photo enables one to describe and perhaps measure the relationships among the components at that one moment. However, on the basis of a still picture, one has no idea about how stable relationships are or how they evolved. A motion picture, however, presents a more dynamic and realistic view of relationships of components. By watching a motion picture, one can tell how relationships have changed over time and perhaps be better able to predict how they will change in the future.

There is a significant need for more motion pictures of stress and work. Any researcher and manager is well aware that studying relationships in organizational settings involves some variables remaining stable and others undergoing significant change. Cross-sectional research is not able to capture the dynamic changes in stressor intensity, meaningfulness, and frequency. The consequence is that interpreting results is inevitably problematic (Kimberly, 1978). Managerial reliance on still pictures is fraught with problems because of the changes regularly occurring in the world of managers.

These suggestions are not listed in any order of priority; all of them seem to be important. Further interest and research on stress and work will have import. For *behavioral science,* it will offer opportunities to learn more about stressors and the role they play at work, home and in the community; for *medical science,* it can increase our ability to predict and understand the stress and disease link; for *practicing managers,* it will provide strategies for managing stress and using positive stress to achieve optimum performance.

REFERENCES

Dohrenwend, B.J. and B.P. Dohrenwend, eds. *Stressful Life Events.* New York: John Wiley and Sons, 1974.

Hinkle, L.E., Jr. "A study of the precursors of acute and fatal coronary heart disease." Public Annual Report, Cornell University Medical College, NHL1 70–2069, February 1, 1973.

Holmes, T.H. and R.H. Rahe. "The social readjustment rating scale." *Journal of Psychosomatic Research* 2 (1967): 213–218.

House, J.S. "Occupational stress and coronary heart disease: A review and theoretical integration." *Journal of Health and Social Behavior,* 15(1974): 12–27.

Ivancevich, John M. and Michael T. Matteson. "Longitudinal organizational research in field settings." *Journal of Business Research,* August 1978.

Jenkins, C.D. "A comparative review of the interview and questionnaire methods in the assessment of the coronary-prone behavior pattern." In *Coronary Prone Behavior.* T.M. Dembroski et al., eds. New York: Springer-Verlag New York, Inc., 1978 71–88.

Rose, R.M., Jenkins, C.D. and M.W. Hurst. "Air traffic controller health change study." Federal Aviation Administration Contract, Department of Transportation, 1978.

Glossary

Arousal Theory of Motivation—the notion that once optimum arousal (activation) is achieved, individuals are more receptive to the external stimuli in the environment at the time.

Behavioral Medicine—a new field that emphasizes the need for biochemical scientists, physicians, and behavioral scientists to join together to study 1) psychosocial factors contributing to disease; 2) methods for assessing health problems; and 3) strategies for treating and rehabilitating physical disorders.

Behavioral Science—a body of systemized knowledge pertaining to how people behave, what is the relationship between human behavior and total environment, and why people behave as they do.

Biofeedback—a technique, usually involving the use of some type of instrumentation, in which the user attempts to learn to control various bodily functions such as heart rate, body temperature, and blood pressure. It has been used successfully in relaxation training.

Cerebral Cortex—the section of the brain that is chiefly responsible for initiating the stress response sequence.

Cholesterol—a fatlike substance that may collect on the linings of coronary arteries and lead to narrowing of the artery. There is strong evidence that stress increases the production of cholesterol.

Context—the social and physical environment in which a stressor may be found.

Darts Disease—an affliction resulting in painful swelling of the hands. It is caused by a variety of factors, most commonly by prolonged exposure to vibration.

Diseases of Adaptation—a phrase coined by Dr. Hans Selye. Diseases of adaptation are those that are thought to arise at least partially as a result of the body's attempt to adapt to change, hence they are stress related. Examples include ulcers, hypertension, headaches, and coronary heart disease.

Distress—sometimes erroneously used as a synonym for *stress*. Distress refers to "bad" or disruptive stress and should be distinguished from eustress.

Economic and Financial Stressors—stressors related to inflation and the difficulty of maintaining a standard of living.

Endocrine System—a glandular system that plays an integral role in the stress reaction, primarily through the production and release of hormones. The most important glands regulated by the endocrine system are the adrenals.

Extraorganizational Stressors—stressors that are initiated off the job, such as family relationships, financial conditions, and residential attributes.

Eustress—a term coined by Dr. Hans Selye to describe "good" stress, that is, stress that results in positive outcomes such as creativity and intrinsic satisfaction.

Family Stressors—a conglomeration of conditions generated by child rearing problems, marital conflict, and other family issues and situations.

General Adaptation Syndrome—the defense reaction activated in response to a stressor. It consists of three distinct phases of alarm, resistance, and exhaustion. The G.A.S. is responsible for the increase in adrenalin production, heart rate, and blood pressure that accompany stress.

Homeostasis—as applied to stress, the term signifies a balance of an individual's internal environment. Homeostatic mechanisms are those which maintan internal equilibrium.

Hypothalamus—the part of the midbrain that is partially responsible for regulating emotions. Most importantly, in terms of stress, it activates the autonomic nervous system.

Inadequate Group Support Stressors—a group stressor that occurs when there is little sharing of opinions and emotions among a group's membership.

Intergroup Conflict Stressors—a group stressor that occurs when conflict or antagonism exists between two or more groups.

Intragroup Conflict Stressors—an internal group stressor that occurs when group members are antagonistic toward each other.

Lack of Cohesiveness Stressors—a group stressor related to forces that pull a group member away from other members.

Leadership Influence Stressors—the actions, style, and procedures of a leader that function as stressors for some individuals.

Locus of Control—a term that refers to people's perceptions of the extent to which they feel that control over external events is either within or outside their power to influence. Locus of control is a potential moderator of the stress response.

Measurement—the rules for assigning numbers to objects in such a way as to represent quantities of attributes.

Medical Research Approach—measurement that uses historical, biochemical, and physiological data to perform a patient diagnosis.

Muscle Monitoring—a relaxation technique in which the individual focuses attention on tense muscles and learns to relax them. Eventually the relaxation process becomes automatic.

Optimum Arousal Performance—the point at which peak performance is achieved.

Organizational Climate Stressors—an organizational stressor that is generated by the interaction of the people, structure, policies, and goals of an organization.

Organizational Structure Stressors—an organizational stressor caused by the structural arrangements and power-authority hierarchy of an organization.

Organizational Territory Stressors—an organizational stressor caused by instrusions into or the disorganization of an employee's personal space (e.g., work area, work programs, group area).

Preventive Management—a philosophy that emphasizes identifying and correcting environmental and job problems which are potential stressors before they become organizationally and individually pathological.

Psychosomatic Medicine—the practice of medicine that studies the relationship between psychological processes of behavior and somatic structures of bodily organs.

Race and Class Stressors—sociopsychological conditions created by the race and class of a person.

Raynaud's Disease—a condition in which the hands become unusually sensitive to cold. It can be precipitated by prolonged exposure to vibration.

Reliability of a Measure—the ability to generate the same value on a test-retest schedule or other statistical reliability check. If the measure is repeated at two different times, there is said to be high reliability.

Relocation Stressors—an antecedent to stress created by relocating from one residence to another.

Residential Stressors—residential features such as orderliness, safety, cleanliness, and transportation, and their interpretation by an individual. A person's perception of these attributes determines whether they become stressful.

Role Ambiguity—uncertainty as to the scope of one's job.

Role Conflict—conflict that results when compliance with one set of role pressures makes compliance with another set difficult or impossible.

Shift Work Stressors—a stressor generated by the work schedule. Since most people are attuned to daylight activities, working on afternoon or evening shifts can be a stressor.

Standardized Measures—a measure employed by different individuals who obtain the same or similar results.

Stress—an adaptive response, mediated by individual characteristics and/or psychological processes, that is a consequence of any external action, situation, or event that places special physical and/or psychological demands upon a person.

Stressor—any event, situation, or person that an individual may encounter in the environment and which requires change or adaptation on the individual's part. Also, that stimulus which elicits a stress response.

Task Characteristic Stressor—a stressor generated by the poor arrangement and motivational impact of such task attributes as task variety, autonomy, and feedback.

Technology Stressor—an organizational stressor that is created by technological arrangements, limitations, or equipment.

Tolerance of Ambiguity—a characteristic of an individual allows that person to feel at ease in ambiguous or unstructured situations. Tolerance of ambiguity is thought to moderate the stress response.

Transcendental Meditation—a meditative technique advocated by the Maharishi Mahesh Yogi, it requires no particular philosophic commitment and is practiced by many as a stress relieving device.

Triglycerides—like cholesterol, triglycerides are fatty substances found in the blood. They are thought by some to be an important contributing factor to artery disease.

Type A—a personality type characterized by a hard-driving and competitive orientation toward events and situations, it is thought to be implicated in coronary heart disease. The opposite of Type A is Type B.

Type B—a personality type characterized by a relaxed, calm, and collected approach to events. Type Bs are thought to experience much less stress than their Type A counterparts, although there is no universal agreement on this point.

U-Shaped Relationship—a U-shaped relationship between arousal and performance. Performance increases as arousal increases to an optimum point and then decreases.

Validity of a Measure—the degree to which the measure actually indicates what it is supposed to be measuring.

Vulnerability—personal characteristics such as age, sex, and emotional predispositions that determine in part the extent to which a stressor will result in a stress response.

Work Overload—a condition of being overloaded either quantitatively or qualitatively. Quantitative overload occurs when an individual has too much work to do or insufficient time to complete required work. Qualitative overload occurs when individuals feel they lack the skills, abilities, or competencies to do their jobs.

Index